LANDMARK

Black Forest

Grant Bourne & Sabine Körner-Bourne

Grant Bourne and his wife Sabine met on a Kibbutz way back in 1982. Their shared passion for travel has since taken them through much of Europe, Asia, Africa and the Near East. Now living in Germany's lovely Rhine Valley, the authors frequently visit the Black Forest for walking holidays or to go cross-country skiing.

Grant and Sabine have written travel guides and articles in both English and German. They have also written a walking guide to the Bavarian Alps. On their web site readers can inform themselves about the latest developments affecting travel in the Black Forest and much else besides:
http://members.xoom.com/grantbourne/BlackForest.htm

Acknowledgements

The authors are most grateful to the various tourist offices for their generous help. We would also like to extend special thanks to the VFG in Baden-Württemberg for their helpful advice on fishing permits and to Sylvia for the great time we had in Altglashütten.

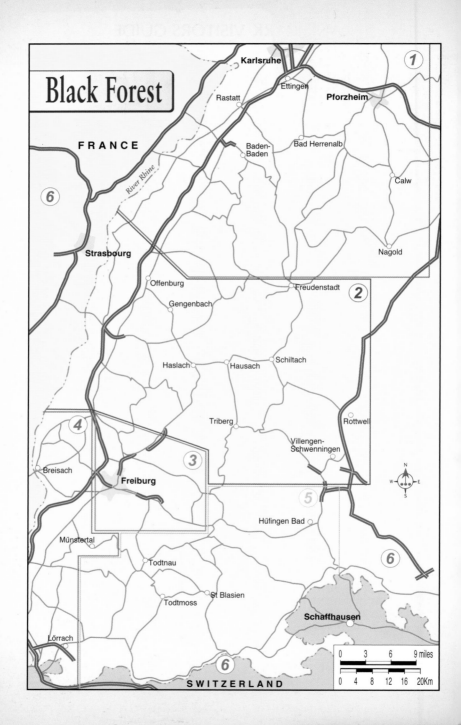

Black Forest

FRANCE

Karlsruhe
Ettingen
Rastatt
Pforzheim

Baden-Baden
Bad Herrenalb

Calw

Nagold

River Rhine

Strasbourg

Offenburg
Freudenstadt

Gengenbach

Haslach
Hausach
Schiltach

Triberg
Rottwell

Villengen-Schwenningen

Breisach

Freiburg

Hüfingen Bad

Münstertal

Todtnau

St Blasien
Todtmoss

Schaffhausen

Lörrach

SWITZERLAND

| 0 | | 3 | | 6 | | 9 miles |
| 0 | 4 | 8 | 12 | 16 | | 20Km |

N
W — E
S

Black Forest

• CONTENTS •

*I*ntroduction

Covering an area of 2,300sq miles (6,000sq km), of which two-thirds is forested, the Black Forest is Germany's largest wooded region. Mountainous in character its picturesque hills and valleys have attracted foreign visitors for over a century. Many have been drawn by the beautiful

natural scenery, made accessible by around 14,300 miles (23,000km) of walking trails that criss-cross the region from north to south. Others have come to benefit from the health-giving mineral waters of the spa towns that dot the western borders and northern area.

Most visitors to the region are pleasantly surprised by a cuisine that has been influenced by those of adjacent Alsace (France) and Switzerland. In fact few places in Germany can boast so many gourmet restaurants, so many outstanding chefs. It almost goes without saying that an evening meal can be washed down with local wines that belong to the very best that Germany has to offer.

As if all this was not enough the Black Forest offers cultural sights par excellence; a magnificent minster in Freiburg and romantic monastery ruins at Hirsau and Allerheiligen. Scattered along the valleys are lovely half-timbered villages and many hill-tops are crowned with castle ruins. For lovers of rural culture and folk traditions there are picturesque Black Forest farmhouses, cuckoo clocks and the Swabian-Alemannic Carnival with its bright costumes and bizarre masks.

Having said all this, it should be remembered that the fleeting impressions of a visitor are just one side of the coin. Steep mountains and narrow valleys were never the easiest places to settle and farm; cuckoo clocks were made and sold to better the meagre income of a rural population, not simply to thrill the hearts of souvenir collectors. Wars and famine lie behind the visible remains of castles and cathedrals. In modern times cluttered highways and pollution cast shadows over the time-worn clichés of idyllic, untouched landscapes propagated by glossy travel brochures. Even the famous cuckoo clock is as likely to have its origins in distant Taiwan as in some small factory in the woods. Nevertheless the charm is still there, and visitors will long remember the little things that make any holiday; the delicious Black Forest cake tasted in a local café, the cherry brandy that capped an evening meal, or the view over a lonely valley on a summer's afternoon.

History

The history of the Black Forest region is inextricably entwined with that of the nations and regions that surround it. A detailed description of the complex tapestry of events that has been woven in the course of more than 10,000 years (if one really begins at the beginning) would fill many thick volumes. What follows, instead, is a brief chronology that restricts itself to the more important dates that have influenced the course of history in this small region in the heart of Europe.

Prehistory

The Black Forest was an uninhabited region, its mountains were cloaked in dense, virtually impenetrable forest. Stone Age settlements were confined to less difficult terrain on the region's fringes: the Upper Rhine near Freiburg and in the vicinity of Bad Säckingen. Evidence indicates that the very first settlers hunted wild horses and reindeer, and it was not until the Neolithic period (around 3,000 to 1,800 BC) that the stone age hunters turned to agriculture.

Celts and Romans

From 800 BC a people known as the Celts first settled the outskirts of the region, then gradually penetrated deeper into the southern valleys. These Celtic tribes were described by the Greek historian Herodotus as being warlike, with a tendency to drunkenness. In spite of their alleged fondness for the bottle they nevertheless developed a complex culture as archaeological finds in Germany and elsewhere have proved. Having learned to work metals the Celts came to the Black Forest to dig for iron-ore. The remains of some of their settlements have been found at the site of present day Kirchzarten (Tarodunum) and around Breisach and the general area of the Kaiserstuhl, near Freiburg.

In a series of military campaigns around 58 BC the Romans defeated the Celts and gradually entered the area of the Upper Rhine and the Black Forest. The best account of the vanquished Celtic people is contained in Julius Caesar's *De bello Gallico* (The Gallic War).

In the first century AD Roman settlements were founded at Baden-Baden, Badenweiler, Hüfingen, Pforzheim and Rottweil. In this period the Romans built a military road through the Kinzigtal and constructed the *Limes*, a defensive line against marauding Germanic tribes.

Though the Romans came as conquerors, they also brought many benefits to the Celts who lived among them. In general living standards improved and the sons of important officials were able to visit Roman schools – poor farmers' sons were more likely to end up as soldiers. They also introduced grapes to the region and by the second century viticulture had spread to many areas along the Upper Rhine.

Germanic tribes

In the course of the third century Alemannic tribes moved south from north-eastern Germany. In 259 they broke through the *Limes* and pushed the Romans back to the area of Lake Constance (Bodensee). The interior of the Black Forest remained uninhabited.

In 496 another Germanic tribe, known as the Franks, defeated the Alemanni at Zülpich. At first the northern region of the Black Forest, then later the central and southern regions came under their influence.

Monastic foundations

From about 650 the Christianization of the Black Forest began, as mainly Irish monks settled in the southern and western reaches of the region. St Trudpert in the Münstertal was the first monastery on the right bank of the Rhine. Other monasteries or smaller monastic cells were founded at Ettenheimmünster (around 700), Gengenbach (about 725) St Blasien (about 800) and Hirsau (830).

In a ninth century document found at the monastery of St Gallen, in Switzerland, the region is referred to as the *Schwarzwald* (Black Forest) for the first time. The name is only unusual in that it was applied to such a large area; in the German-speaking alpine regions the term 'Schwarzwald' was commonly used in reference to coniferous mountain forests.

Settlement, industry and war

In the eleventh to fourteenth centuries the settlement of the Black Forest gathered momentum. From about 1000 settlers gradually moved into the mountainous interior. A driving force behind this period of colonisation was the emergence of the high nobility, who were to dominate the territorial history of the region for the next few centuries. Among the most powerful families

Lovely half-timbered houses are commonplace in Gengenbach

were the Zähringen dynasty, who founded Freiburg in 1120 (their lineage died out in 1218), the House of Habsburg (for over 400 years, until 1805, Austria was able to control large areas of the Black Forest), the Margraves of Baden and the Princes of Fürstenberg. In concert with the large monasteries these powerful families sought to extend their properties and influence by clearing the virgin forests for the establishment of towns and farmland. An additional impetus for the exploitation of the interior was the discovery of profitable deposits of iron-ore and silver in the mountains.

Traditional costume, Gutachtal

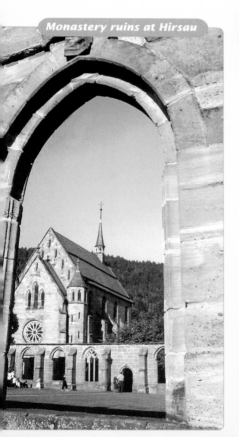

Monastery ruins at Hirsau

In the course of the Reformation, around 1525, a few smaller areas of the Black Forest became Protestant enclaves, but the rest of the land remained Catholic – a situation which has remained unchanged to this day.

Between 1618 and 1648 the Thirty Years' War ravaged the Black Forest; farmlands were laid waste, mining stopped and many towns and villages were depopulated. Grimmelshausen wrote his novel *'Adventures of a Simpleton'* in 1668, based on his experiences of this war.

The seventeenth century saw the emergence of small settlements in the northern Black Forest that lived from forest-based professions such as lumbering, log rafting and glassmaking. By the eighteenth century log rafting and the traditional glassmaking industry had reached the height of their importance. Having begun as a cottage industry in the seventeenth century, the manufacture of clocks shifted to the factory methods of mass production in the nineteenth century.

In 1720 the Saltpetre Wars began when the abbot of St Blasien decided to curtail the special rights enjoyed by the inhabitants of the Hotzenwald (southern Black Forest) and reduce them to the status of serfs. Three revolts had to be crushed before the wars ended in 1755.

In 1803 the monasteries were secularised and church property was appropriated by the State. Under Napoleon's territorial reforms (Napoleon's successful campaign against Prussia enabled him to take control of large chunks of German territory) the Black Forest was divided between the House of Baden and the House of Württemberg.

From war to stability

In 1846 the construction of a railway line between Mannheim and Basle, through the Upper Rhine valley, provided the basis for the gradual development of tourism in the region.

In 1848 revolutions swept through Europe as a reaction against the economic distress and lack of democratic rights that characterised the post-Napoleonic era. In Germany the Grand Duchy of Baden was one of the hot-beds of liberal agitation. It was here, on the 12 April 1848, that Friedrich Hecker called for the establishment of a German Republic. In 1849 it came to fighting and Grand Duke Leopold of Baden was forced to flee. Hecker and the other revolutionary leader, Gustav Struve, attempted to establish

a republic in Baden, as a stepping stone to a united Germany. Their hopes were dashed, however, when Prussian troops came to the aid of the grand duke and finally crushed the revolution.

In 1918 after the abdication of Grand Duke Friedrich I of Baden and King Wilhelm II of Württemberg, the states of Baden and Württemberg emerge as democratic republics.

In World War II a number of Black Forest towns including Freiburg, Freudenstadt and Pforzheim were heavily bombed. At the end of the war American and French forces occupied the region.

The most important events in the peaceful years of the latter half of the twentieth century were of a mainly administrative nature. In 1952 the states of Baden and Württemberg (between which the Black Forest was divided), along with Württemberg-Hohenzollern, were joined to form the federal state of Baden-Württemberg. Between 1971 and 1974 local government was centralised around larger towns, which then managed the municipal affairs of surrounding towns and villages. These reforms were designed to cut administrative costs and resulted in towns with double names like Baiersbronn-Tonbach and Baiersbronn-Mitteltal.

Arts, Culture & Entertainment

Though most people come to the Black Forest to enjoy the beautiful natural scenery, the region also has a lot to offer in respect of cultural activities and museums – the most important museums are referred to in the tour descriptions. For instance, what could be more inspiring than listening to the strains of one of Bach's organ concertos within the walls of an ancient monastery? In June and July concerts are held in the monastery at Hirsau, classical music is performed at various times throughout the year at St Trudpert, in the Münstertal, and during the summer months the magnificent monastery church of St Blasien is the venue for the **Internationale Sommerkonzerte**. Those with a preference for modern avant-garde music can visit the **Donaueschinger Musiktage** in October, whereas friends of jazz will be able to listen to top musicians from Europe and America at the **Jazz Festival** (April) in Villingen-Schwenningen.

Of course it is the region's two big cities that can offer the most varied selection of entertainment. In Freiburg the cultural calendar is packed with events ranging from performances of ballet and modern dance to the staging of the **Internationales Zelt-Musik-Festival** in summer (June-July). Here one can listen to an exciting mixture of jazz, rock and classical music. Karlsruhe is also able to entertain it guests with operas, musicals and performances of classical music by internationally renowned artists. In May visitors can experience the delights of Baden's highly acclaimed cuisine at an open-air food festival known as the **Brigande-Feschd**. An important feature of Karlsruhe's cultural scene is the **Tollhaus**, a performing venue that was once a slaughterhouse! The building's excellent acoustics make it popular for rock and jazz concerts, but a disco and other events are held here as well.

Throughout the year one can expect some festival to be taking place in some town or village, somewhere in the Forest. In December traditional **Christmas markets** are held in just about every larger town, in January the entire region celebrates **Fasnet** (carnival), whereas wine festivals are held in the wine-growing region of Baden (the area along the Rhine) from June through to September. In the summer months many of the tourist resorts also arrange **Heimatabende**, that is evenings of traditional folk-dancing and songs.

Flora

Covering an area of 2,300sq miles (6,000sq km), of which two-thirds is forested, the Black Forest region is the largest area of continuous forest in Germany. Medieval monks, who were also the first to settle the interior, called these inhospitable mountains the *Silva nigra* (Black Forest). Today that name is more accurate than ever: around 80 per cent of the forest is composed of dark conifers, only 20 per cent of the total area is covered by deciduous trees. Just over 150 years ago the percentage of conifers stood at no more than 55 per cent. In other words the present composition of the forest is a direct result of centuries of human settlement and interference in the ecology of the region.

Among the few places where visitors can get an idea of the original vegetation are the areas of upland moor in the northern Black Forest (Hohlohsee) and in the Hotzenwald, in the southern Black Forest. For the most part one generally finds larger areas of deciduous forest in the south and at altitudes of between 1,650 and 3,300ft (500-1,000m).

The changing forest

To get a picture of the original forest vegetation one has to travel back some 10,000 years to the end of the last Ice Age. As the ice and snow slowly retreated the tundra-like landscape was at first covered by low growing bush vegetation. Gradually trees such as birch and pine started to appear on the mountain slopes. They were followed by a mixed oak forest that also included ash, elm and lime trees. As the climate got damper around 4000 BC large areas were covered by beech and pine. These were to be the predominant species in the upper regions until about 1000 AD, when settlement of the Black Forest gathered pace. The large areas of forest that disappeared during the colonising process were later replaced by fast growing firs. Today the fir, which in the original forest played only a minor role, is by far the most common type of tree.

Landscape near Gengenbach

Fauna

With all those trees it is not surprising that the Black Forest offers bird-watchers plenty of avian subjects for their binoculars. Among the more common species are coal tits, crested tits, black woodpeckers, tree-creepers, goldcrests and wood pigeons. Rarities include golden eagles, nutcrackers and the large capercaillie. Moving away from the higher forests an especially interesting area for bird-watching is the Taubergiessen Nature Reserve, north of Freiburg. Here one can find a great variety of waterfowl, many of which are migratory. In respect of plumage the kingfishers are the prettiest inhabitants of this riverine landscape, but huge flocks of bean geese, as well as such rare birds as the curlew, and Montagu's harrier, will keep wildlife enthusiasts busy for hours. The bee-eater, a bird otherwise more common in southern Europe, can be observed in the vicinity of the Kaiserstuhl, just west of Freiburg.

Visitors from North America will, no doubt, be somewhat disappointed by the lack of variety among the larger mammals. The last bear was shot in 1750, the last wolf was bagged in 1819 near the Mummelsee, and the last time anyone saw a lynx was way back in 1780. There are, however, plenty of deer and wild pigs, as well as badgers, foxes and hares. In the vicinity of the Feldberg and Belchen one can also see chamois. After having been exterminated they were reintroduced in the 1930s. A good overview of the fauna that was once present in the region is offered by the Bergwildpark Steinwasen, a zoo specialising in native animals between Kirchzarten and Todtnau.

Environmental issues

The average visitor probably would not notice it, but one of the gravest problems facing the Black Forest at present is *Waldsterben*. This is the term the Germans use to describe the gradual dying of the forests due to pollution. It is estimated that around 40 per cent of the region's trees are severely damaged. The first to suffer were the conifers and, later, various species of deciduous tree. The exact causes of Waldsterben are by no means fully understood, but aerial pollutants which lead to 'acid rain' are suspected to play a major

Black Forest in spring

role. Here the main culprit is not heavy industry, as many might expect, but car exhaust fumes.

The phenomenon was first brought to the attention of the public in the 1980s, when forestry experts noted that many conifers were shedding an unnaturally large amount of needles and, in some places, whole groups of trees had inexplicably died. It was the publicity surrounding this problem that accelerated the adoption of unleaded fuel and catalytic converters (all new cars sold in the country must be equipped with three-way catalytic converters) in Germany and sparked off a discussion about a speed limit on the motorways – which has yet to eventuate. Attempts to remedy the problem on a local level include the closing of the road to the Belchen summit on weekends and holidays (since 1990), the introduction of a 70km (just over 43mph) speed limit on the Schwarzwaldhochstrasse (B500) in 1995 and encouragement of the use of public transport. Happily the forest's condition has stabilised over the last few years, though no one can say exactly why and to what extent the above measures have helped.

But as was already suggested at the start of this topic, one usually has to be an expert to recognise the symptoms of Waldsterben, and for most the forests seem as unblemished and picturesque as ever. Especially on weekends people pour into the mountains from the outlying towns and cities to enjoy the possibilities for outdoor recreation. Unfortunately their sheer number at certain popular destinations has become a big problem in itself; too many cars, too much littering, and severe erosion caused by cyclists and hikers leaving the marked paths.

Conservation success

That both the needs of the natural environment and those of the tourists who have come to enjoy it can be satisfied, is proved by the example of the capercaillie on the Feldberg. These large, rare birds still manage to find the kind of habitat they need to survive in the general area of the mountain summit. In order to make sure it stays that way the local authorities have moved cross-country ski circuits and walking tracks away from their breeding areas. By concentrating recreational activities in certain, less critical areas, it is possible for the capercaillie, and other wildlife to remain undisturbed, while ensuring that skiers and hikers can still have their fun. In addition a ranger has been employed not only to make sure that people do not stray into restricted areas, but also to educate them on the need for nature conservation.

Food and drink

Centuries of cross-cultural influences have left their mark not only on the language and traditions of the Black Forest but also on its cuisine. This is most obvious in the wine-growing towns and villages bordering the Rhine, where cooking is regarded as a fine art, as in France, and dining out is part of the lifestyle. With this in mind it is small wonder that the Forest is regarded as a regional culinary paradise, attracting gourmets and wine-lovers from far and wide.

Food

However, one need not fear that a meal with a glass of wine will empty one's wallet. Though the Black Forest has borrowed some of the ingredients for its cooking from the Swiss and French, it has not put the same price on it. Dining out in a good local restaurant is significantly cheaper than it is across the border. Even if one decides against one of the famed gourmet establishments, one can be usually sure of a good meal. In fact those who wish to sample dishes cooked in the traditional way will find that an ordinary *Gasthaus* offering *Gutbürgerliche* (home-style) or *Badische Spezialitäten* (traditional cooking from the Rhine region) one of the best bets.

The Black Forest can offer dozens of delicious specialities but one of the most commonly served (in nearby Alsace as well) is the *Flammkuchen*. This consists of a base of thinly rolled yeast dough upon which a mixture of crème fraîche, onions and chopped bacon is sprinkled. Baked in an oven like a pizza it is often eaten as a snack, but some are so large they would be more than enough for lunch or dinner. Other specialities include *Spätzle* and *Knöpfle*, both of which are a kind of pasta served with main meals, *Schäufele* (smoked shoulder of pork) and *Flädelsuppe* (a broth with strips of pancake added to it). Often eaten with a glass of *Federweisser* (new wine) is a slice of *Zwiebelkuchen* (onion tart).

Of course with all those mountains and woods many restaurants also offer wild game on their menus. Depending on the season one can expect venison, wild pork, rabbit or wild duck and partridge. A real classic is *Schwarzwald Forelle* (Black Forest trout), which is offered throughout the region, but especially in restaurants found along the mountain valleys.

Something else which is offered in many restaurants is a cold snack known as a *Vesper*. This usually consists of a variety of German sausages, thinly cut slices of Black Forest ham and a few slices of bread served on a round wooden board. Often a glass of schnapps is served with it. Originally Vesper was only eaten in the afternoons, after a day's work, but now it can be eaten at any time of the day.

Those who are doing their own cooking will find the local street-markets (where the vegetables are freshest) and the various supermarkets quite reasonably priced. Worth trying if one can find a good *Metzger* (butcher) is the famous *Schwarzwälder Schinken* (Black Forest ham) – ask locals or at the Tourist Office for possible tips. If it is properly prepared (beware of the vacuum-packed varieties in tourist shops) this smoked ham can taste very good. The best quality hams need to be cured for at least 4 months or even better a whole year.

Drink

Though the Germans are most fond of their coffee (preferably strong) many also drink tea, either black or with a squirt of lemon-juice. Visitors who like milk with their tea or coffee will find that the restaurants and cafés usually offer it as evaporated milk – one can always try and *(cont'd on page 20)*

Cafes and restaurants line Freiburg's Münsterplatz

A simple but delicious lunch consisting of Flammkuchen with a glass of wine is as typical of Alsace as it is of the Black Forest

Calw, Northern Black Forest

FAMILY HOLIDAYS IN THE FOREST

Happy children generally mean happy parents and if the whole family enjoyed its holiday they are more likely to come back again some time. This is a fact that many tourist resorts in the Black Forest have long since recognised. In a competition held in the state of Baden-Württemberg (to which the Black Forest region belongs), to decide which towns offered the best facilities for family holidays, 9 of the 12 winners came from the Black Forest: Baiersbronn, Feldberg, Grafenhausen, Lenzkirch, Lossburg, Schluchsee, Schönwald, Seebach and Unterkirnach.

The above mentioned towns offer, among other things, organised activities for children, price reductions for families and some even have (during the summer holiday season) a baby-sitting service. Also important is that they have a wide range of reasonably priced accommodation, away from busy roads. However, many other towns like Hinterzarten and Wolfach also offer organised activities for children, along with hotels that especially welcome families.

A tip

Enzklösterle, in the northern Black Forest (Route 3, Chapter 1), offers visiting families free kindergarten facilities for children aged between 3 and 6 years. More information about these and other towns offering 'family friendly' facilities can be obtained from the Schwarzwald Tourismus-verband (see FactFile).

Swimming at Nagoldstausee

ask for *frische Milch* (fresh milk) instead. In cafés it is becoming more common to offer *Milchkaffee* (like the French *café au lait*), which is made with milk instead of water and is much less strong than normal percolated coffee. *Kaffee Haag*, a brand of decaffeinated coffee, is also widely available. Herbal tea is known in German as *Kräutertee*.

Wine and schnapps have been dealt with elsewhere but it is worthwhile mentioning the local beers, which are also very good. Among the most well-known local brands are *Alpirsbacher Klosterbräu* (northern Black Forest) and *Fürstenberg Pilsner*, a good pils (lager) beer from the vicinity of Donaueschingen. Worth sipping in the Freiburg area is beer bottled by the Riegeler brewery. For their popular *Felsen Pils*, and other beers, they use spring water that is so pure it requires no further treatment before being added to the other ingredients. Note that in restaurants and bars beer is served chilled but not ice-old. Fresh from the tap is *'vom Fass'*.

Geography & geology

The Black Forest region is part of the federal state of Baden-Württemberg, in south-western Germany. The region stretches 100 miles (160km) from north to south and 18 to 37 miles (30 to 60km) from west to east. To the west it is bordered by Alsace, in France, to the south by Switzerland. Adjoining the region to the east is an area of hills known as the Swabian Alb (or Jura). Flowing along the area bordering Switzerland and France is the river Rhine.

The present mountains of the Black Forest and those of the Vosges, to the west of the River Rhine, owe their existence to the gargantuan forces that formed the Alps and caused what is now the Upper Rhine Plain to slowly sink a total of 8,200ft (2,500m). The sinking of such a large mass of rock resulted in the accumulation of tremendous pressure in the earth's crust, which was compensated for by pushing the rock layers that bordered the fault (the Vosges and the Black Forest) upwards. This process began some 45 million years ago and the deep valley that it produced has long since been filled with sediments carried by the Rhine and its tributaries.

'What goes up must come down' is a law that seems to apply to geological processes as much as it does to gravitation. Apart from the wind and rain that immediately began gnawing at the mountain peaks, the greatest leveling factor was the last Ice Age, which began some 2 million years ago. Large glaciers covered the region, gouging out valleys and rounding once craggy peaks. Relics of this period of glaciation are the small tarns (glacially formed lakes) in the northern Black Forest and the lakes known as Titisee, Schluchsee and Feldsee in the south.

As far as the underlying rocks are concerned the bedrock is mainly composed of granite and gneiss, with broad bands of red sandstone appearing in the north and east. The southern region is bordered by a narrow band of more fertile limestone. As has already been mentioned, the mountain tops are characteristically rounded with the highest peaks being in the south. The highest of all, in a range that only achieves modest altitudes, is the

Feldberg. Peaks in the northern part of the Forest have an average height of around 2,000ft (606m).

Politics

Germany is divided politically into sixteen *Länder* (federal states) and the Black Forest is a mountain region within the federal state of Baden-Württemberg. Baden-Württemberg is further divided into four administrative districts, two of which divide the Black Forest between them: Nordbaden with its capital at Karlsruhe and Südbaden with its capital at Freiburg.

Traditionally Baden-Württemberg is politically conservative and the CDU (Union of Christian Democrats) has held power on its own, or in coalition with the SPD (Social Democrats) or FDP (Free Democrats), since the state came into existence in 1952. The present state government is led by a coalition between the CDU and FDP. The capital of Baden-Württemberg is Stuttgart.

Economy

The forest has always been one of the region's major assets and in earlier times the dark woods provided a livelihood for charcoal-burners, pitch-makers and the strapping men who once floated great rafts of logs down the rivers for eventual sale in far-off Holland. These old professions have long since disappeared, but forestry and woodworking continue to play a significant role in the local economy.

Traditional crafts that have survived the passage of years include glassblowing (though it is of only minor significance today), woodcarving and the manufacture of cuckoo clocks. It was from the cottage industries of woodcarving and cuckoo clock manufacture that the factory based clock-making industry was able to develop in the nineteenth century. The most important modern clock-making factories are found today in Schramberg and Villingen-Schwenningen. It was the firm of Junghans in Schramberg that developed the world's first radio-controlled wristwatch in 1990 – a long step forward from the rustic, wooden cuckoo clock!

Agriculture is a significant factor in the valleys and on the plains and slopes bordering the Rhine. Most obvious for the visitor are the extensive vineyards which cover a total of 58,000sq miles (15,000ha), making this wine-growing region the third largest in Germany. Market gardening and fruit growing are also widespread. Around places like Bühl in the north, and the Kaiserstuhl in the south, are large orchards of plums, cherries and apples. The higher regions are generally reserved for grazing dairy cows and cattle rearing.

After its beginnings in the nineteenth century tourism has grown to become the most important economic factor in the region. At first it was restricted to the thermal and mineral springs at places like Baden-Baden and Badenweiler, but with improved road and rail connections it has long since spread throughout the entire Forest. With around 6 million visitors per year the Black Forest is one of Germany's most popular holiday destinations.

A picturesque corner of Oberkirch

The northern Black Forest is a region strewn with ancient monastery ruins, lonely mountain lakes and idyllic valleys. Here the clear streams can still tumble unhindered over green, moss-covered boulders and isolated wayside inns entice with rustic interiors and local specialities.

It is also a region of contrasts; in the far north is the busy city of Karlsruhe, once the residence of the powerful margraves of Baden; in the mountainous central area the larger towns are absent, only small villages dot the forested flanks of the lower slopes. On the western and eastern fringes, old spa towns attract with their spacious parks and health-giving thermal pools. In places like Baden-Baden, where taking the waters has been a tradition since Roman times, the pools are housed in luxurious buildings of truly palatial dimensions. Here every visitor can feel like a king, at least for an hour or two. Last, but not least, a trip along the northern section of the Baden Wine Road will reveal the sunny side of the mountains; quaint little villages surrounded by vineyards and plum and cherry orchards that transform the slopes into a sea of blossom in the spring.

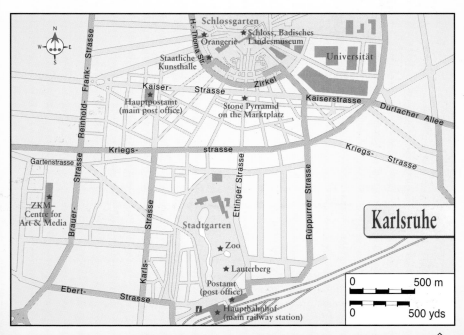

Route 1 — BAROQUE TOWNS OF THE NORTH (circular route)

Karlsruhe

At the northern edge of the Black Forest the small city of **Karlsruhe** (population: 276,000) is first stop for those who travel south from Frankfurt's international airport. It is nationally important as the seat of the highest German courts; the Bundesverfassungsgericht (Federal Constitutional Court) and the Bundesgerichtshof (Federal Court of Justice). There are a number of other government institutions located here as well but those who fear a stuffy city populated by hordes of brief-case swinging civil servants need not fear; Karlsruhe University, and several other tertiary institutions, bring with them the typically relaxed atmosphere associated with most university towns.

Though primarily known for its important trade fair, Karlsruhe has much to offer visitors in the form of some outstanding museums, an excellent zoo, an extensive cultural programme, many good restaurants, and a wide range of accommodation from youth hostel and camping ground to first-class hotels. No less important, it serves as a strategic location for excursions to various places of interest in the northern Black Forest.

Schloss

A glance at a map of Karlsruhe reveals the city's most characteristic feature; in the middle of the city 32 streets radiate from the **Schloss** (palace), like the ribs of a fan. This distinctive example of Baroque town planning reflects the absolutist ideals of the time. When Margrave Karl Wilhelm of Baden-Durlach founded Karlsruhe in 1715, he had the illustrious example of Versailles in mind. According to this model a palace should be placed in the middle of a town and all streets should lead to it. This stressed its dominant position and the power of the rulers who lived there. The creator of this symbol of princely self-aggrandisement now lies buried below a **stone pyramid** in the Marktplatz (Market Square), not far from the Schloss.

Today the Schloss houses the **Badisches Landesmuseum** (Baden State Museum) with impressive collections on pre- and early history, Egyptian, Greek and Roman art, folklore, and an interesting collection of war trophies brought back from the Turkish campaigns of Margrave Ludwig Wilhelm of Baden (also known as 'Louis the Turk'). A visit here can be combined with the ascent of the **Schlossturm** (Schloss Tower), as it allows an excellent bird's-eye view of the town's fan-shaped plan.

The Schloss lies in the middle of the **Schlossgarten**, a spacious park in the English manner. On muggy days in summer it is a popular retreat for the locals, who come to cool off under the trees, or to go for a ride on a miniature railway known as the **Schlossgartenbähnle**. At the south-west edge of the park is one of Germany's principal picture galleries, the **Staatliche Kunsthalle** (State Art Gallery).

Staatliche Kunsthalle & Orangerie

Housed here are important works of early German painting, along with French and Dutch paintings from the seventeenth and eighteenth centuries. Artists represented include Grünewald (the creator of the famous altar in Colmar), Grien, Dürer, Holbein the Younger, Lucas Cranach, Rubens, Rembrandt and Caspar David Friedrich. The landscape painter Hans Thoma, who was director of the gallery from 1899-1919, has a section to himself. Nearby, in the **Orangerie**, is the modern department with works by such artists as Gauguin, Courbet, Cézanne, Kandinsky, Kokoschka, Miro and Otto Dix. Interesting for families is the **Kindermuseum** (Children's Museum) with an arts and crafts and painting room.

Zoo

In 1865 a group of local poultry farmers bought a swampy section of land near the present main railway station and populated it with their geese, ducks and pheasants. Later various species of deer were added and, as time went by, all sorts of exotic animals joined them. Today the genesis from chicken shed to zoological garden can be described as a great success. In beautiful park surroundings you can now admire 150 different species from all over the world.

Apart from viewing polar bears, lions and elephants you can also paddle boats on the park's waterways, play mini-golf or let the kid's burn off excess energy in the adventure playground. All in all, the zoo is a great place to relax after doing *(cont'd on page 28)*

Where Art Meets Cyberspace
ZKM – Centre for Art and Media

Located in what used to be a munitions factory, the huge **ZKM** complex consists of two museums and a Mediathek. Opened in 1997 it is, without a doubt, a highlight of any visit to Karlsruhe. It is a hands-on museum in the best sense of the word, with numerous interactive displays that invite both adults and children alike to explore the world of modern art in a way not possible in most museums. In the **Medienmuseum** (Media Museum) you can cycle through virtual worlds, stimulate growth in real plants or participate in an interactive art gallery. The **Museum für neue Kunst** (Museum of Contemporary Art) is one of the biggest media art collections in the world. Along with contemporary paintings, sculptures and photography, are the works of important media artists like Nam June Paik, Garry Hill and Bill Viola. After a walk through the museums you can sit down in the **Mediathek** and listen to electronic music or watch one of a thousand works of modern video art.

The Westweg (West Route) is the most popular and most ambitious long-distance walk through the Black Forest.

In a minimum of 11 days the hiker traverses approximately 175 miles (280km) of mountainous terrain between Pforzheim in the north-east and Basle (Switzerland) in the south-west. This strenuous route takes you along dark forest trails, through farm meadows, past lonely upland moors and mountain lakes. On its journey south the trail also ascends the region's highest peaks (Feldberg, Belchen and Blauen), all of which offer grandiose views towards the Swiss Alps and over the Rhine plain to the Vosges mountains in France. A total of 19,700ft (6,000m) is climbed, with the lowest point at Hausach (781ft/238m) and the highest on the Feldberg (4,898ft/1,493m). For the most part one is alone with nature; of the 14 small towns and villages that lie along the route a few are only touched on their outskirts.

Though this walk includes no peaks of alpine magnitude, some sections involve a series of steep ups and downs that require a good degree of fitness. Those who want to do the entire walk in the usual 11 days should bear in mind that each day one has to cover distances of between 13 and 20 miles (21 to 33km). That means walking for 6 to 9½ hours at a stretch. If you are unfit and are also lugging a heavy pack that can be a bit uncomfortable.

FOOT – THE WESTWEG

However, you do not have to be an Olympic athlete to complete this walk. If time is not a problem then it is much more comfortable to do the walk in say 14 or 15 days. This gives you more leisure to enjoy the scenery and chat with other walkers along the trail. Those with limited time can of course just do parts of the route, perhaps saving the rest for another holiday. Particularly attractive is the stretch between Mummelsee and Hotel Alexanderschanze (Kniebis).

Accommodation on the walk is in mountain-top hotels or cosy bed and breakfasts (*Privatzimmer/Pension*) in the small towns along the way. Some of these places offer *Wandern ohne Gepäck* (walking without luggage), which is by far the most comfortable way to do the Westweg. The *Gasthöfe* offering this service will deliver your gear to the next place where you plan to spend the night. Usually there is a set price (it can range from 20 to 80 German marks) for the luggage transport, which means that it is cheaper if you are in a group. A compromise would be to only take advantage of this service on particularly long or rugged sections of the walk. It can also be a good idea to post a package with fresh clothes to a hotel (notify them of your intentions first!) at the end of the walk. Cardboard boxes for this purpose can be bought at German post offices.

The various stages for the 11-day walk are:

- Pforzheim to Dobel, 13^1/$_2$ miles (22km);
- Dobel to Forbach, 15^1/$_2$ miles (25km);
- Forbach to Mummelsee, 15 miles (24km);
- Mummelsee to Kniebis, 14 miles (23km);
- Kniebis to Hausach, 20^1/$_2$ miles (33km);
- Hausach to Schonach, 13 miles (21km);
- Schonach to Thurner, 18 miles (29km);
- Thurner to Feldberg, 14 miles (23km);
- Feldberg to Multen, 15 miles (24km);
- Multen to Kandern, 18 miles (29km);
- Kandern to Basle, 15 miles (24km).

Those who want to discover the region's most secluded spots will have to put on their walking boots

(cont'd overleaf)

The whole route is clearly waymarked by a red diamond on a white ground. Nevertheless, good walking maps are useful for finding short-cuts or identifying alternative routes. The best are those published by the Landesvermessungsamt Baden-Württemberg in conjunction with the Schwarzwaldverein (Black Forest Walking Club). They have a scale of 1:50,000 and 5 *Blätter* (sheets) are required for the complete walk: **Karte des Schwarzwaldvereins Blatt 1** Karlsruhe – Pforzheim; **Blatt 2** Baden-Baden – Hornisgrinde; **Blatt 5** Freudenstadt – Schramberg; **Blatt 7** Triberg – Donaueschingen; **Blatt 8** Belchen – Wiesental.

Detailed information on the various types of accommodation and luggage transport on the Westweg can be obtained (at a moderate cost) from Touristik Nördlicher Schwarzwald (see FactFile). The Westweg is also described in the book *Walking in the Black Forest* by Fleur and Colin Speakman, published by Cicerone Press.

a round of the city's museums. What is more, you also have a great view over Karlsruhe from atop a hill within the zoo's precincts known as the **Lauterberg**.

Ettlingen

Just to the south of Karlsruhe is Ettlingen, a pleasant town which Margravine Augusta Sibylla of Baden-Baden (the wife of Louis the Turk) chose as the site for a **Schloss**. Now used as a concert hall, the former Schloss chapel was decorated by the best fresco painter of his time, Cosmas Damian Assam. His ceiling fresco depicts the life and death of Saint Nepomuk with the lavish detail and bright hues so typical of Baroque art. Also located in the Schloss are two art galleries, a local history museum and a collection of valuable Chinese and Japanese arts and crafts.

Apart from the Baroque Rathaus, with its 164ft (50m) high tower, other buildings of note include the

Was Aeneas here?

Virgil, author of the Latin classic '*The Aeneid*', would have been surprised and Homer certainly knew nothing about it: an inscription on a wall of the **Rathaus** (Town Hall) claims that the town was founded in 1111 BC by Trojans under the leadership of Aeneas. Well, even the town authorities consider this a bit unlikely and readily admit that it was just an attempt by the theologist and Latin scholar Caspar Hedio (1494-1552) to borrow some of the glory of ancient Greece for his home town. It is true, however, that the Romans were here as excavations have uncovered the remains of a small settlement.

St Martinskirche (in its present form eighteenth century), and the lovely half-timbered houses at Kirchplatz 2-4. The fountain with a figure of St George on it in front of the Rathaus is from the late Gothic period. St George has been revered since the time of the crusades and often appears in southern Germany as patron saint of town market rights.

Though the majority of visitors come to Ettlingen during the popular festival of classical music held in the Schloss in summer, it would make a nice alternative base for those who prefer something smaller and quieter than Karlsruhe. From May an added attraction is the historic steam train that runs along the **Albtalbahn** (Alb Valley Line) from here to Bad Herrenalb.

Pforzheim

Pforzheim is reached on the road going via **Ellmendingen**. The modern face the town now presents to visitors offers little in the way of picturesque sights: in one night of intensive bombing in 1945 over 17,000 people died and the town was almost completely flattened. Twin town is Guernica, in Spain, a place that suffered a similar fate in 1937. Today Pforzheim has international importance as a place where gold, silver and gems are fashioned into exquisite necklaces, rings and other objects of personal adornment. The town exports its costly wares to over 160 countries, thus accounting for 80 per cent of the overseas jewel trade in Germany.

In a town where gold and jewels are of such overriding importance it is not surprising to hear that the **Schmuckmuseum** in Reuchlin-Haus is the most important museum. On display here are rings, brooches and necklaces from antiquity to the present day. Especially interesting is a collection of rings spanning some 4,000 years. One of the most valuable was worn by Pharaoh Amenhotep III.

Those who want to see how watches and jewels are made can visit the **Technisches Museum** at Bleichstrasse 81. At the **Edelstein-Ausstellung Schütt** you are not confined to just looking at all the valuables made from precious and semi-precious stones, you can buy them. It is conveniently located just opposite Reuchlin-Haus.

A worthwhile detour south-east from Pforzheim is to **Tiefenbronn**. Here the Catholic **Pfarrkirche St Maria Magdalena** is the outstanding attraction. Inside the parish church are wall paintings and stained glass windows from around 1400, but it is above all the altar painting (1432) by Lukas Moser that is of interest. Considered the most beautiful example of late Gothic painting in southern Germany, it is the only one of his works to have survived. Depicted on the altar are scenes from life of Mary Magdalene.

South to Bad Herrenalb

Continue south from Pforzheim to Neuenbürg, on the B294, then go via Straubenhardt to **Marxzell-Pfaffenrot**. Located here, in what used to be a sawmill, is the **Fahrzeugmuseum** (Motor Vehicle Museum). With a collection of over 70 vintage cars and more than 200 motorcycles most old-timer fans will be kept happy for quite awhile. Highlights include a 1957

Northern Black Forest

Badisches Landesmuseum
Staatliche Kunsthalle
and Orangerie
Zoo
ZKM

Karlsruhe

B293 · Bretten · B35 · Maulbronn

B294

Schloss

FRANCE

Freiheitsmuseum
Schloss
Wehrgeschichtliches Museum

Ettlingen · A8

Langensteinbach · B10

Caracalla-Therme
Casino
Friedrichsbad
Kloster Lichtental
Roman Bath
Stadtgeschichtliche Sammlung
Stiftskirche
Trinkhalle

Schloss Favorite
and Eremitage

Rastatt

A5

Fahrzeugmuseum
Kuppenheim

Kloster Frauenalb
Klosterkirche
Spielzeugmuseum

Ellmendingen
Marxzell-Pfaffenrot
Neuenbürg

Edelstein-Austellung
Schütt

Pforzheim

Kloster Frauenalb
Bad Herrenalb

Pfarrkirche St Maria
Magdalena · Tiefenbronn

Nouvelle
Schömberg

Bad Liebenzell

Rheinmünster-
Schwarzach

Baden-Baden

Varnhalt · Lichtental
Steinbach
Neuweier

Gernsbach · Palais Thermal
Bad Wildbad ★
Wildsee &
Hornsee ★

Calmbach · Schömberg
B296

Oberreichenbach · Hirsau

Klostermuseum

B296

Bühl

Affental

Alt-Windeck
Bühlerhöle
Sand

Ottersweier

Lauf

Kaltenbronn
Hohlohsee
Forbach
Enzklösterle

Hirsau

Achern

Sasbachwalden

Schwarzenbachtalsperre
Raumünzach

Bad Teinach-
Zavelstein

Hermann-Hesse-Mus
Museum der Stadt C

Calw

Kentheim

Kappelrodeck
Waldulm

Hornisgrinde
★ Mummelsee

Poppeltal

Neubulach

Besucherbergwerk
'Hella-Glück-Stollen'

B296

Wildberg

Ottenhöffen
Heimatmuseum

Oberkirch · Lautenbach · Allerheiligen

★ Wildsee
Ruhestein

Schwarzenburg

Museum

Nagoldstausee

Altensteig

B28

Nagold

B28

Durbach

Oppenau

Mitteltal
Zuflucht

Kloster
Tonbach Reichenbach

Erzgrube
Kälberbronn

Baiersbronn

B28

Offenburg

B28 · Freudenstadt

Mercedes-Benz 220 with 100hp and a 1930 Model A Ford coupé with 40hp. Apart from all this there are also old trams, tractors, locomotives and other technical devices to be seen.

Appropriately enough the museum is dedicated to the memory of Karl Benz (1844-1929), the inventor behind the name of Germany's world-famous Mercedes-Benz motorcars. In 1885 he built the first car with an internal combustion engine. In the 1990s Daimler-Benz merged with the American Chrysler Company to form Daimler-Chrysler, one of the largest automobile firms in the world. Though Benz was born in Karlsruhe his family originally came from this small Black Forest village.

Kloster Frauenalb

Further south from Marxzell are the ruins of the Benedictine **Kloster Frauenalb**. For over 600 years the nuns of Frauenalb were the rulers of Marxzell and the surrounding communities. As was often the case in past centuries the Kloster was not only a place of worship, but also controlled large estates, therefore making the abbess a person with considerable power. The local villages were not only obliged to pay tithes (usually in the form of agricultural produce)

Baroque Schloss at Karlsruhe

The nicely situated spa town of **Bad Herrenalb** is quickly reached from Frauenalb. Of historic interest in the middle of town is the ruin of

but were also under the abbess's jurisdiction. All this came to an end when the Kloster was secularised in 1803 and became the property of the state of Baden. After being used as a cloth factory, then a brewery, a large part of the building complex was destroyed by fire. Still impressive are the ruins of the monastery church, which was built in the Baroque style by Peter Thumb (1681-1766), one of the most famous architects of his time.

an old Cistercian **Klosterkirche** (monastery church) from the twelfth century. These ruins, along with the photogenic **Hotel Post**, and some noble-looking Art Nouveau villas, would justify at least a short stop. However, if time permits it would also be worthwhile having a look at the **Spielzeugmuseum** (Toy Museum). Housed in one of the town's Art Nouveau villas, the museum has an excellent collection of dolls' houses and other toys. Especially remarkable is a doll's kitchen from 1890, made of oak, and with a stove that can actually be heated! On the last weekend in August there is a *Bahnhofsfest* (Railway Festival), a major attraction of which are rides on the Albtalbahn steam train.

Kuppenheim lies just to the southeast of Rastatt. From Bad Herrenalb the town is reached via Gernsbach (for a description see Route 3) on the B462. Though there is nothing of interest to see in Kuppenheim itself, a short detour from town will bring you to **Schloss Favorite.**

Schloss Favorite

This small Baroque Schloss (1710-12) was built as a summer residence for Margravine Sibylla Augusta of Baden, a few years after the death of her husband Margrave Ludwig Wilhelm I (Louis the Turk). The main interest of the building itself lies in its magnificently furnished interior. Although the Margravine intended to devote herself to religious contemplation at this retreat, she did not find it necessary to dispense with her lavish way of life. Sumptuously decorated rooms that are especially worthy of attention include the **Speisesaal** (dining hall), the **Prunkküche** (kitchen) and the living chambers. Also noteworthy is a valuable collection of porcelain and Bohemian glass. In the ground-floor kitchen there are some fine tureens made of faience, a kind of tin-glazed earthenware from France.

Near the Schloss, which is situated in a lovely park, are four **cavalier's houses** and the **Eremitage** (hermitage). Devout as she was the Margravine used to visit the hermitage from time to time to do penance. As though to make up for the pomp of her living quarters, it is decorated in a rather sombre fashion with various religious motifs.

Rastatt

In **Rastatt** it is once again a **Schloss** (1697-1705) belonging to Louis the Turk and his wife that forms the central attraction. Like many potentates of his time the Margrave wanted to reproduce the splendour of French châteaux in his own domain. The result was a Baroque Schloss that was the first and most exact copy of Versailles to be built in Germany. A (guided) tour through the opulently furnished rooms, with their intricate stuccowork and magnificent ceiling frescoes, offers a glimpse into a world of extravagant luxury. The stucco figures representing Turkish prisoners of war in the **Festsaal** (festival hall) are reminders of the Margrave's glorious victories against the Ottoman Turks.

On the ground-floor of the Schloss are two museums, though it is probably the **Wehrgeschichtliches Museum** (Museum of Military History) that is of most interest to foreign visitors. Here one can see everything from medieval halberds to modern weapons of war. In a large diorama is a representation of the battle at Slankamen (1691), which was fought against the Turks. Also of interest is a large-scale model of a trench from World War I. The **Freiheitsmuseum** (Freedom Museum) is dedicated to the liberation movements which have occurred in German history. Particular emphasis is given to the Revolution of 1848, as it was in Rastatt that the revolutionaries were finally defeated.

From Rastatt the B3 leads back to Ettlingen and Karlsruhe. However, those who wish can take the road south to join the start of **Route 2** at Baden-Baden.

Route 2 NORTHERN SECTION OF THE BADEN WINE ROAD AND THE BLACK FOREST SUMMIT ROAD (circular route)

Baden-Baden

Spring is a good time to visit this spa, which lies nestled between forested hills. At this time of the year the large crowds have not yet arrived and, if the weather is fine, the town is bathed in a clear, soft light that best complements its dignified buildings and spacious parks. There are

Baden-Baden's history

The Romans were the first to appreciate the healing qualities (and warmth) of the town's springs which gurgle up from the depths at a temperature of 156°F (69°C). Below the imposing structure of the nineteenth century **Friedrichsbad** are in fact the restored remains of a **Roman bath** from the first to third centuries. However, a visit here need not end with a dry excursion into antiquity, as the Friedrichsbad houses one of the most splendid mineral baths in Europe. Here visitors can bathe away their aches and pains in a luxurious setting that recalls the town's heyday in the 'belle époque', when kings and emperors took the waters in what was styled 'Europe's Summer Capital'.

It may seem strange that such a small Black Forest town, populated as it was by simple farmers and tradesmen, became a preferred haunt of the rich and famous. The explanation lies in the aftermath of the French Revolution. French nobility, fleeing the guillotine, found the town's surroundings congenial and decided on it as their place of exile. In 1830 a second wave arrived, this time to escape a cholera epidemic in Paris. These cultivated aristocrats laid a solid basis for the establishment of a genteel spa town. The building of a casino in 1838 heralded the spa's rise to international prominence. Illustrious guests included Otto von Bismarck, Brahms, Wagner, Nietzsche, and even Queen Victoria spent time here. With the visit of Kaiser Franz-Joseph of Austria, the Russian Czar Alexander and Napoleon III in 1863 Baden-Baden attained the height of its fame.

Though the spa is no longer a meeting place of European princes and diplomats, it still has an aura of exclusiveness about it. The rich have not left, in fact more millionaires live in Baden-Baden than anywhere else in Germany. Even today there are still plenty of top-class hotels, like **Brenner's Park-Hotel**, awaiting the arrival of visitors with heavy wallets. A walk around town reveals that shops selling expensive Italian suits and Rolex watches are common enough. But wealth is not flaunted to the extent that visitors need feel uncomfortable. It is more often only glimpsed in the form of a Porsche parked by a noble restaurant, an old lady with her two pedigree dogs, or an expensive price-tag in the window of an otherwise modest shop front.

numerous hot springs in the Black Forest around which spa towns have grown, but none of them have become as famous as Baden-Baden. In this respect things have not changed much since the time when Mark Twain made his visit, back in the 1870s. In '*A Tramp Abroad*' he wrote:

'Baden-Baden sits in the lap of the hills, and the natural and artificial beauties of the surroundings are combined effectively and charmingly. The level strip of ground which stretches through and beyond town is laid out in handsome pleasure grounds, shaded by noble trees and adorned at intervals with lofty and sparkling fountain-jets.'

Sightseeing

Perhaps the best way to get a feeling for the place, is to first go for a short stroll through the park flanking the **Lichtentaler Allee**. It begins at Goethe Platz, in the middle of town, near the theatre and Kurhaus. Planted with exotic trees and flowers it is especially pretty in spring, when the rhododendrons are in flower. Over the years artists, princes and kings have walked this path, which follows the Oos stream to **Lichtental**, about 1 mile (1.6km) away. On the opposite bank of the river there are a number of noble-looking health clinics and hotels in park-like settings.

Kurhaus and casino

The **Kurhaus** (1821-22) with its attached casino is the town's focal point. From the outside the **casino** looks rather disappointing; painted a bright white and with neo-classical columns fronting it, it does not seem to justify its reputation as being the world's most beautiful place to lose money. On entering,

Baden-Baden's health-giving mineral waters can be tasted at the Trinkhalle

Pleasant cafes provide a break from sight-seeing

however, one is almost over-whelmed by the splendid interior with its magnificent paintings, chandeliers, sculptures and rooms decorated in red and gold.

Though the casino can be visited on a guided tour in the mornings it is best experienced at night, when the gaming-tables are opened. Nobody is required to gamble, all that is necessary to enter is a suit and tie for the men and appropriate dress for women (no jeans). Equipped with a glass of champagne you can thus admire the interior and watch the guests trying their luck at games like blackjack, baccarat and roulette. It was here, in Germany's oldest and largest casino, that Fyodor Dostoyevsky, himself a compulsive gambler, gathered impressions for his novel *'The Gambler'*.

Trinkhalle

The Trinkhalle is only a short walk through the park from the Kurhaus and casino. Its impressive façade is composed of Corinthian pillars that provide support for a 295 ft (90m) long covered walk, a sort of monu-mental porch in front of the main building. Its walls are decorated with large murals illustrating scenes from local myth and legend. Inside visitors can try the health giving waters, just as Mark Twain did, when he visited Baden-Baden in the 1870s. Here he proved himself no better than any other tourist and ended up paying far too much for his glass of warm medicinal water.

Caracalla-Therme

If you would rather swim in the local waters than drink them, then the best address is the **Caracalla-Therme**. Only a short walk from the town's pedestrian zone this is one of Europe's most attractive pool and bath complexes – there is even an exact copy of the Caracalla-Therme in Japan. It was built in the 1980s to replace the old Augustabad. Indoor and outdoor pools, thermal pools, saunas and solariums, together with a stylish interior, provide all the ingredients necessary for a few relaxing hours.

Stiftskirche & Neues Schloss

On the Marktplatz, close to the Friedrichsbad, is the **Stiftskirche** (collegiate church). The interior is dominated by an 18ft (5$^1/_2$m) high sandstone crucifix (1467) by the Dutch master Nikolaus von Leyden. Also of interest are some impressive tombs in the choir, the most splendid of which belongs to Margrave Ludwig Wilhelm I (1655-1707). He was also known as Louis the Turk because of his victorious campaign against the Turks in 1683. Appropriately enough his tomb is decorated with emblems and allegories relating to his greatest military success.

The climb up to the **Neues Schloss** (1437) is rewarded with lovely views over town. The castle was once the residence of the margraves of Baden, but they moved their seat to nearby Rastatt after marauding French troops ransacked Baden-Baden in 1689. Located here is the **Stadtgeschichtliche Sammlung** (Municipal Historical Collection), which includes archaeological finds from the days of Roman settlement.

The outskirts of town

The castle ruins of **Burg Hohenbaden** (also known as Altes Schloss) stand on a hill called the **Battert**, on the northern edge of town. From the tower there are great views over Baden-Baden, the Rhine lowlands and as far as the Vosges mountains. The castle courtyard has quite a romantic feel to it and if you are feeling hungry there is also a restaurant here.

Also a good place for views is the **Merkur** (2,191ft/668m), a hill a short drive east of town. The name derives from a Roman votive tablet, dedicated to the god Mercury, that was discovered here. The quickest way up is with the funicular, but there are plenty of waymarked trails to the top for those who prefer to walk.

Along the Baden Wine Road (Badische Weinstrasse)

Leaving Baden-Baden on Fremersbergstrasse (following the Baden Wine Road from town) in the direction of **Varnhalt** one enters a small wine-growing region known as the **Baden-Badener Rebland**. Along with Varnhalt the other wine-growing villages here are **Steinbach** and **Neuweier**. Each of these villages possesses a rural charm of its own, in stark contrast to the more worldly flair of Baden-Baden itself. Wines produced here include Riesling, Spätburgunder and Weissherbst, a rosé wine. All three villages have the right to fill their wine into the *Bocksbeutel* , as this wide, rounded bottle is known. Otherwise this is only permitted in Franconia, in Bavaria. Good restaurants, idyllic surroundings, and plenty of opportunities to sample the local wine, might tempt many visitors to stay a little longer than they planned.

An interesting detour west of Steinbach is to the **Klosterkirche** (monastery church) at **Rheinmünster-Schwarzach**. Built in the thirteenth century this Romanesque church has been restored to its original, medieval form. Visitors used to the sombre grey stone found in many churches will be surprised by the vivid tones that have been used here to decorate the capitals. The relief depicting Christ Enthroned on the main portal is a common motif in this area.

From Neuweier continue towards **Bühl**, on the way passing the vineyards surrounding **Affental**, which produce the renowned Affentaler Spätburgunder. There is nothing of exceptional interest for the visitor to see in Bühl itself, but the environs are pleasant and restaurants like Gude Stub and Die Grüne Bettlad are outstanding. The mild climate provides not only perfect growing conditions for wine but also for fruit, such as the locally prized *Bühler Frühzwetschge* (plums).

Alt-Windeck

Gourmets with a foible for castle ruins will appreciate a stop at **Burgruine Alt-Windeck**, which lies only a short distance south-east of Bühl. The castle was built in the thirteenth century, but was already abandoned by the middle of the fifteenth century. Perched on a hill, the ruins are surrounded by vineyards, and provide a perfect setting for the excellent restaurant located here. From the castle terrace, which is accessible to everybody, there are wonderful views over the Rhine lowlands and, if the air is clear, as far as the Vosges mountains and Strasbourg in France.

From Alt-Windeck the Wine Road descends to the outskirts of **Ottersweier**, then turns left in the direction of **Lauf**. The intensively cultivated hill country through which it now threads its way is known as the **Ortenau**. It is a fertile region given over to orchards, tobacco fields and of course the vineyards which contribute so much to its charm. Often windy, at times quite steep and narrow, the road offers ever-changing vistas at just about every bend. One's eye is constantly wandering from the forested slopes of the Black Forest mountains, rising to the east, to the broad plain of the Rhine to the west.

Around Achern

Shortly after leaving Lauf the road passes **Achern**, a town chiefly interesting as the starting point for a steam train journey on the historic **Achertalbahn** (see under the heading Steam Trains in the Fact File). From here it is worth making the brief detour to **Sasbachwalden**. Among the many pretty villages the Ortenau has to offer, this is one of the prettiest. In 1967 it was voted the loveliest village in the state of Baden-Württemberg. A stroll down the main street with its impressive half-timbered houses, will convince most that the judges made a good choice. As red as the geraniums growing in the window-boxes is the local Spätburgunder wine, known as *Saschwaller Roter*. This excellent drop can be tried in one of the many local restaurants – there are over 30 to choose from!

Another interesting detour in the vicinity of Achern is to **Ottenhöfen**, just to the south-east of Kappelrodeck. This pleasant holiday resort is the terminus of the Achertalbahn and can also offer visitors one of the most enjoyable walks in the Ortenau, the **Mühlenweg** (Watermill Trail). (*See box overleaf*)

The Mühlenweg at Ottenhöfen

This trail goes through some of the loveliest scenery in the Achertal, passing on its way a good half-dozen restored watermills. Particularly photogenic is the old **Bühler Mühle**, where walkers can get refreshments on summer weekends.

A feature of the walk is the opportunity to buy schnapps from the farmers en route. In this respect it is a good idea to have a handful of small change, as some of them have set up little self-service *Probierstände* (schnapps tasting stands) near their homes. Apart from schnapps you can also buy home-made liqueurs, *Apfelmost* (apple cider) and fruit juices. All in all it is a great idea, but how long it will last is another question. It seems a few dishonest people have stolen both glasses and whole bottles of kirsch from these wayside stands. Another problem has been the stealing of fruit from the orchards; some trees have been picked almost bare, a big problem for part-time farmers who rely on the extra income they earn by distilling schnapps.

The entire circular walk covers around 9 miles (14.5km) and takes 4 hours. It is waymarked by a white M on the trees and wooden signposts marked 'Mühlenweg'. Starting point is the Tourist-Information (they can provide hikers with maps) in the **Kurpark**. Though interesting at any time of the year, this walk is especially beautiful in late summer and autumn.

Vineyards at Ortenau

Oberkirch

Oberkirch, further south on the Wine Road, is reached via **Kappelrodeck** and **Waldulm**, two charming towns known for their premium quality red wines. Wine also plays a role in Oberkirch but it is as the home of Hans Jakob Christoffel von Grimmelshausen (about 1622-1676) that the town enjoys some measure of fame among the literary-minded. He was the author of '*Simplicissimus*', a picaresque novel regarded as one of the greatest literary works of the seventeenth century. The author lived, for a time, in the suburb of **Gaisbach**, where he worked as innkeeper at the **Gasthaus zum Silbernen Stern**, which still stands to this day.

If a glass of schnapps at Grimmelshausen's *Gasthaus* is not enough, then consider buying a bottle as a souvenir from a shop in town. Nowhere in Germany are there so many schnapps distilleries as here:

an impressive total of 891! One of them is the **Oberkircher Winzergenossen-schaft** (Wine Co-operative), though their real speciality is wine. In fact the *Grauburgundersekt* (champagne made from Pinot Gris grapes) they produce enjoys such a good reputation that a few bottles have even been sent to the White House, in Washington.

As far as sights are concerned the town itself is pleasant enough for a stroll; you can visit the **Heimatmuseum** (Local History Museum) to learn more about Grimmelshausen or, if you are romantically inclined, you can walk up to the **Schauenburg** (twelfth century), a castle ruin that rises high above town. Grimmelshausen worked here for a while as a bailiff, before he moved down to Gaisbach to open his small inn. Now there is a restaurant set amidst the ruins, from where there is a lovely view over the Rhine lowlands.

Grimmelhausen's *'Simplicissimus'* – a Tale of the Thirty Years' War

'*Der abenteuerliche Simplicissimus Teutsch*' was first published in 1668 and was an immediate success. Set against the background of the Thirty Years' War it is both a realistic and satirical account of those unsettled times. Many of the incidents described in the novel are based on Grimmelshausen's own experiences of the war and the peace that followed. He was kidnapped by Croat troops as a boy (like the novel's hero, Simplizius), served in both the Imperial and Swedish armies and later worked as a bailiff, a town clerk and innkeeper in the Black Forest. One of his later novels, '*Die Landstörtzerin Courasche*' (1670), served as an inspiration for another tale of the Thirty Years' War, Bertolt Brecht's '*Mother Courage*'.

'*Simplicissimus*' is ranked alongside such picaresque masterpieces as '*Don Quixote*' and '*Gil Blas*'. It can be recommended to anybody who is curious as to what life was like in those tumultuous times, when nearly all of Europe was embroiled in war and whole regions were depopulated – as was the Black Forest. A number of modern translations are available, for instance '*Adventures of a Simpleton*' (translated by Walter Wallich, Ungar Pub. Co. ISBN 0804462291).

In nearby **Lautenbach** the pilgrimage church of **Mariae Krönung** is also well worth a look. Consecrated in 1488, it is one of the few Gothic churches in this region that have remained relatively unchanged over the centuries. The choir altar (about 1496) is of special interest. Art historians still debate as to whether or not Matthias Grünewald (see Colmar) was involved with the painting of the altar's wings. Also of note are the fifteenth century stained glass windows, the choir stalls and the **Gnadenkapelle** (1485). A glance upwards reveals the beautiful net-vaulting of the ceiling.

Touring note

From Oberkirch the Wine Road continues south via Durbach to Offenburg (see Route 5, Chapter 2). The present tour, however, continues southeast to **Oppenau** on the B28. From here two steep, curvy roads leave the B28 and climb up to the Schwarzwald-Hochstrasse (B500). Those who wish to visit Kloster Allerheiligen and the nearby waterfall can take the left fork. The right fork up to the Hochstrasse offers no particular sights but once on the B500 it is worth stopping at **Hotel Schliffkopf** for some great views from the **Schliffkopf** summit.

Kloster Allerheiligen

Set in a lonely valley, surrounded by forest, the ruins of **Kloster Allerheiligen** are touched by the romance of a bygone age. Founded at the end of the twelfth century the former Premonstratensian monastery was once a place of pilgrimage and learning. Within its stone walls generations of monks followed the austere dictates of their order. They wore white robes, went bare-foot, ate no meat and vowed to live a life of poverty. Their secluded monastic life came to an end, however, when the monastery was secularised in 1803. Not long after the monks left lightening struck; fire gutted the buildings and later they were used as a stone quarry. All that is now left are the still impressive ruins of the monastery church, one of the earliest examples of Gothic architecture in Germany.

Only a short distance away from the ruins the **Allerheiligenfälle** (Allerheiligen Waterfalls) drop 328ft (100m) over a series of seven cascades to the valley below. A steep path leads downhill alongside the falls through a landscape that Mark Twain described as '...*a mixture of sylvan loveliness and craggy wildness.*' As both the falls and Kloster ruins are popular attractions during the busy summer period (there was already a hotel catering to tourists at the ruins when Twain made his visit in the late 1870s), the best time to visit would be in the early morning or late afternoon.

The Black Forest Summit Road (Schwarzwald-Hochstrasse)

The Schwarzwald-Hochstrasse (B500) is joined at **Ruhestein**, as the mountain saddle on the pass road between Achern and Baiersbronn is known. The name (*Ruhe* means rest and *Stein* is stone) recalls how difficult it once was to cross this mountain range. There was, in fact, once a large flat stone on the pass, where travellers dropped their heavy loads after the tiring climb from either Baiersbronn or the Seebach valley. It was removed in the first half of the twentieth century to make way for a new road.

There are many good walks that can be undertaken from Ruhestein, but one of the most interesting leads to the **Wildsee**. The tarn (it is of glacial origin) is situated in a nature reserve where the forest has been left to itself, thus allowing scientists to study how a forest biotope would develop without human interference. The quickest way up from the saddle is to take the chair-lift from **Gasthaus Ruhestein** (a hotel) to the start of a short path that goes through upland moor. Shortly before the trail descends to the lake you pass the grave of Dr. Julius Euting (1839-1919), from where there is a great view down to the dark waters of the Wildsee. The doctor did much to develop this region for walking and it was his wish to be buried here, at the spot he loved most. If the chair-lift is taken only one way the walk takes an hour, otherwise 40 minutes or so are sufficient.

Bühlerhöhe

From Mummelsee (*see box overleaf*) the B500 winds its way past the hotels Unterstmatt and Sand to reach the most exclusive of them all, **Schlosshotel Bühlerhöhe** . Built in 1914 it was thoroughly renovated in the 1980s by its new owner, the industrialist Max Grundig. He spent 180 million German Marks to make this hotel one of the noblest in Germany. Guests have included the first German Chancellor Konrad Adenauer and, more recently, tennis-ace Boris Becker. The cuisine is excellent, the prices exorbitant, but if you just want to stop in for coffee

Ruins of Kloster Allerheiligen

Mummelsee

At an altitude of 3,376ft (1,029m) the Mummelsee is the highest, largest (9sq miles/3.7ha) and deepest (56ft/17m) tarn in the Black Forest. Once quite remote its gloomy waters fired the imagination of lonely wanderers and woodsmen, who imagined they could hear voices rising from the depths. It is therefore hardly surprising that legends evolved about spirits and water nymphs (known as *Mümmeln* in German, though the term *Mummel* also refers to the yellow waterlily) that dwelled in its waters. The German novelist and poet Grimmelshausen even devoted a few chapters to this underwater world in his masterpiece *'Simplicissimus'*. However, with the building of the B500 the lake lost much of the charm of its seclusion. On busy weekends the shores are crowded with day-trippers and paddle-boats ply the otherwise still waters. Though the *Mümmeln* have, no doubt, long since packed their bags for quieter realms, visitors can check theirs into the hotel on the lake shore. Then, in the evening, when the souvenir stalls are closed and the boats are tied to the shore, a stroll around the lake might just recapture a bit of the romance of yore.

Having just decried the B500 for spoiling the tranquillity of the Mummelsee it is perhaps fair to mention that it does have its advantages. Those without the benefit of a car can easily reach the tarn by bus from either Freudenstadt or Baden-Baden. The buses run most regularly on weekends and if the weather is fine the trip is worth it as there are plenty of good walking tracks in the vicinity. One leads up to the long, flat summit of the **Hornisgrinde**, at 3,819ft (1164m) the highest point in the northern Black Forest. On the way there is a good view down to the lake and at the top the views are even better.

and cake then this taste of luxury is quite affordable.

After leaving Bühlerhöhe a scenic stretch of road winds its way down to **Lichtental**. Here one can visit **Kloster Lichtental**, a medieval Cistercian nunnery. It still functions as a nunnery but the Gothic **church** (1248) and the **Fürstenkapelle** (1288) are both open to public view. From here it is only another 2 miles (3.3km) back to Baden-Baden.

Route 3 FROM BADEN-BADEN TO THE GROSSE ENZ AND MURG VALLEYS

Gernsbach

Gernsbach lies only 5 miles (8km) to the north-east of Baden-Baden. Situated in the still densely wooded Murgtal (Murg Valley) the town was once an important base for the rafting of logs down to the Rhine. From the fourteenth to the nineteenth century the local timber trade, and therefore rafting, was firmly in the grip of the *Murgschifferschaft* (Murg Boatmen's Guild). The guild owned huge tracts of forest and provided employment and prosperity for the townsfolk. Though rafting logs ceased to be of importance in the nineteenth century the timber industry is still present in the form of a saw-mill, a paper-mill and Germany's only **Papiermacherschule** (School of Paper Manufacture).

A testament to the guild's erstwhile importance is the former **Rathaus** (1617) in the Marktplatz. This impressive late Renaissance building was once the private home of a wealthy timber merchant and guild member. Apart from that Gernsbach also has many lovely old half-timbered buildings that can be admired in the course of a stroll through the old quarter of town.

The route now follows the B462 a short way south to **Hilpertsau**. From here it branches left to follow a narrow, windy road via **Reichental** up to Kaltenbronn. In summer this pretty stretch of road is popular with both mountain-bikers and motorcyclists – something which is true of many of the Black Forest's smaller mountain roads.

Upland Moors near Kaltenbronn

At **Kaltenbronn** it is worth stopping to explore one of the two upland moors in the vicinity. Both can be reached from the large car park just above Gasthaus Sarbacher – coming from Hilpertsau you will get to the car park first. The larger area of protected moor (both are in nature reserves) is to the north-east and surrounds two small lakes known as the **Wildsee** and the **Hornsee**. Boardwalks go past both lakes and should be used as they not only help to keep your feet dry but also protect the sensitive moor flora from being trampled. From the car park to the Wildsee and back requires about an hour.

Hohlohsee

The **Hohlohsee**, to the south-west, is closer but it is a fairly stiff climb alongside a stream before you reach it. Again a boardwalk passes the lake and a number of benches have been provided for those who need a rest after the climb. Characteristic of the flora of this nutrient-poor area are the scrub-like dwarf pines and cotton grass that grow close to the lake shore. One of the rarest plants to be found here is the insect-eating sundew, which flowers in July and August. As for animal life it should consist mainly of small birds, dragonflies and other insects; however ducks have now invaded these lakes, attracted by visitors who feed them. Their excrement has had the effect of fertilising the lake shores, resulting in the appearance of dandelions and other plants that are starting to take over the fragile ecosystem. Signs therefore request all visitors to refrain from feeding the ducks, or throwing away food in the area. A short distance further on from the Hohlohsee is the **Kaiser Wilhelm-Turm**, a lookout tower which is worth climbing for some great views.

On to Baiersbronn

From Kaltenbronn follow the road via Sprollenhaus to **Enzklösterle** on the River Grosse Enz. Continue along the river to **Poppeltal**. Those who have children with them might like to pause here for a ride on what is claimed to be Germany's longest summer toboggan-run, the **Riesenrutschbahn**. On either a single or a two-seater toboggan you can slide 5,000ft (1,500m), in a series of five giant curves, down a mountain-side. The kids will love it! Note that it is only open if the weather is fine. At the foot of the toboggan-run there are also other amusements such as a merry-go-round and a miniature train.

If whizzing down slopes is not your thing, then continue on past Poppeltal until the B294 is reached. The B294 is now followed south to the turn-off to Kloster Reichenbach and Baiersbronn.

Baiersbronn

At first appearance **Baiersbronn** has nothing special to offer visitors. The only real sight, as such, is the former monastery church at **Kloster Reichenbach**, a village that now belongs to Baiersbronn. However, more people overnight in the town and environs than anywhere else in the Black Forest. This probably has a lot to do with the excellent tourist facilities (the town makes a special effort to cater for families), the mild, healthy climate and the attractive surroundings. In fact Germany's largest rural community (nine other villages belong to the Baiersbronn administrative district) includes six lakes and over 680 miles (1,100km) of waymarked trails within its densely forested boundaries. But fresh air and hills are things that most other rural Black Forest towns can offer as well; what really makes Baiersbronn unusual is the exceptional niveau of the local cuisine.

Gourmet fare

Baiersbronn's gastronomic fame rests on the outstanding reputation of the chefs at Hotel Traube in **Tonbach** (3 miles/4.75km from Baiersbronn), Hotel Bareiss in **Mitteltal** (2½ miles/4km) and at Hotel Sackmann in **Schwarzenberg** (11 miles/18km). Gourmets come from all over Germany (and not a few from nearby France and Switzerland as well) to sample dishes that have been praised by the French gourmet bibles '*Guide Michelin*' and '*Gault Millau*'. Happily these top addresses have also helped raise the standards of other, less expensive restaurants in town – so if money is short, one can still be quite sure of a good meal. Apart from great food, what further adds to the exclusive aura of Baiersbronn is the fact that Hotel Traube and Hotel Bareiss are now counted among the ten best hotels in the world.

Walks around
Baiersbronn

A chance to lose some of the calories gained in Baiersbronn's restaurants is offered by a walk (3 hours return) to **Huzenbacher See**. This small tarn can be reached by following the Seebach stream south-west from **Huzenbach**, a village which lies $8\frac{1}{2}$ miles (14km) north of Baiersbronn, in the Murg valley – this route along the B462 follows the **Schwarzwald-Tälerstrasse** (Black Forest Valley Road). The tarn is one of seven that still remain in the northern Black Forest and like the others has its origins in the last Ice Age, which ended in central Europe about 10,000 years ago. Adding much to the charm of the lake and its picturesque location are the waterlilies that cover its surface.

A circular walk to the **Sankenbach Falls** covers a distance of roughly 7 miles (11km) and takes $2\frac{1}{2}$ hours. From **Hotel-Restaurant Krone**, in the middle of town, walk towards the Bahnhof (railway station) and then follow the waymark Z3. Two small bridges are crossed, after which the trail begins climbing out of town. On leaving the last few houses pass a small Schnapsbrennerei (distillery) and continue towards the woods. After crossing under a chair-lift the trail enters the woods and climbs in the direction of Kniebis (signposted). Every now and again you should see the Z3 waymark, but pay attention as there are many other trails branching off this route. An elevation known as the **Gruberkopf** is reached after around three-quarters of an hour. Go past the **Wasenhütte**

Wildsee, near Kaltenbronn

The walk to Sankenbach See can
also be done with children

(forest hut) and
eventually you will come
to a turn-off (to the right)
marked by a blue
diamond with a vertical
white line in the middle –
also signposted
'Sankenbachfall-Kniebis'.
This waymark is now
followed to an asphalt
road (also the waymark
K6 along here) which in
turn is followed a short
distance downhill. At the
point where you see the
signpost 'Sankenbachfall',
and see the blue diamond
again, the track descends
steeply. On reaching
another small asphalt
road turn right. At the **Wasserfallhütte** (another hut) the trail turns
left and continues descending.

Not long after passing the Wasserfallhütte the trail reaches the
waterfall. This is the prettiest stretch of the walk. At the top section of
the **Sankenbach Falls** it is possible to dam the water with a wooden
'gate' and then, when sufficient water has gathered in the small rock
basin, one can open it with a lever and watch the water gush down
over the rocks. This 'instant waterfall' is great if you have children
with you; they can either dam the stream up top, or wait a little
further down for the spectacular effect of a sudden torrent of water,
spilling over a precipitous rock face – the spot where they can wait is
marked by wooden benches. At the bottom of the falls is the pretty
Sankenbachsee, a small lake (tarn) of glacial origins. This is a good
place for a picnic.

Return to Baiersbronn by following waymark R16 around the
southern shores of the lake (coming from the Falls go right) and then
walk along the Sankenbach stream, in the direction of the
Rotwildgehege (red deer enclosure).

The road back to Baden-Baden

Continuing in the direction of Forbach a detour from the B462 at **Raumünzach** leads up a steep, windy road to the **Schwarzenbachtalsperre** (Schwarzenbach Dam). In the 1920s, when it was built for the generation of electricity, it was Germany's highest dam (213ft/65m) and the lake it created is one of the largest in the Black Forest. Something of an achievement for its time (never before had cast concrete had been used in a dam of this size in Germany), the top of the dam is 1,250ft (380m) long and 20ft (6.2m) wide. At its base the dam wall has a width of 157ft (48m). Around 380,000cu yards (290,000cu m) of concrete and stone were used in its construction.

On hot summer weekends the lake itself is crowded with rowing-boats, swimmers and wind-surfers. Many interesting trails lead into the surrounding forest, for instance to a very pretty tarn known as **Herrenwieser See** and to the Nature Reserve **Hoher Ochsenkopf**. For those who want to linger longer in the area there is a camping ground and youth hostel at **Herrenwies**.

Up until 1790 there was no road running through the Murg gorge, a particularly narrow section of the valley between Schönmünzach and Gernsbach. Here the softer rock (gneiss) that is found around Baiersbronn and Klosterreichenbach gives way to harder granite. For those entering the valley from the north Forbach was literally 'the end of the road' (*see below*).

It is only another 7½ miles (12km) to Gernsbach from Forbach and from there it is only a short drive back to Baden-Baden. An interesting alternative is the twisty country road via Bermersbach (10½ miles/17km). It is quite scenic, passes a couple of pleasantly secluded restaurants on the way, and enters Baden-Baden via the old monastery town of Lichtental.

Forbach

Today Forbach is served by both road, rail and trail – the oldest long-distance walk through the Black Forest, the Westweg (*see pages 26-8*), runs through town. Apart from its lovely location in this narrow part of the Murg valley, the town's main attraction is a **Holzbrücke** (covered wooden bridge) over the River Murg. It was built in 1954, using an earlier bridge from 1776 as a model. With a length of 131ft (40m) it is the largest bridge of its type in Germany.

Route 4 THE VALLEYS OF THE NAGOLD AND ENZ (circular route)

Calw

The first thing that strikes non-German speaking visitors to the town is its name. How on earth does one pronounce that odd assemblage of consonants and a solitary vowel? Lucky are those who are asking directions and have a map handy. They can just point. Otherwise the English speaking tongue is forced to render the name pronounceable by conjuring up what it perceives to be the missing vowel before the 'w' or 'right' consonant at the end. The results are at the very least amusing, some might even be highly imaginative. But those who do not want to be sent off in the direction of Cracow might try this: an approximation of Calw's pronunciation is to pronounce the 'c' as in cake and the 'alw' as in Alf.

The town was an important trading place in the Middle Ages, with flourishing industries such as cloth weaving and tanning. Rafting was also an important profession (as elsewhere in the Black Forest) and many of the fir trees felled here were bound together to be floated to Holland, where they were used as ships' masts. The old part of town preserves a number of lovingly renovated half-timbered houses from the seventeenth and eighteenth

A strained relationship: Hermann Hesse and Calw

Calw is famed as the birthplace of Nobel Prize winning novelist and poet Hermann Hesse (1877-1962). He is, without doubt, one of the most internationally acclaimed and popular German writers of the twentieth century. Though Hesse loved his home town the feeling was not always mutual. The young Hesse stood out in a community that praised hard work and had a conservative outlook on life. In his youth he was considered something of a lazy good-for-nothing, who preferred to write poems and go fishing (from the Nagold Bridge), rather than do something 'useful'. The fact that he did not fight in World War I, and that novels like *'Demian'* and *'Narziss und Goldmund'* were viewed as immoral, hardly endeared him to the town's upright citizens. It took the Nobel Prize and a donation of money before the town softened its attitude. He was made an honorary citizen in 1947 and eventually (over ten years later and after much debate) a school was named after him.

In 1990 a **Hermann-Hesse-Museum** was finally established in the historic Haus Schütz, on the Marktplatz – prior to this memorabilia relating to the author were located in the Municipal Museum. The museum documents the great author's life from his beginnings in provincial Calw to his final days in Switzerland. Also to be seen is an exhibition of Hesse's water-colour paintings.

**Left:
Zalvenstein's
lovely Kurpark
harmonises
perfectly with
the
surroundings**

**Below: The work
of craftsmen in
the Black Forest
is prominent in
the many
carved wooden
signs**

centuries. **Haus Vischer** (1790) contains the **Museum der Stadt Calw** (Municipal Museum) with exhibits relating to pre-history, domestic life in the nineteenth century and folklore. Also of interest is the **Nagold Bridge** (1400), with its small Gothic chapel, and the **Rathaus** (1673) in the Marktplatz.

Hirsau

The romantic monastery ruins of **Kloster Hirsau** are only a short drive north of Calw. In its heyday, in the eleventh century, the Benedictine monastery exerted considerable influence and power. It was the German base for the spread of the Reform Movement that had its origins at the great Burgundian abbey of Cluny. This movement aimed to counter secularisation and to re-establish the power of the church against worldly authority. The monastery was also important for its role in encouraging the colonisation of the northern reaches of the Black Forest. Around 1200 its many possessions included 31 villages, 40 churches and 70sq miles (18,000ha) of fields and vineyards.

The French destroyed the Kloster in 1692, so there is not a great deal left except for the ruins of the once massive church (1081-1091), the Gothic cloister (1425-94) and the Marienkapelle (1508-16), which houses a museum. In the sixteenth century a Renaissance-style hunting lodge was built within the monastery complex, but it also suffered at the hands of the French. In summer popular open-air performances are held in the Kloster ruins. A nature trail near the car park, opposite the Kloster, leads to an animal enclosure with deer and wild boar.

Along the Nagold Valley to Altensteig

At **Kentheim**, on the B463 (Bäderstrasse/Spa Road), just south of Calw is one of the region's oldest churches. Built around 1000 the church is rather plain-looking from the outside but the interior contains some interesting wall frescoes from the fourteenth and fifteenth centuries. They depict the life of Christ, along with scenes from the lives of various saints.

A bit further south a worthwhile detour can be made to **Bad Teinach-Zavelstein**. Of greater interest is **Zavelstein** (as in many other parts of Germany, the two towns were joined in the 1970s for administrative purposes), once renowned as the smallest town in the old state of Württemberg. Originally the town consisted of only one street with twelve houses, a church and a castle. The town has retained its lovely old houses and the old **Burg** also remains, if only as a ruin. From the 92ft (28m) high castle keep there are wonderful views over the surrounding countryside.

Probably the best time to visit Zavelstein is in spring. From about the middle of March until the beginning of April the fields around town are covered with millions of violet-blue crocuses. Though these crocuses (*Crocus napolitanus*) now grow wild around here they are not native but actually originate from the area of the Mediterranean. A trail known as the **Krokusstrasse** leads around the flowers, which are protected within a 128-acre (52ha) nature reserve.

To the south-west, near **Neubulach**, is a silver mine (signposted 'Besucherbergwerk') that can be visited daily during spring and summer. Silver and copper mining began here in the eleventh century and only stopped in 1924. The mine's tunnels reach a depth of 200ft (60m) and can be followed (guided tour) for a distance of 1,300ft (400m). Because the moist air is completely free of dust and pollen the tunnels are also used for treating patients suffering from asthma and bronchitis.

Back on the B463 **Wildberg** is known for what is supposed to be the oldest folk festival in the northern Black Forest: the Wildberger Schäferlauf (Shepherds' Contest). As the name implies it all centres around sheep and since 1723 it has taken place nearly every two years. The next festival takes place on the third Sunday in July in 2002. The town itself is also of interest and traces of its 700 year-old history can be seen in the castle ruins, remnants of the medieval town wall and the wooden **Rathaus** (1480).

Nagold lies 6 miles (10km) further south of Wildberg. Unfortunately the overall picture of the town is somewhat spoiled by a number of ugly modern buildings. However, the half-timbered houses in the old part of town come to the rescue and do, in the end, add a touch of romance to the place. Especially notable is the hotel **Alte Post** (1697), which is also a good place to try regional cooking. The **Remigiuskirche** (tenth and twelfth centuries) has some Gothic wall frescoes, while above town **Burg Hohen-Nagold** (thirteenth century) has been a ruin since it was destroyed in the Thirty Years' War.

Altensteig

From Nagold the Bäderstrasse (now the B28) winds its way along the River Nagold to **Altensteig**. The town is much acclaimed as having one of the most picturesque townscapes in the northern Black Forest. The houses of its medieval *Altstadt* (old quarter of town) are clustered on the steep slopes below the **Altes Schloss** (thirteenth century), like vassals paying tribute to their mighty lord. A well signposted circular walk, the so-called **Historische Meile** (historic mile), leads up past ancient half-timbered houses, through narrow alleyways, to the castle. Located here is a local history museum, with interesting exhibits concerning once typical professions in this part of the Forest.

Continuing on from Altensteig leave the Bäderstrasse (B28) and take a minor road south-west towards the **Nagoldstausee** (man-made storage lake). It follows an especially attractive stretch of the Nagold valley, past old mills and fishponds, to the lake. Swimming

Frog Design

Of interest is the fact that medieval Altensteig is home to a very modern industrial design company. '*Frog Design*' is one of the most innovative companies in its field and their designs have pepped up products as diverse as the Melitta coffee machine and Apple Macintosh computers. That they have the outstanding knack of being able to combine functionality with aesthetics is proved by the fact that some of their works are displayed at the Museum of Modern Art in New York.

Grosse Tannen Nature Reserve

This 32-acre (13ha) nature reserve offers a rare glimpse of what the Black Forest may have looked like before the intervention of man. Growing here are the tallest pine trees in the Forest, some of which are between 200 to 250 years old and up to 164ft (50m) high. Though the majority of trees in the region are now firs, the original forests were composed of pine and beech. A trail leads through the reserve and you will be able to recognise the pines by the fact that their cones point upwards – those of fir trees point downwards. At the entrance to the reserve is an adventure playground.

To get to the reserve take the road south-east from the Nagoldstausee in the direction of Kälberbronn-Hallwangen. It is situated on the outskirts of **Kälberbronn**, at the exit to **Grömbach**.

and other water activities are only permitted in the vicinity of **Erzgrube**. This small village was established as a lumberjack and log-rafting settlement around 1700. At the beginning there was only a pub for forest workers, but that was enough to attract other settlers to the area.

The road back to Calw

From Erzgrube take the road right (north-west) along the River Nagold to **Besenfeld** on the B294. After **Urnagold** you have the choice of either following the River Grosse Enz (Bäderstrasse) via Enzklösterle to Bad Wildbad, or you can stick to the B294 and follow the River Kleine Enz up to **Calmbach**. From here turn left and south to the spa town of Bad Wildbad. Both routes are scenic, but the B294 is perhaps a bit quicker to drive.

Bad Wildbad is, like most spas in the area, a well-manicured place with a lovely park and gardens. Its chief attraction is the very noble **Palais Thermal**, formerly known as the Graf-Eberhard-Bad, that was established over 150 years ago. This luxurious thermal bath has a magnificent interior that seems to come straight from the Arabian Nights; decorative tiles, wall frescoes, sculptures and palms all help to create a peaceful, exotic atmosphere.

A pleasant excursion from the middle of town is the ride up to the **Sommerberg** (2,625ft/800m) with the *Bergbahn* (funicular railway). Up top there are, apart from good views, several cafés and restaurants and dozens of walking trails. In winter there is some good cross-country

skiing here as well.

The B296 provides a direct link back to Calw via **Oberreichenbach**, but if time allows it is worth continuing on the B294 to **Höfen**. From here go right, via **Schömberg**, to Bad Liebenzell.

Bad Liebenzell

Bad Liebenzell is a pleasant little spa town with curative springs that are used for healing rheumatism and various circulatory problems. The town has a long tradition as a spa, as already in 1403 baths had been built to utilise the warm health-giving waters. Bubbling up from a total of seven springs, these waters have a temperature ranging between 73°F and 80°F (23°C and 27°C). Even those who are not taking a cure are free to use the **Paracelsusbad** (mineral baths), or to take a stroll through the gardens of the Kurpark.

Rising high above town is **Burg Liebenzell** (thirteenth century), a castle destroyed by the French in 1692. It was rebuilt in the 1950s and now serves as a youth hostel and seat of the 'International Forum', a meeting-place for young people from all over the world. The 110ft (34m) high castle keep is accessible to everybody, however, as is the restaurant with its lovely views over the Nagold valley.

One of the best known walks from town is that through the **Monbachtal**. The walk goes through a narrow, romantic gorge and is clearly waymarked. It takes about 30 minutes to walk through the gorge itself, but the entire circular walk via Monakam (some restaurants here) back to Bad Liebenzell would require about 3 hours.

Wine and Schnapps

Wine

Wine has been grown along the sun-kissed slopes facing the Rhine since Roman times and, as might be expected, the local wine-growers have had plenty of time to perfect their art. In fact the European Union has designated the vineyards here as belonging to the category 'Zone B'. In this same category are the famous French wine-growing regions of Alsace, Champagne, Savoy and the Loire Valley. What this means is that the wine produced between Baden-Baden and Lörrach has to meet stricter quality standards than wine grown in other areas of Germany, such as along the Moselle.

The four wine-growing areas in the Black Forest are (from north to south): the **Ortenau** between Baden-Baden and Offenburg, the **Breisgau** between Lahr and Freiburg, the **Kaiserstuhl** to the north-west of Freiburg and **Markgräflerland** between Freiburg and Basle.

The most common variety of grape cultivated in the region is Müller-Thurgau, followed by Blauer Spätburgunder (Pinot Noir), Grauburgunder (Pinot Gris) and, in Markgräflerland, Gutedel (Chasselas, known in Switzerland as Fendant). Though white wine varieties predominate, a quarter of the total wine-growing area is given over to the reds. Especially good red wines come from the Ortenau. Here visitors should try the famous *Affentaler* Spätburgunder (with a monkey on the bottle) and the delicious *Hex von Dasenstein* Spätburgunder (witch riding a broomstick on the label), which is grown around Kappelrodeck. One of the best white wines is the Grauburgunder (formerly known as Ruländer) grown around the Kaiserstuhl. Riesling fans will find the vineyards surrounding Varnhalt, near Baden-Baden, of interest.

Opportunities to try wine abound along the Baden Wine Road (see Chapters 1 and 4), visitors just need to look out for signs advertising *Weinprobe* (wine tasting) or *Weinverkauf* (wine sales). Usually if you buy your wine direct from the vineyard you get to taste it beforehand for free.

Schnapps

The Black Forest's farmers have had the right to distil their own *Obstschnäpse* (fruit brandies or schnapps) since at least the seventeenth century. Around 14,000 of these small private distilleries are scattered around the region and two-thirds of all commercial distilleries in Germany are found in the Forest as well. A reason for such a high concentration of distilleries lies, no doubt, in the mild climate of the Upper Rhine valley, which has always provided ideal growing conditions for the wide variety of stone fruits used in the local brandies.

Common to all the best schnapps varieties is the use of only the very best fruit. Even a small quantity of over-ripe plums or cherries can ruin a good schnapps. Also important for high quality is an alcohol content of not less than 45 per cent. A schnapps which has less cannot develop its full aroma. In the case of a good *Kirschwasser* (cherry brandy) this takes about 2 years.

Of all the many kinds of schnapps it is *Kirschwasser* (also known as *Chriesewässerli*) that is held in highest regard. The most exclusive type of *Kirschwasser* is the so-called *Gebirgskirschwasser*. It is made from especially aromatic cherries that grow high in the mountains. Other rarities include *Sauerkirschwasser* and the very expensive *Zibärtle*, which is distilled from wild plums. A speciality of the northern Black Forest is the strong tasting *Topinambur*, or *Rossler*. It is made from the root of a plant originally from Brazil and is valued as a digestive.

Generally speaking it is best to buy your schnapps directly from the farmer rather than in a supermarket – note that many wine growers also offer excellent schnapps. One of the best regions to look for private distillers is the Ortenau, an area otherwise known for its wine. Oberkirch alone, in the Rench valley, can boast around 800 private distilleries but another good pick is Ottenhöfen, near Achern. Here you can follow a trail known as the Mühlenweg and discover several excellent *Schnapsbrennereien* (schnapps distilleries) along the way. Of the commercial distilleries the best include Schladerer in Staufen, Scheibel in Kappelrodeck and Fies in Oberkirch.

And finally: one should drink a fine schnapps at room temperature, or only slightly chilled, otherwise it can easily lose its fruit aroma. Furthermore, like a good cognac, it should be reserved for special occasions and is enjoyed best after a meal. *Zum Wohl!* (cheers!)

ACCOMMODATION

Baden-Baden

Haus am Spörsig $
(Privatzimmer/rooms
in a private house)
Spörsigweg 16, Oberbeuern
☎ (07221) 71440,
Fax (07221) 71400
Located south-east of town,
near Lichtental.

Michaela Markert $
(Privatzimmer/rooms
in a private house)
Fremersbergstrasse 43
☎ (07221) 31620
Facilities for children
and shared kitchen.

Hotel Löhr $$
Lichtentaler Strasse 19
☎ (07221) 26204,
Fax (07221) 38308
Quiet, central location.

Hotel Laterne $$
Gernsbacher Strasse 10
☎ (07221) 3060,   '
Fax (07221) 38308
A picturesque 300 year-old
house in the middle of town.

Brenner's Park-Hotel & Spa $$$
Lichtentaler Allee
☎ (07221) 9000,
Fax (07221) 38772
One of the world's top
hotels, more luxury would
be hard to find.

Baiersbronn

Campingplatz Gasthof Mohren
Schönmünzach
☎ (07447) 360
Camping ground is open
throughout the year.

Campingplatz Tannenfels
Obertal
☎ (07449) 212
Camping ground with
restaurant and shopping
facilities. Also open in winter.

Käthe Batz $
(Privatzimmer/rooms
in a private house)
Mozartstrasse 37
☎ (07442) 5108
Non-smoking, bicycles for hire,
TV in room and English spoken.

Ruth Maurer $
(Privatzimmer/rooms
in a private house)
Pappelweg 4
☎ (07442) 2973
Non-smoking, reductions for
children, TV in room, fridge and
kitchen for guests, holiday flat
available, English spoken.

Hotel-Pension Stöckerhof $$
Reuteweg 1
☎ (07442) 3517, Fax (07442) 50637
Centrally located hotel in the style
of a traditional Black Forest house.
Offered in the *Milchstube* are
products from the hotel's own
farm. English spoken.

Hotel Bareiss $$$
*Gärtenbühlweg 14,
Baiersbronn-Mitteltal*
☎ (07442) 470, Fax (07442) 47320
Counted among the world's top
ten hotels.

Hotel Traube-Tonbach $$$
*Tonbachstrasse 237,
Baiersbronn-Tonbach*
☎ (07442) 4920,
Fax (07442) 492692
Luxury accommodation in one
of the world's top hotels.

Bühlerhöhe

Schlosshotel Bühlerhöhe $$$
☎ (07226) 550, Fax (07226) 55777
Exclusive and expensive.

Calw

Campingplatz Obere Mühle
Calw-Stammheim
☎ (07051) 4844, Fax (07051) 12485
Restaurant, small shop, sauna
and facilities for campervans.

**Terrassencamping
Schwarzwaldblick**
Weidensteige 54
☎ (07051) 12845,
Fax (07051) 20438
Restaurant, children's play-ground,
facilities for campervans. Open all
year.

Gasthaus Waldhorn $
*Calwer Strasse 20,
Calw-Hirsau*
☎ (07051) 58484
Close to Hirsau railway
station and monastery.

Haus Schweickhardt $
(Privatzimmer/rooms
in a private house)
*Kohlerstrasse 6,
Calw-Spesshardt*
☎ (07051) 51338
Kitchen for guests.

Hotel-Garni Alte Post $$
Bahnhofstrasse 1
☎ (07051) 2196,
Fax (07051) 700379
Centrally located,
holiday flat available.

Hotel-Gasthof Rössle $$
Hermann-Hesse-Platz 2
☎ (07051) 79000,
Fax (07051) 790079
Old half-timbered building
in the middle of town.

Gernsbach

Hotel-Gasthof Sternen $$
Staufenberger Strasse 111
☎ (07224) 3308, Fax (07224) 69486

Hotel Sarbacher $$$
Kaltenbronner Strasse 598
Gernsbach-Kaltenbronn
☎ (07224) 2602, Fax (07224) 69486
Comfortable rooms and good
food in the attached restaurant.

Karlsruhe

AZUR Camping Turmbergblick
*Tiegenerstrasse 40,
Karlsruhe-Durlach*
☎ (0721) 497236
Camping ground with on-site
restaurant. Disposal facilities
for chemical toilets.

Gasthaus Zum Goldenen Ochsen $
Schultheiß-Kieferstrasse 28
☎ (0721) 481506
East of inner-city at Grötzingen.

Hotel Augustiner $$
Sophienstrasse 73
☎ (0721) 845580, Fax (0721) 853320
Central location.

Gasthaus Zum Goldenen Lamm $$
Karlsbader Strasse 2
☎ (0721) 947550,
Fax (0721) 9475547
Situated south-east of
inner city at Stupferich.

Hotel Kübler $$$
Bismarckstrasse 37-43
☎ (0721) 1440,
Fax (0721) 144441
Peacefully situated in a park.

Schlosshotel Karlsruhe $$$
Bahnhofplatz 2
☎ (0721) 38320, Fax (0721) 3832333
Noble rooms in palatial
surroundings.

EATING OUT

Baden-Baden

Café König $
Lichtentaler Strasse 12
A popular place with good
coffee and hot chocolate.
Open: daily from 9am-7pm.

Gasthaus Nest $
Rettigstrasse 1
☎ (07221) 23076
Local specialities and Hungarian
cuisine and vegetarian dishes. Also
modestly priced accommodation.
Open: Wednesday to Monday.

Namaskaar $$
Kreuzstrasse 1
☎ (07221)24681
Good Indian food.
Open: seven days a week.

Weinstube im Baldreit $$
Küferstrasse 3
☎ (07221) 23136
Rustic interior, pleasant courtyard
and a good selection of wine.
Open: Tuesday to Sunday.

Restaurant Stahlbad $$$
Augustaplatz 2
☎ (07221) 24569
International dishes and local
specialities. Open: Tuesday to
Sunday.

Zum Alde Gott $$$
Weinstrasse 10,
Neuweier
(to south-west of Baden-Baden)
☎ (07223) 5513
Gourmet dining in a top restaurant. Open: Friday to Wednesday.

Baiersbronn

Gourmet-Restaurant Bareiss $$$
Gärtenbühlweg 14
(at Hotel Bareiss),
Baiersbronn-Mitteltal
☎ (07442) 470
A cheaper alternative to the
gourmet restaurant are the
'Dorfstuben' restaurants, where
one can dine on traditional
Black Forest cuisine in rustic
surroundings.

Restaurant Schlossberg $$$
Murgtalstrasse 602
(at Hotel Sackmann),
Baiersbronn-Schwarzenberg
☎ (07447) 2890
Gourmet cuisine.

Schwarzwaldstube $$$
Tonbacherstrasse 237
(at Hotel Traube),
Baiersbronn-Tonbach
☎ (07442) 492665
Award winning food in one of
Germany's best restaurants.

Bühl

Gude Stub $$$
Dreherstrasse 9
☎ (07223) 8480
Outstanding.
Open: daily, except Tuesday.

Die Grüne Bettlad $$$
Blumenstrasse 4
☎ (07223) 93130
Top dining. Open: daily,
except Sunday and Monday.

Calw

Café-Konditorei Wendland $
Hermann-Hesse-Platz 1
Ice-cream specialities. Open: every
day except Wednesday.

Café-Restaurant Alt Calw $/$$
Im Calwer Markt
☎ (07051) 40933
Centrally located, fish dishes.
Open: Monday to Saturday.

Gernsbach

Gasthof Alte Post $/$$
Bleichstrasse 38
☎ (07224) 3373
Baden, Alsatian and Swabian
cuisine. Open: 7 days a week..

Gasthof Jockers $/$$
Schlosstrasse 4
☎ (07224) 1630
Trout dishes. Open: every day
except Wednesday.

Karlsruhe

Dorfschänke $
Am Künstlerhaus 33
☎ (0721) 557249
One of Karlsruhe's oldest pubs,
with a good selection of vegetarian dishes. Open: 6pm-1am,
7 days a week.

Goldenes Kreuz $$/$$$
Karlstrasse 21a
☎ (0721) 22054
Open: 7 days a week.

Blüthner's $$$
Gutenbergstrasse 5
☎ (0721) 842228
International and French cuisine.
Open: every day except Monday.

Oberländer Weinstube $$$
Akademiestrasse 7
☎ (0721) 25066
A selection of over 700 wines from
the region. Local specialities
served in the romantic courtyard in
summer. Open: closed Sunday.

KARLSRUHE CITY INFORMATION

Area Code: ☎ (0721)

Important Telephone Numbers
Automobile Breakdown Service ☎ (01802) 222222
German Automobile Association (ADAC) ☎ 81040
Emergency Medical (weekends) ☎ 19292
Taxi ☎ 944144

Airlines
The Swiss airline 'Crossair' links Baden regional airport with the
international EuroAirport near Basle. Contact **Baden-Airport** for details
☎ (07229) 66300, Fax (07229) 66309.

Guided Tours and Excursions
Organised tours in and around Karlsruhe can be arranged at the **Karlsruhe
Tourist Office**, Bahnhofplatz 6. They also offer a special bus tour for
children (accompanied by adults) that is specially designed to fit in with
their interests.

Post Office

The **Hauptpostamt** (main post office) is situated at Karlstrasse 217. There is also a post office next to the main railway station.

Trains and Buses

The **Hauptbahnhof** (main railway station) is situated at Bahnhofplatz, near the zoo. The **Busbahnhof** (bus station) is situated nearby. For information about trains and buses in the Karlsruhe region contact the Tourist Office, or inquire at the information counters (*Auskunft*) at one of the stations.

Discount tickets for bus and tramway in Karlsruhe include the **CityKarte**, a 24 hour ticket for two adults and two children under 17, and the **Regiokarte** for trips a bit further afield. The latter ticket is also valid for 24 hours and is great for those who want to visit such destinations as the lovely Alb valley, Baden-Baden and Pforzheim without a car. Inquire at the Tourist Office for further details.

Those who intend to stay at least one night in Karlsruhe can call the **Tourist Office** (☎ 35530) and they will arrange a discount train ticket to the city. They also offer reasonably priced weekend packages that include hotel accommodation, free rides on public transport within the city and reduced entrance prices to the museums.

PLACES TO VISIT

Altensteig

Museum
In the Altes Schloss (Old Castle)
Open: Wednesday 2-4pm, Sunday 11am-12noon and 2-4pm. During summer open until 5pm.

Baden-Baden

Caracalla-Therme
Römerplatz 1
The pools here offer plenty of fun for the entire family.
Open: daily 8am-10pm.

Casino
Kaiseralle 1(in the Kurhaus)
One need not be James Bond to enjoy the splendid interior of this gambling temple. However, house rules dictate that men dress like him. Open: daily guided tours from 10am-12noon. Casino opens for gambling from 2pm-2am.

Friedrichsbad
Römerplatz 11
Mineral pools in luxurious surroundings. Open: Monday to Saturday 9am-10pm, Sunday and public holidays 12noon to 8pm.

Kloster Lichtental
Hauptstrasse 40,
Lichtental
Open: Tuesday to Sunday (as the opening times may vary inquire at the Tourist Information in Baden-Baden beforehand).

Roman Bath
Römerplatz 11
(under Friedrichsbad)
Open: Good Friday to 31 October, daily 10am-12noon and 1.30-4pm.

Stadtgeschichtliche Sammlung
Schlossstrasse 22
(in Neues Schloss)
Exhibits on local history go back to the days of the Roman Empire. Open: Tuesday to Sunday 10am-12.30pm and 2-5pm.

Stiftskirche
Marktplatz
Open: outside church services.

Trinkhalle
Kaiserallee
Open: daily 9.30am-6pm.

Bad Herrenalb

Kloster Frauenalb
On road between Marxzell and Bad Herrenalb
Open: always open.

Klosterkirche
Middle of town
Ruins of a medieval monastery church. Open: always open.

Spielzeugmuseum
Klosterstrasse 2
Very good toy museum. Open: Tuesday to Sunday 2.30-5.30pm, weekends and public holidays 10am-12noon and 2.30-6pm.

Bad Liebenzell

Paracelsusbad
Bahnhofstrasse
Attractive mineral pool complex. Open: Monday to Saturday 8am-9pm, Sunday and public holidays 8am-8pm.

Bad Wildbad

Palais Thermal
Middle of town
Beautiful thermal pool complex. Open: Monday to Friday 2-10pm, Saturday, Sunday and public holidays 10am-10pm.

Calw

Hermann-Hesse-Museum
Marktplatz 30
Open: Tuesday to Sunday 11am-5pm, Thursday 11am-7pm

Museum der Stadt Calw
In Palais Vischer/Bischofstrasse 48
Pre-history and exhibits relating to Calw. Open: April to October, Sunday 2-5pm.

Ettlingen

Schloss
Middle of town
Art galleries and museum. Open: Tuesday to Sunday 10am-5pm. Guided tours through chapel at 2pm Saturday and Sunday.

Hirsau

Klostermuseum Hirsau
Calwer Strasse 6
Exhibits on the history of Kloster Hirsau and a model of the monastery complex. Open: April to October, Tuesday to Sunday 2-5pm; November to March, Saturday and Sunday 2-5pm. The monastery ruins can be viewed at any time.

Karlsruhe

Badisches Landesmuseum
In the Schloss
Impressive collection of antique art. Open: Tuesday and Thursday to Sunday 10am-5pm. The **Schossturm** (tower) has the same opening times.

Staatliche Kunsthalle and Orangerie
Hans-Thoma-Strasse 2
Art galleries with a special children's section in the Orangerie. Open: Tuesday to Friday 10am-5pm, weekends and public holidays 10am-6pm.

Zoo
Main entrance near railway station
Open: May to September, 8am-6.30pm, in the winter months open from 9am.

ZKM
Lorenzstrasse 19
This complex contains two fascinating museums devoted to art and media. Open: Wednesday to Saturday 12noon-8pm, Sunday 10am-6pm.

Kuppenheim

Schloss Favorite and Eremitage
Favoritestrasse,
Förch (west of Kuppenheim)
Baroque palace with a beautiful interior and set in a lovely park. Open: 16 March to 30 September, Tuesday to Sunday 9am-5pm; 1 October to 15 November, Tuesday to Sunday, 9am-4pm. Guided tours through park and Eremitage Saturdays at 11am and 2pm.

Marxzell-Pfaffenrot

Fahrzeugmuseum
Albtalstrasse 2
Interesting collection of vintage cars and motorcycles. Open: daily 2-5pm.

Neubulach

Besucherbergwerk 'Hella-Glück-Stollen'
Old silver mine. Open: April to October, Monday to Friday 10am-12noon and 2-4pm, Saturday, Sunday and public holidays 10am-5pm.

Oberkirch

Heimatmuseum
Hauptstrasse 32
Local history and memorabilia concerning Grimmelshausen. Open: Tuesday and Thursday 3-7pm, Sundays 10.30am-12.30pm and 2-5pm.

Pforzheim

Edelstein-Austellung Schütt
Goldschmiedestrasse 6
Here one can buy the necklaces and rings on display. Open: Monday to Friday 9am-5pm, Saturday 9am-1pm. No entrance fee.

Schmuckmuseum
Jahnstrasse 42
A collection of rings, necklaces and other valuable accessories that have been used as adornment over the centuries. Open: 10am-5pm. Closed Monday. No entrance fee, except from 3 July to 5 September.

Technisches Museum
Bleichstrasse 81
How watches are made and more.
Open: Wednesday 9am-12noon
and 3-6pm, every second and
fourth Sunday in the month
10am-12noon and 2-5pm.
No entrance fee.

Rastatt

Freiheitsmuseum
Herrenstrasse (in Schloss)
Dedicated to liberation movements that have taken place in
Germany's history. Open: Tuesday
to Sunday throughout the year,
9.30am-5pm Entrance is free.

Schloss
Herrenstrasse 18
Baroque palace with a sumptuously
decorated interior.
Open: guided tour through Schloss
from 1 April to 31 Oct-ober 10am-
5pm; 1 November to 31 March
10am-4pm Tours take
place on an hourly basis.

Wehrgeschichtliches Museum
Herrenstrasse (in Schloss)
A museum of military history.
Open: throughout the year,
Tuesday to Sunday 9.30am-5pm.

Schömberg

Nouvelle Schömberg
Bergstrasse 44
Well-equipped swimming pool
complex. Open: daily 10am-9pm,
Monday 1-7pm

Tiefenbronn

Pfarrkirche St Maria Magdalena
Church with interesting frescos and
windows. Open: May to October,
daily 1.30-4.30pm; November to
April, Saturday and Sunday 1.30-
3pm.

*Romantic monastery
ruins of Kloster Hirsau,
near Calw*

TOURIST INFORMATION OFFICES

Achern

Achern-Schwarzwald-Information
Hauptstrasse 1
☎ (07841) 29299,
Fax (07841) 25552

Altensteig

Städtisches Verkehrsamt Altensteig
Rosenstrasse 28
☎ (07453) 6633,
Fax (07453) 3249

Bad Herrenalb

Tourismusbüro
Bahnhofplatz 1
☎ (07083) 500555,
Fax (07083) 500544

Bad Teinach-Zavelstein

Kurverwaltung Bad Teinach-Zavelstein
*Otto-Neidhardt-Allee 6,
Bad Teinach*
☎ (07053) 8444,
Fax (07053) 2154

Bad Liebenzell

Kurverwaltung Bad Liebenzell
Kurhausdamm 4
☎ (07052) 4080,
Fax (07052) 408108

Bad Wildbad

Reise- und Verkehrsbüro Wildbad GmbH
König-Karl-Strasse 5-7
☎ (07081) 10280,
Fax (07081) 10290

Baden-Baden

Tourist-Information Baden-Baden
Augustaplatz 8
☎ (07221) 27520001,
Fax (07221) 275202
Open: April to October, Monday to Friday 9.30am-5pm, Saturday 9.30am-3pm.

Baiersbronn

Baiersbronn Touristik
Rosenplatz 3
☎ (07442) 84140,
Fax (07442) 841448
Open: April to October, Monday to Friday 9.30am-1pm and 2-6pm, Saturday, Sunday and public holidays, 10am-12noon.

Bühl

Tourist-Information Bühl
Hauptstrasse 41
☎ (07223) 935332,
Fax (07223) 935339

Calw

Stadtinformation Calw
Marktbrücke 1
☎ (07051) 968810,
Fax (07051) 968877
Open: Monday to Friday 9am-12.30pm and 2-5pm, Thursday 2-6.30pm, Saturday 9.30am-12.30pm.

Ettlingen

Stadtinformation Ettlingen
Schillerstrasse 7-9
☎ (07243) 101221,
Fax (07243) 101430

Enzklösterle

Kurverwaltung Enzklösterle
Friedenstrasse 16
☎ (07085) 7516,
Fax (07085) 1398

Forbach

Tourist-Information Forbach
Stried 14
☎ (07228) 2340,
Fax (07228) 2997

Gernsbach

Verkehrsamt Gernsbach
Igelbacherstrasse 11
☎ (07224) 64444,
Fax (07224) 64464
Open: Monday to Friday 8am-
12noon, Thursday 8am-12noon and
2-6pm, Friday 8am-1pm.

Karlsruhe

Stadtinformation
Karl-Friedrich-Strasse 22
Downtown branch of
Karlsruhe Tourist Office.
☎ (0721) 35534376,
Fax (0721) 35534389
Open: Monday to Friday 9am-6pm,
Saturday 9am-1pm.

Verkehrsverein Karlsruhe e V
Bahnhofplatz 6
☎ (0721) 35530,
Fax (0721) 35534399
Open: Monday to Friday 9am-6pm,
Saturday 9am-12.30pm.

Nagold

**Stadtverwaltung/
Verkehrsamt Nagold**
Marktstrasse 27
☎ (07452) 6810,
Fax (07452) 681230

Neubulach

Kurverwaltung Neubulach
Marktplatz 13
☎ (07053) 969510,
Fax (07053) 6416

Oberkirch

Tourist-Information Oberkirch
Eisenbahnstrasse 1
☎ (07802) 82241,
Fax (07802) 82179

Ottenhöfen

Tourist-Information Ottenhöfen
Allerheiligenstrasse 2
☎ (07842) 80440,
Fax (07842) 80445

Pforzheim

Tourist-Information Pforzheim
Marktplatz 1
☎ (07231) 1454560,
Fax (07231) 1454570

Rastatt

Stadtinformation Rastatt
Barockresidenz (Schloss)
☎ (07222) 972462,
Fax (07222) 972180
Open: Monday to Thursday
8.30am-12noon and 12.45-
4.30pm, Friday 8.30am-12noon
and 12.45-3pm.

Wildberg

Städtisches Verkehrsamt Wildberg
Marktstrasse 2
☎ (07054) 20122,
Fax (07054) 20126

Central
2 Black Forest

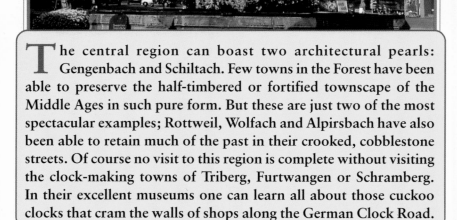

T he central region can boast two architectural pearls: Gengenbach and Schiltach. Few towns in the Forest have been able to preserve the half-timbered or fortified townscape of the Middle Ages in such pure form. But these are just two of the most spectacular examples; Rottweil, Wolfach and Alpirsbach have also been able to retain much of the past in their crooked, cobblestone streets. Of course no visit to this region is complete without visiting the clock-making towns of Triberg, Furtwangen or Schramberg. In their excellent museums one can learn all about those cuckoo clocks that cram the walls of shops along the German Clock Road.

Towns and townscapes aside, there is just as much to discover in the countryside, whether it be the famous waterfall at Triberg or the lonely Glaswaldsee (lake) near Bad Rippoldsau. A cycle trip from Gengenbach, for instance, leads to rustic country inns (*Bergvesperstuben*), where one can snack on home-baked bread and enjoy an unhampered vista of green fields and cows. Local traditions and magnificent old Black Forest farmhouses can be discovered at the Vogtsbauernhof open-air museum. Those who visit in winter can not only go cross-country skiing, but can also enjoy the spectacular carnival parades in such places as Rottweil and Elzach. At these festivals ancient customs are kept alive in a way seldom found elsewhere in Germany.

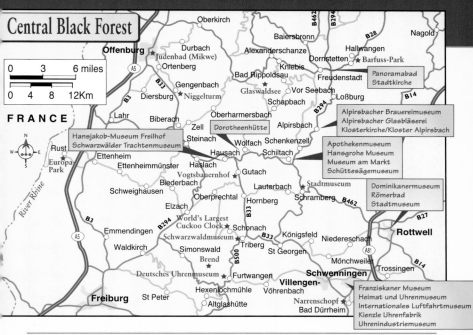

Route 5 — A Round Trip from Gengenbach

Gengenbach

Set against a backdrop of vineyards, hills and forest is the beautifully preserved old town of Gengenbach, in the Kinzig valley. A visit here is to take a step back in time. Cobblestone streets, beautifully restored half-timbered buildings and medieval town gates evoke the past in a way that is scarcely matched by any other town in the Forest. In summer the town is at its most idyllic, then the streets and houses are decorated with what is an almost tropical profusion of flowers.

It would be a shame to just pass through Gengenbach. Anybody who decides to pause a few days will not regret it. Even at the height of the season the town is remarkably free of large tourist crowds. On balmy summer evenings life takes place on the street, just like in Mediterranean lands. People either settle down at one of the inviting outdoor restaurants, or gather to chat on the market square. Old-fashioned street lamps illuminate the historic shop fronts. On some evenings a night watchman takes visitors around the local historical highlights. Carrying a lantern and chanting as he goes, he always draws a crowd. In the mornings another quaint touch is added as the gardener does his rounds, watering the flowers with the aid of his horse-drawn watercart.

A stroll around town can begin in front of the **Rathaus**, an elegant building that adds a very dignified air to the spacious Marktplatz in front. From here there is a lovely view down Victor-Kreuz-Strasse to one of the medieval town gates, the **Obertorturm**. There are a number of pretty half-timbered houses lining this main street, but it is worth exploring the little side-streets and alleyways as well. Particularly idyllic is **Engelgasse** with its charming old houses that date from the eighteenth century. A couple of inviting wine cellars can be found along Hauptstrasse.

Not far from the Rathaus is the former Benedictine abbey and the **Stadtpfarrkirche St Martin**. Though in parts Baroque on the outside (the church tower) the stunning interior has been converted back to its original Romanesque style. Brightly painted as it is, it is a fascinating attempt to recreate an authentic medieval church interior. The neo-Romanesque paintings were executed in the late nineteenth century using historical models – St Blasll cathedral in Braunschweig and St Michaelskirche in Hildesheim, among others. Nowhere else in southern Germany is there any equivalent.

For a great view over town and the surroundings walk up to the chapel on the **Bergle**, a hill with vine-covered slopes a mere 15 minutes walk from the Rathaus. If you are more in the mood for something a little less strenuous you can climb the **Niggelturm** instead. The view over town is also good and it is only a short stroll away from the Rathaus, near the end of the Hauptstrasse. Built in the fourteenth century it was originally a defensive tower, as can be seen by its impressive bulk. Later it was used as a prison and then a storage room. These days it has risen in the world again and has been transformed into a museum with exhibits relating to the town's lively carnival (*Fasnet*) celebrations.

Zell am Harmersbach

Zell, in the picturesque Harmersbach valley, is only a short drive south of Gengenbach. It was once one of the smallest of the so-called *Reichstädte*. In earlier times these were towns that owed direct allegiance only to the Kaiser, not to local lords, as was otherwise the case. Many towns symbolised this status by building a fountain with the figure of a knight in their market square – the sixteenth century fountain in Gengenbach's Marktplatz is a good example of this.

An attractive feature of town is the busy Hauptstrasse (main street), which is lined with many lovely old buildings, including some fine-looking houses in Art Nouveau style. Apart from this Zell is best known as being the home of **Zeller Keramik**, the makers of high-quality crockery with the famous *Hahn & Henne* (rooster and chicken) motif. Established in 1794 they were the first company in Germany to produce stoneware using methods developed by Josiah Wedgwood, in England. At their factory outlet in town it is possible to buy their products at greatly reduced prices.

Haslach

That the broad Kinzig valley was a preferred invasion route for French armies in the seventeenth and eighteenth centuries is confirmed by the history of **Haslach**, south of Zell on the B33. Having already ransacked Gengenbach in 1689 they put Haslach to the torch in 1704. Most of the many old half-timbered buildings visitors can see today are therefore a product of the time shortly thereafter.

Haslach was the home of Heinrich Hansjakob (1837-1916), a popular writer, politician and priest, who set all his stories in the region he loved so well. One of Hansjakob's driving interests was the preservation of the Black Forest's old folk traditions. He often complained about the fact that country girls were so easily influenced by current fashion trends, only too readily putting their traditional costumes aside. His recommendation to those girls who wanted to uphold tradition was to 'avoid, tease and make fun of' those who had been tempted by modern tastes.

It may have been of some consolation to Hansjakob that his home town has set up an interesting museum (**Schwarzwälder Trachtenmuseum**) with folklore costumes from all over the region. It is located in the former **Kapuzinerkloster** (Capuchin monastery). Those who are interested will find that Hansjakob has his own **Hansjakobmuseum** in the Hansjakobstrasse.

Elzach

Old traditions are alive and well in **Elzach**, a climatic health resort south of Haslach on the B294. This small town is famed for its lively, quite spectacular *Fasnet* (carnival) celebrations. Highlight of the festivities, which can be traced back to 1530, is the procession of *Schuttig* (masked fools) on Shrove Sunday and Shrove Tuesday. Dressed in bright red costumes, their faces hidden by demonic masks, they dance and caper through the streets, sometimes stopping to strike at hapless onlookers with a *Saublodere* (inflated pig's bladder tied to the end of a stick). Young women 'attacked' by Schuttig in this way can feel privileged; age-old tradition has it that they can expect to raise a large family.

Hemingway at Oberprechtal

Hemingway fans might consider an excursion to **Oberprechtal**, just north-east of Elzach, in the lovely Elz valley. While on an angling holiday with his wife and friends he had some unpleasant experiences with German innkeepers. At one place they refused him and his companions accommodation, at another he was dismayed by the sour wine and dirty surroundings. He found the beer good though, and his unfriendly reception is probably explained by the fact that he visited Germany not long after the country's defeat in World War I. Gasthaus Zur Sonne and Zum Rössle, both of which Hemingway visited, still stand. Apart from these establishments there are also a number of other inviting-looking places to eat and sleep in this (despite Hemingway's experiences in the early 1920s) pleasant little town.

From Elzach a country road (*Landstrasse*) runs in a north-westerly direction via **Biederbach** and **Schweighausen** to Ettenheim. Just

A mountain —— bike tour

The following cycle tour (it requires roughly $4^{1}/_{2}$ hours and lots of energy if the weather is hot) is best done with a mountain bike – the three-gear 'touring bikes' are cheaper to rent, but it is a struggle to climb those hills with them. Bicycles can be hired at Gengenbach's Tourist Information. They also have suitable maps and suggestions for other cycle tours or walks in the area. A good choice of map is the *Atlasco Wanderkarte Lahr – Haslach* 1:30,000 as it shows both walking and cycling tracks.

One of the most charming features of this ride is that it takes you past a number of rustic old *Bergvesperstuben*. These are places where the farmer has bettered his income by selling simple snacks to passers-by. Usually located away from the main roads, they offer good home cooking at very reasonable prices. At some places they even make their own schnapps. It is well worth trying if the opportunity arises.

Leave Gengenbach in the direction of **Haigarach**. Eventually you will come to a road climbing steeply uphill towards **Pfaffenbach**. Part of this road is covered with loose gravel and it is a hard slog to the hut at **Pfaffenbacher-Eck** (1,791ft/546m). Just before the hut, turn left, and go downhill along another gravel road, following waymarks 7 and 8. After passing a car barrier, come to an asphalt road which leads down to **Ernsbach**, a rural settlement consisting of nothing more than a few scattered farmhouses. At the point where the cycle trail reaches the turn-off to **Störgeist,** continue downhill following waymarks 6, 7, and 8 and the red pyramid to reach **Nordrach** in the valley.

At **Gasthaus-Pension zur Post**, on the main road, turn left, go past the turn-off to the **Puppenmuseum** (Doll Museum) and then turn right in the direction of **Schottenhöfen.** *Vesperstuben* passed on the way include **Flackeneinkehr** (closed Tuesdays), **Mühlstein** (closed Mondays) and **Bächlehof**. On the way downhill to Zell you will pass the **Schnaps-Brennerei Anton Schwarz**, where it is possible to buy fruit brandy. The main road to Zell is reached at **Gasthof Adler**. Those who wish could

before Ettenheim it might be worth pausing for a look at the pilgrimage church of St Landolin, in **Ettenheimmünster**. Landolin was an Irish monk and missionary who, according to legend, was murdered on this spot by a pagan hunter. Inside the church are some lovely altars, a beautifully restored Silbermann organ and a ceiling fresco depicting the legend.

Ettenheim

Ettenheim once belonged to the bishopric of Strasbourg and this inevitably meant that the town was often embroiled in the many feuds

Gengenbach provides an ideal base for cycle tours in the surrounding countryside

continue directly into Zell, but note the road here is very busy.

From the *Gasthof* turn left, then pass a *Haltestelle* (bus stop), immediately after which you turn right, in the direction of **Hochstall**. Cross over the railway lines and now continue in the direction of **Schreilergrund** (signposted). This section is partly waymarked by a G. Once you reach the railway line again in **Zell** you will pass an old steam locomotive, from where a pictogram of a bicycle is followed into the middle of town.

The road out of Zell turns left (south-west) and passes **Gasthof zum Gröbenhof**. Just after the *Gasthof* cross the road and then follow the cycle path in the direction of Biberach – Haslach (signposted). Once you arrive at a road bridge turn right, following the blue diamond towards **Biberach**. On the outskirts of town turn right into Waldstrasse and follow the signposts back to Gengenbach.

of that city's prince-bishops. Though it suffered more than its fair share of war and plundering over the centuries, the town has nevertheless managed to rescue a good deal of the past into the present. In fact Ettenheim's most impressive feature is the very picturesque ensemble of Baroque buildings clustered below the parish church of **St Bartholomäus**. Inside this late-Baroque church is the tomb of Cardinal Rohan of Strasbourg (1734-1803) who, along with other members of his family, played an important role in French history. Forced to leave Strasbourg in the aftermath of the French

Revolution he spent the last years of his life here in exile.

Only 5 miles (8km) west of Ettenheim, near the village of **Rust**, are two important attractions; the Europa-Park and Naturschutzgebiet Taubergiessen. Those wishing to spend more time in the area will find that accommodation is on average cheaper in Ettenheim than it is in Rust or at the Europa-Park.

Taubergiessen Nature Reserve

Entangled water courses, verdant meadows and a dense, almost jungle-like forest alive with the sound of birds: this is what the Rhine landscape must once have looked like before the river's flow was regulated by dikes and dams some 150 years ago.

Europa-Park

In spite of the fact that Disneyworld near Paris is only a few hours drive away, the older Europa-Park has lost none of its attraction. The largest and most popular of Germany's theme parks was set up in 1975 by the Mack family. Established in 1781 the family business had long specialised in the construction of fairground architecture and circus equipment before they turned their attention to the development of an amusement park. And it seems that they made a good job of it: over sixty attractions lure young and old in ever increasing numbers to the park. What adds to its popularity is the fact that prices are comparatively moderate (entrance price includes all attractions) and food in the park's many restaurants is both good and varied – an important fact when one bears in mind that most people spend the entire day here.

Those who wish to see all that the park has to offer will require at least two days. In the course of a mini-tour through Europe (each section of the park has a European country as its theme) visitors can take a roller-coaster ride in the 'Quartier Français', go bobsledding in the Alps and, the biggest thrill of all, race down at a speed of 50mph (80kph) from the top of the Euro-Mir tower to the rustic charm of the 'Russian Village'. Apart from the many thrill rides one can also visit the revolving multimedia theatre 'eMotional', with its spectacular laser-light show, or enjoy one of the many variety shows. If all this is not enough there are also various concerts and festivals that take place throughout the year.

After a long day enjoying the park's many attractions most families are probably going to be exhausted. Of course the park's operators have thought about this. What better to way to end the day than with a meal in medieval surroundings (Knights' Banquet), or to the accompaniment of can-can dancers at La Cigale restaurant? Your bed for the night could be in a medieval Spanish castle (Hotel Castillo Alcazar), or at the equally Spanish Hotel El Andaluz. Those who have brought their own accommodation with them will find a large caravan park is situated nearby.

The **Naturschutzgebiet** (nature reserve) covers an area of 4,000 acres (1,600ha) and stretches for some 6 miles (10km) along the Rhine. It is home to hundreds of different species of plants and animals, many of which are endangered or rare elsewhere in Europe. In autumn and winter the reserve is an important sanctuary for migratory birds, some of which spend the entire winter here, while others merely pause on their way further south. However, summer is also a good time for hobby ornithologists to visit. At this time of the year there are close to 120 species of birds nesting in the reserve.

Those who want to explore the reserve can do so on foot or by boat. Tours of the waterways that dissect the reserve are conducted by the local fishermen. The trip by punt takes about 1 hour and can be booked at the Tourist Office in Rust or it can be arranged directly with the fisherman – some addresses are included in the Fact File under Sports and Pastimes. These boat trips are not only good value but they are also the best way to experience the essentially riverine nature of this unique landscape.

Apart from the tour by punt, which is the highlight of any visit to the Taubergiessen, visitors can also follow one of the various circular trails through the reserve. The *Orchideenweg* is a 4 mile (6.5km) way-marked trail that leads through a section of the reserve known for the abundance of wild orchids – 22 species are found here. The *Kormoranweg* (4 miles/6.5km) is especially interesting for bird-watchers as they will have plenty of opportunities to observe rare waterfowl. Another waymarked path is the *Schmetterlingsweg*. In summer it is possible to see numerous species of butterfly along this 1 mile (1.6km) route. An interesting alternative would be to combine sections of these trails in a much longer walk. Maps and walking tips are available at the Tourist Information in Rust.

Moving on

For a short stretch the B3 between Ettenheim and Offenburg takes the same route as the Baden Wine Road, which was followed (going in the opposite direction) as far as Oberkirch on Route 2. But rather than take the Wine Road's somewhat circuitous route via Diersburg and Gengenbach to Offenburg remain, instead, on the B3.

Offenburg

The town is an important traffic junction and for those journeying by train it offers access to the lovely Kinzigtal (Kinzig Valley), to Freiburg further south and to Strasbourg in France. The **Schwarzwaldbahn** (Black Forest Railway) trip to Villingen starts here too. Known for the numerous tunnels and viaducts along the way this is one of the most picturesque rail journeys in Germany. Those who wish could continue from Villingen to the attractive old town of Konstanz, on Lake Constance (Bodensee) – for a description of Konstanz see Chapter 6.

Anybody entering town from the railway station might, at first, be a little disappointed with the place. Nondescript buildings flank a busy road on the five-minute walk to the middle of town – on leaving the station turn left and follow Hauptstrasse. However, at the time of writing a good deal of construction work was going on and, with a little luck, the town planners might show a surer hand than they have in the past.

Historic buildings around Hauptstrasse & the Fischmarkt

Having said this, appearances do improve as you near the pedestrian zone section of Hauptstrasse. Though a few modern department stores still disturb the overall picture, many attractive old buildings remain to convey at least a touch of the romance that the average tourist associates with 'Old Germany'. Photogenic buildings along Hauptstrasse include the **Rathaus, Hotel Sonne** and the **Einhorn-Apotheke**, a lovely old chemist's shop that dates from 1772.

The Ölberg (Mount of Olives), Offenburg

Baroque buildings are a feature of Ettenheim's pretty Altstadt

Just off Hauptstrasse is the Fischmarkt, another pedestrian zone. This is also a pretty part of town, with some nice old buildings such as the **Hirsch-Apotheke** and the **Salzhaus** (Salt House, 1786). If you leave the Fischmarkt along Steinstrasse you will come across a number of pleasant looking cafés and restaurants. In warm weather they invariably place tables outside. The **Judenbad** (Jews' Bath or *Mikwe*) is located at Glaserstrasse 8, a street running parallel to Steinstrasse. It dates back to the thirteenth century and is one of the few underground ritual baths left in the region. In order to view the Mikwe you will have to join one of the guided tours around town arranged by the Tourist Office.

The Baroque **Heilig-Kreuz-Kirche**, to the north-east of the Rathaus, is certainly worth a look but the main interest focuses on a sculpture outside. The **Ölberg** (Mount of Olives, 1524) is considered to be the town's most valuable work of art. A closer look at this beautifully detailed work will reveal that the bailiffs who are approaching Jesus and the Disciples are wearing costumes and weapons characteristic of the sixteenth century.

There are a number of other historic buildings scattered around

On the Wine Road

In the vicinity of Offenburg there are a number of charming old wine-growing villages. **Durbach**, on that stretch of the Wine Road linking Oberkirch with Offenburg, is one of the prettiest of them all. The main street is lined with quaint old houses and the little stream that runs alongside it further enhances the idyllic atmosphere of the place. If you have not managed to sip the local wine elsewhere then you will hardly find more conducive surroundings for doing so than here. The best addresses in town are Hotel Ritter and Hotel Rebstock, both of which are noted for the quality of their wine and food. Those who want to buy wine direct from the grower can drive up to nearby **Schloss Staufenberg**. There is also a *Weinstube* here, so the wine can be tasted before it is bought. The Schloss is open for sales from: 8am-12noon and 1-5pm Monday to Friday, 9am-12noon Saturday.

town and those who want to know more should visit the **Stadtinformation** (Tourist Office) at Gärtnerstrasse 8. It is only a short walk from the Rathaus along Kornstrasse. Those with a car will find there is parking space in the Marktplatz just opposite. Apart from a good selection of material on the region in general, they also have a useful pamphlet that includes a town plan and a guide (in English) to all places of interest.

A nice way to drive back to Gengenbach, whether from Durbach or Offenburg, is to take the road via **Rammersweier, Weierbach** and **Fessenbach** to **Ortenberg**. All these villages have picturesque corners and you will pass one inviting-looking restaurant after the other. Above Ortenberg is the imposing **Schloss Ortenberg**. It was rebuilt in the nineteenth century in the manner of an English castle and now houses a youth hostel.

Route 6 THROUGH THE KINZIG AND WOLFACH VALLEYS (circular route)

Freudenstadt

Like Offenburg the town of Freudenstadt is an important road and rail junction. This fact, together with its central position, makes it an excellent base for those who want to explore the northern and central regions of the Black Forest using public transport.

Marktplatz

To this day the Marktplatz remains Freudenstadt's most important attraction. There are prettier market squares elsewhere in Germany, but its sheer size has made it a focal point for all who visit. Unfortunately a busy road separates it into an upper (Oberer Marktplatz) and a lower (Unterer Marktplatz) market square, making it impossible to appreciate as a whole.

At one corner of the lower market square is the Protestant **Stadtkirche**. This church is unusual in that it consists of two naves meeting at right angles, thus giving the building a distinctive L shape. In earlier times the men sat in one nave, the women in the other. Though they could not see one another the preacher could, as his pulpit was situated at the point where the naves converge. From the church's once rich furnishings three valuable pieces remain: a beautifully carved cross from the sixteenth century, a Romanesque font with a frieze of entwined animals and a carved lectern from the same period.

Recent additions to the lower market, which has been partly landscaped as a park, are the many small fountains set in a paved area. An expensive project, it at first raised the ire of the locals, until they discovered that their kids just loved playing among them. In contrast to the green of the lower market the broad, paved expanse of the upper market is a favourite place for staging festivals and concerts. At one corner is the **Rathaus**, with its distinctive tower. A couple of good restaurants in the vicinity include the Ratskeller and Gasthof Jägerstüble. Also located on the

Duke Friedrich builds a town in the woods

In the sixteenth century the spot where the town now stands was covered by a gloomy pine forest. There were no roads to speak of, at the most a few simple trails frequented by woodsmen or hunters. But the local ruler Duke Friedrich I of Württemberg had plans for this particular patch of forest. In 1599 he placed the architect Heinrich Schickard in charge of a project to build a town from scratch, right in the midst of these 'daunting woods'. His reasons for doing so were manifold, the decision no princely whim. One important factor was that by creating a town here he could provide better living conditions for the men working in his silver mine at Christophstal. Also influencing the decision was the fact the town would provide a new home for Protestant refugees fleeing persecution in Catholic Austria – the duke was a supporter of the French Huguenots. It was perhaps a happy coincidence that there were also miners among these refugees.

The town that the duke envisaged was to have a large, empty rectangular space in the middle where, at a later date, he proposed to build a Schloss. His plans in this respect were never realised but this explains why the present market place has such extraordinary dimensions – covering an area of 11½ acres (4.73ha) it is only a bit smaller than the Place de la Concorde in Paris. The rest of the town was also built according to a rigorous geometrical pattern, somewhat in the manner of a board game. It is this remarkable town plan, still clearly visible on modern-day maps, that establishes Freudenstadt's historical significance. Friedrich's town was the first in Germany to be designed in such a fashion. More than a hundred years later followed Karlsruhe, Ludwigsburg, Mannheim and Schwetzingen.

Practical man that he was Duke Friedrich had hoped to create a town that could compete with Frankfurt as a base for trade and industry. Alas, the Plague and the Thirty Years' War put an end to these ambitious hopes. It was not until the advent of tourism at the end of the nineteenth century that the town's fortunes improved. The clear, fresh air attracted many visitors and the town earned the title of *Luftkurort* (climatic health resort). However, at the end of World War II disaster struck again. In April 1945 the town was largely destroyed by French soldiers. All the buildings lining the present Marktplatz had to be rebuilt after the war.

upper market is the post office, next to which there is a large underground car park.

Excursions from Freudenstadt

A pleasant excursion from Freudenstadt can be made to the small medieval town of **Dornstetten**, which lies a short distance to the east. Though the Marktplatz here is a lot smaller than its counterpart in Freudenstadt it is certainly a lot cosier and more peaceful. There are a number of superb half-timbered buildings lining the market and other places of historical interest can be seen in the course of a signposted walk around town.

The fountains on Freudenstadt's huge Marktplatz are a big attraction for the kids

Dornstetten's Marktplatz is a lot smaller, but also a lot cosier than Freudenstadt's

Hauptstrasse, Wolfach

Bare-foot Park

One of the more unusual attractions in the vicinity is to be found in nearby **Hallwangen**. The recently opened **Barfuss-Park** (Bare-foot Park) has been especially designed with the interests of families with small children in mind. Here the parents and the kids can kick off their shoes (lockers are provided) and stroll around a 1½-mile (2.4km) circuit consisting of various surfaces like sand, mud and pebbles. Entrance to the park is free and there is a place to wash your feet before you leave.

Along the Kinzig Valley

The B294 curves its way south from Freudenstadt, on its route through the lovely Kinzig valley. The Kinzig river actually originates near **Loßburg**, just south of Freudenstadt. It flows south as far as Schiltach, from where it turns west until, by Haslach, it bends north-west to finally reach the Rhine near Offenburg – this western section of the Kinzig valley is described in Route 5 (see above).

Alpirsbach

The first place of interest along this route is **Alpirsbach**. Here the main attraction is a **Klosterkirche** (basilica) that was attached to the old Benedictine monastery. This Romanesque building dates back to the eleventh century and has remained surprisingly pure in style over the centuries, in spite of some additions from

the Gothic period. The cruciform ground plan and relative lack of embellishment in the church interior, show the influence of Hirsau. Concerts are held in the Gothic cloister during the summer months.

Monastery Brewery

For those who have worked up a thirst, it might be deemed fortunate that the old Benedictine monks were not only good at building churches but also at brewing beer. The **Alpirsbacher Klosterbräu** (Monastery Brewery) is adjacent to the monastery buildings. Here they still brew beer using traditional methods that are centuries old. Both the brewery and the **Brauereimuseum** (Brewery Museum) can be visited as part of a guided tour by prior arrangement. Otherwise the product can be tested at one of the town's many inns.

Schiltach

In **Schiltach** tourism has long since replaced such old trades as log-rafting (the last raft was floated on the Kinzig in 1894) and tanning as the most important source of income. Romantic cobbled streets, lined by row upon row of beautifully restored half-timbered buildings, make this town one of the loveliest in the Black Forest. The prettiest section of town is perched on a hill slope around the Marktplatz. Located here is the Renaissance **Rathaus** (1594) which, like many other buildings in Schiltach, was built after a devastating fire in 1590. The paintings on the façade date from 1942 and are typical for the Nazi period. In the old **Gerberviertel** (Tanners' Quarter), near the river, is the **Äussere Mühle** (1557), the town's oldest half-timbered building. Good views over town can be had from the **Häberlesberg**.

Those with an interest in the history of the place have ample opportunity to deepen their knowledge in one of Schiltach's four museums. The **Apothekenmuseum** (Pharmacy Museum) is situated in a building that up until 1985 was, in fact, a pharmacy. All sorts of interesting things are on display here, for instance a device for straightening crooked noses! At the **Hansgrohe Museum** visitors can learn all about bathroom design and how 'washing oneself' has developed over the ages. The firm, which manufactures bathroom articles, actually started business in Schiltach way back in 1901. The remaining museums are the **Schüttesägemuseum** (history of log-rafting in the Kinzig valley) and the **Museum am Markt** which offers an overview of the town's eventful history.

Wolfach

Wolfach is situated at the point where the River Wolfach meets the Kinzig. In the late Middle Ages not only the town, but also a large chunk of the Kinzig valley, and all the Wolfach valley, were controlled by the Counts of Fürstenberg. Their seventeenth century **Schloss**, situated in the middle of town, now houses various district authorities along with a Heimatmuseum (local history). Running north from the Schloss is Hauptstrasse, where those with a car can park. It has been spruced up in recent years and, with its restaurants and shops, is now one of the most pleasant parts of town. One of the more imposing buildings to found here is the **Rathaus** (1892), which was rebuilt after a fire in Renaissance style.

Glassworks

The biggest attraction which Wolfach has to offer is the **Dorotheenhütte** (glassworks), at the southern end of town. Glassblowing has been practised in the Black Forest for centuries and this is probably the best place to see it done. Here they really do make and sell their own lead crystal glassware, the glassblowers are not just performing for the tourists. Those who wish can even have a try at glassblowing themselves. The finished product is yours to keep, though if you prefer something a bit more professional there is plenty to choose from in the shop at the front of the building.

Apart from watching the glassblowing demonstrations it is also worth strolling through the attached glass museum. Here visitors are given an insight into over 2,000 years of glassmaking history. Among the various articles of glassware on display is an ornamental set of lead glass commissioned by the Shah of Iran, shortly before he was deposed in 1979. In the **Weihnachtsdorf** (Christmas Village) visitors have the opportunity to buy typical German Christmas decorations, no matter what the time of year.

The road back to Freudenstadt

South of Wolfach on the B33, near Gutach, is an outstanding open-air museum known as the **Vogtsbauernhof**. This museum is devoted to the rural culture of the Black Forest and features original buildings from various parts of the region. For more details refer to Route 7 (see below).

From Wolfach this route follows a scenic road through the Wolftal (Wolf Valley) back towards Freudenstadt. At **Vor Seebach**, shortly before Bad Rippoldsau, it is possible to make a detour to the lovely **Glaswaldsee**. After about 2½ miles (4km) the steep, narrow road brings you to a car park. From there it is about another 20 minutes to the tarn along a steep track.

The small lake (the term 'tarn' refers to its glacial origin) lies within a nature reserve at an altitude of around 2,750ft (840m) above sea level. Surrounded by a dense stand of fir trees, and with a steep rock wall towering over 325ft (100m)

high behind it, it makes a romantic spot for a picnic snack. The present name (it was once known as 'Wildsee') is a reference to the fact that glass-works existed near here in the sixteenth century. The return walk downhill takes only 10 minutes.

At **Bad Rippoldsau** one can either go left in the direction of **Kniebis**, or right in the direction of Freudenstadt. Both roads are equally scenic, though the route via Kniebis on the Black Forest Summit Road (this stretch is along the B28) is slightly longer. Kniebis is a popular winter sports resort, with some good cross-country skiing in the vicinity. Just up the road the **Hotel Alexanderschanze** is a reminder that the area around Kniebis was once of some military importance. *Schanze* is the German term for a redoubt (fortification) and there were several of these near Kniebis, including the well-preserved example at Alexanderschanze. It was, like most of the other fortifications in the Black Forest, part of a defensive system erected against invading French troops in the seventeenth and eighteenth centuries.

A pleasant detour from the Wolftal can be made to the Glaswalsee

Black Forest —— —Farmhouses

There is something vaguely medieval about the *Schwarzwaldhaus* (Black Forest farmhouse); its huge (originally thatched or with wooden tiles) hipped-roof, sloping down almost to the ground, appears like a kind of helmet, with the windows at the front peeping Darth Vader-like from under the frontal fringe of roof – those not familiar with *Star Wars* might be reminded of the helmet with raised visor worn by the knight in Dürer's engraving *Knight, Death, and the Devil*. Its design, and the shape of the rest of the building, was a response to the local geography and the Forest's raw climate, which in winter often forced the farmers of yore to spend long periods indoors. As to the reason why the roof is so large the simple answer lies in the fact that it provided shelter not only for the family (the grandparents often lived here as well) but also the farm animals, their fodder and the farm machinery; in other words the house was both a dwelling and barn in one.

Although they share certain basic characteristics, such as the fact that they were all mainly wooden constructions, traditional Black Forest houses were by no means identical throughout the region. There are in fact seven basic historical types, each of which differs according to the kind of landscape and climatic conditions found in its particular area. For instance the so-called *Schauinslandhaus*, which was situated in an area exposed to strong winds and extreme weather, had a roof which extended far enough to shelter the farmer even if he had to walk around the house in stormy conditions. Even the well was covered by the roof, so (in the days before

(cont'd overleaf)

The Vogtsbauernhof farmhouse at the Vogtsbauernhof open-air museum

running water) nobody had to get wet. Depending on how well-off the farmer was, there were also a number of ancillary buildings surrounding the main house. They might include a flour mill, a bakehouse and even a small chapel – a proper church was not always within easy reach.

In the old days the dining-room cum lounge was the social focal point of the house. Situated at ground level it was, apart from the kitchen, the only room that was heated. In winter the entire family, including farmhands, would gather here to chat around the tiled stove, repair tools, or perhaps take a midday snooze. In niches around the stove apples and pears were baked, or linen sacks filled with cherry pips were warmed up as bed warmers for the night – the bedrooms were, after all, without heating.

In a corner of the dining-room, near the window, was the so-called *Herrgottswinkel*. In this niche hung a crucifix and a statue of the Virgin Mary. In Protestant homes they placed a Bible here instead. This corner of the room was also where one usually found the dining-room table. Here the family would eat their frugal meals consisting perhaps of thin broth, dumplings or potatoes with sauerkraut and a bowl of lettuce or chard – a kind of beet.

Compared to the relative comfort of the dining-room the rest of the house was somewhat less idyllic. The kitchen was dark and smoky and by no means a pleasant place to work. The smoke rose almost unhindered to the roof, curing the ham and sausages that hung in its path and coating the wooden ceiling with soot. Though not exactly a healthy environment, it did at least have the side effect of protecting the wood, and fodder in the hayloft above, from insect pests.

The parents had it a bit more comfortable than the rest of the household when they retired for the night. No doubt shivering, and clutching linen sack bed-warmers to their breasts, they were able to climb into a large, often prettily decorated four-poster bed known as a *Himmelbett*. It offered a measure of protection against draughts and its wooden 'ceiling' (the 'Himmel' or 'heaven') caught the bugs that fell from the roof beams.

The traditional forms of these farmhouses, which nestle so prettily in the countryside to this day, can be studied in more detail at the Vogtsbauernhof museum near Gutach (see Route 7). Those who want to get a taste of life on a modern farm can take advantage of *Urlaub auf dem Bauernhof* (farm holidays), which are offered throughout the region. Here guests will notice that even though the modern farmhouses are now equipped with all modern conveniences, the basic layout of the house has remained unchanged: under the huge roof at least half the building is taken up by cow stalls and the hayloft.

Route 7 — THE GERMAN CLOCK ROAD (circular route)

Triberg

One of the most visited towns in the Black Forest is Triberg with its famous waterfall. In summer the place is swarming with tourists from all over the world and those who like it quieter will probably prefer to base themselves somewhere else. However, the advantages of such a well-known destination include the good facilities and the likelihood that English is spoken in most shops and hotels.

Anybody strolling along the town's steep main street cannot fail to notice that cuckoo clocks not only were, but still are, an important economic factor. Apart from the cheap battery-operated versions found in many of the souvenir shops, there are some impressive examples of hand-carved cuckoo clocks at the appropriately named **House of a Thousand Clocks**. Another good address for souvenir hunters is **Hubert Herr's Uhrenfabrik** (Clock Factory), which is also located in Hauptstrasse. He guarantees that you will get the genuine article from his shop, not the plastic imitations offered elsewhere.

Triberg Waterfall

Germany's highest waterfall, the Triberger Wasserfälle, has been a tourist attraction since the nineteenth century and interest in this natural spectacle shows no sign of dwindling. Every year more than half a million people come to view the Gutach as it plunges a total of 535ft (163m) in seven stages. However, not all of these visitors have come just because the waterfall is so picturesque; for some an equally important reason is that a stroll alongside it is so healthy. It seems that as the water froths over the granite rocks it ionises the air, which is of benefit to people suffering from high blood pressure and respiratory problems. It takes about half an hour to walk to the top of the falls from the main entrance at the top of Hauptstrasse.

Another important attraction that Triberg has to offer is the pilgrimage church of **Maria in der Tanne** (1699-1705). Although rather plain from the outside the church has a magnificent Baroque interior. It gets

---

World's largest cuckoo clock

If none of the cuckoo clocks in Triberg are big enough for your liking, then you will have to drive a short way in the direction of **Schonach**. Located here is what used to be the world's largest cuckoo clock. There is now a larger one on the road to Hornberg, though many claim that the former record-holder is still the most interesting – at least as many people regard both, and those like them, as mere tourist gimmicks. The cuckoo that pops out between 9am and 6pm measures roughly 35in (90cm) and weighs 44lbs (20kg). If you have always wondered how a cuckoo 'lives' between calls, you can also enter its abode at the above times.

its name from a carved Madonna figure that has been incorporated into the high altar. Said to have miracle-working properties, the carving was once located in the hollow of a *Tanne* (pine tree) that grew outside town.

Black Forest Museum

Not far from Triberg Waterfall is the excellent **Schwarzwaldmuseum** (Black Forest Museum), which concerns itself above all with the various trades and industries that were once practised in the region. On display here are traditional costumes, wood carvings, clocks and what is claimed to be the largest collection of barrel-organs in Europe. Of particular interest is a model of the spectacular Black Forest Railway, which runs between Offenburg and Villingen-Schwenningen, touching Triberg on the way. A major feat of engineering, this railway overcomes the difficult terrain en route with a total of 36 tunnels.

Furtwangen

Furtwangen lies south of Triberg, on the scenic B500. Like Triberg this town has long been one of the strongholds of the Black Forest clock industry. Clock-making here had its origins in the bad old days when the poor Black Forest farmers had to supplement their meagre incomes by making and selling those cuckoo clocks that have since become so famous. The first Black

German

The most important museum of its kind in Germany, the **Deutsches Uhrenmuseum** (Clock Museum) deals not only with the history of clock-making in the Black Forest, but with the phenomenon of time and how it is measured in general. Appropriately enough a tour of the exhibits begins chronologically with elementary clocks and sundials, then moves on to Renaissance clocks, wristwatches and the electronic measurement of time.

A highlight of the museum is, of course, the world's largest collection of antique Black Forest clocks. Here collectors can study the classic form of the beloved *Kuckucksuhr* (cuckoo clock), while others might be surprised to

Forest clock was supposedly constructed in Furtwangen around 1640, but the first clock with a cuckoo did not appear on the scene until around 1738. These facts, and much more besides, are documented in the town's main attraction, the German Clock Museum *(see above)*.

Excursions from Furtwangen

A popular excursion from Furtwangen is north-west to the look-out tower on the **Brend** (3,771ft/1,149m), one of the peaks on a ridge that stretches between Furtwangen and Elzach. If the weather is good the views extend as far as the Swiss Alps and towards France. In winter the locality is especially good for cross-country

Clock Museum

know that not all Black Forest clocks came with cuckoos. Just as typical for the region, though not so well-known overseas, are the so-called *Schilduhren* (shield clocks). The faces of these clocks were usually painted with floral motifs and remained quite popular up until the nineteenth century.

Though visitors can tour the museum at their own pace it is worthwhile joining one of the free guided tours. On such a tour one can see demonstrations of how clocks with movable figures worked and hear one of the museum's mechanical organs being played. One clock that can only really be appreciated when it is operating is, for instance, the *Knödelfresser* clock. It was made in 1870 in nearby Vöhrenbach and features a plump mechanical figure ravenously consuming dumplings. Other automatons in this style include one with a butcher who hits an ox on the head when the clock strikes the hour and another with a criminal who is punctually beheaded every hour, on the hour – it all depended on what the customer found amusing! Also interesting is the *Deutsche Reichskolonialuhr* (Clock of the German Colonial Empire, 1905), which showed the different times in all of Germany's old colonies. It had as a motto 'the sun never sets on our land'.

For those who do wander about on their own the museum publication 'Black Forest Clocks' gives interesting background information on this section of the museum. The illustrated booklet is not expensive and might be a useful investment for anyone who actually plans to buy a cuckoo clock.

Hexenloch water-mill

skiing, though snow-boarding and downhill skiing are also possible in the area.

Just a short distance further north is the source of the River Breg (*Bregquelle*), a main tributary of the Danube. From here to the point where the Danube enters the Black Sea it is exactly 1,430 miles (2,302km). Close by is the Romanesque **Martinskapelle.**

Mill in the Witches' Hole

The **Hexenlochmühle** (Mill in the Witches' Hole) is situated to the south-west of Furtwangen in a beautiful, densely-forested little valley. This old sawmill with its two waterwheels is, perhaps, one of the most photogenic in the entire Forest. Built in 1825 the mill has been in the possession of the same family since 1839. Though no longer used as a sawmill (milling timber ceased to be profitable for the family business some twenty years ago), the two wheels are still used to generate energy for a small clock-maker's workshop. The hand-made clocks produced here, along with many other souvenirs, are available in the shop now inside the mill.

Villingen-Schwenningen

From Furtwangen a pleasant country road leads via Vöhrenbach to the twin town of Villingen-Schwenningen. The two towns, which are separated geographically, were joined for administrative purposes in 1972. With its largely intact medieval town wall and numerous historic buildings, it is above all Villingen that is of interest to visitors. On top of this, carnival celebrations (*Fasnet*) have a very long tradition here and are among to the most spectacular in the entire region.

The town's medieval character is best savoured on a leisurely stroll through the Altstadt. Those in need of refreshments will find that most of the cafés and pubs are located along Färberstrasse and Rietstrasse. The latter is part of a pedestrian zone, close to the main sights, and with a good view towards a thirteenth century town gate known as the **Riettor.**

Situated on the Münsterplatz is the late Gothic **Altes Rathaus** (Old Town Hall), an attractive building which now houses a local history museum, and the **Münster Unserer Lieben Frau.** The minster was originally built in Romanesque style in the twelfth century. After a town fire in 1271 parts of the church were rebuilt in the Gothic manner and then, in the eighteenth century, large sections of the interior were redone in the Baroque style. Of interest inside is, among other things, the fourteenth century Nägelin crucifix.

The **Franziskaner Museum** is located in what used to be a Franciscan monastery. It contains an interesting collection of sacred art, as well as finds from an important Celtic burial site on the outskirts of town. Particularly interesting is the **Schwarzwaldsammlung** (Black Forest Collection). On display here are the original interiors of various historic Black Forest dwellings, for instance a Black Forest kitchen and the interior of an inn from 1799. All in all the collection gives a good overview of daily life and folklore in the region.

Schwenningen

Once, Schwenningen was able to claim that it was the largest clock manufacturing town in the world. In 1934 there were 25 factories with 14,000 workers, who produced 50,000 clocks a day. Even in the 1960s the situation still looked good with the town producing 8 million clocks per year. But then in the 1970s cheap imports from Asia burst the bubble and though the clock-making industry is still important (the emphasis is on wall and alarm clocks) it now accounts for a much smaller proportion of the workforce.

Anybody who prefers a German wall clock to a Japanese wristwatch can satisfy their desire by visiting the **Kienzle Uhrenfabrik**, the town's largest clock factory. Here visitors can get some good deals on quality clocks and wristwatches from their factory shop. It is located at Eichendorffstrasse 29.

On to Rottweil

Bad Dürrheim lies to the south of Schwenningen and has some significance as being the only saline spa in the Black Forest. The waters here are meant to be good for curing a number of illnesses but you do not have to be sick to visit the attractive **Solemar** baths complex. An artificial waterfall and indoor saltwater pools might make a trip here worthwhile on a rainy day. Also of interest in town is the **Narrenschopf**, a museum devoted to the tradition of the Swabian-Alemannic carnival. Here one can see beautiful, often bizarre masks and costumes from all over the region.

From Bad Dürrheim the German Clock Road weaves its way north on minor country roads, via **Trossingen**, to eventually reach Rottweil. A much quicker route, especially for those who have omitted Schwenningen and Bad Dürrheim from their itinerary, is to take the B523 and then the B27 north.

Schwenningen's museums

Clocks are obviously an important topic at the **Heimat- und Uhrenmuseum** (Local History and Clock Museum). Housed in a half-timbered building built in 1697 the museum has a good collection of painted Black Forest clocks, along with a clock-maker's workshop. In the local history section is a collection of farmhouse furniture from the period of the Thirty Years' War to the middle of the nineteenth century.

The **Uhrenindustriemuseum** (Clock Industry Museum) is mainly concerned with the technical side of clock manufacture. It is located in what used to be the factory of the Württembergische Uhrenfabrik, a company that closed down in 1984. All the machines on display are still fully operable.

At Schwenningen's aerodrome (*Flugplatz*) is another interesting museum, but this time it is concerned with flight. The **Internationales Luftfahrtmuseum** (International Aviation Museum) has a collection of over 40 planes. They include a Mig 15, a Starfighter and an Antonow 2. Adding to the interest is the fact that you can go for a flight in one of the old-timers.

Rottweil

Apart from *Fasnet*, Rottweil also has much to offer in the form of its well-preserved **Altstadt**. Hobby photographers will appreciate the picturesque rows of houses from the sixteenth or eighteenth centuries with their distinctive bay windows – the street to look for is Hauptstrasse, where you can also see the imposing Schwarzes Tor. No less photogenic are the artfully designed wrought-iron signs hanging in front of many inns and shops. They have been a feature of the town since 1560, when a law was passed making them obligatory for all local *Gasthäuser*. Quite striking is the **Lorenzkapelle** (fourteenth and fifteenth centuries) with its magnificent late Gothic tower. Those who expect to find a medieval Gothic interior on entering will be disappointed however, as it was redone in the Baroque style in the eighteenth century.

Rottweil's most important church is the **Heilig-Kreuz-Münster** (thirteenth to sixteenth centuries). There are several fine altars to be seen here but it is the late Gothic crucifix on the high altar that makes it one of the minster's most valued treasures. Some contend that it is a work by Veit Stoss, one of the greatest artists of his period. In any case it reflects in dramatic fashion the merging of Gothic and Renaissance styles; the stylised curls of the beard and the portrayal of suffering echo the spirit of Gothic art, whereas the powerful, athletic body is suggestive of the Renaissance. Also outstanding is a late Gothic fresco showing the Madonna and Child.

Museums

The main attraction in the **Dominikanermuseum** is the Roman *Orpheus* mosaic. This, and other Roman finds from excavations in and around Rottweil, give a good

Carnival Time

The most interesting time to visit Rottweil is during the period before Lent, when carnival (*Fasnet*) celebrations take place. Rottweil's carnival is one of the oldest and most famous in south Germany. The overall impression is that of a genuinely traditional festival, not something simply put on for tourists.

Highlight of the festivities is a costumed procession known as the *Narrensprung* (Parade of Fools). It always begins at the **Schwarzes Tor** (Black Gate) on Rose Monday and is repeated the following day Shrove Tuesday.

Black Forest Farmhouse at the
Vogtsbauernhof open-air museum

picture of daily life in *Arae Flaviae*, as Rottweil was known in Roman times. Also of interest is an important collection of Gothic sculpture.

More of the town's antique past can be seen at the open-air museum **Römerbad** (Roman Bath). The Roman baths are the most significant archaeological discovery yet made in Rottweil. They cover an area of 148 x 138ft (45 x 42m) and were probably built around AD 110/120, during the reign of the Emperor Trajan.

The **Stadtmuseum** (Municipal Museum) provides an insight into the day to day life of Rottweil's ordinary citizens between 1750 and 1870. Everything is covered from work and leisure, to the exercise of religious belief. Of particular interest is a model of the famous Rottweil carnival procession (Narrensprung) and a group of fools (as the individual figures in the parade are known) dressed in original costumes. At Christmas visitors can

view an exquisitely carved eighteenth century Christmas manger.

Moving on

This tour follows the B462 from Rottweil direct to Schramberg. The Clock Road takes a rather circuitous route, first returning south via **Niedereschach** to **Königsfeld**, after which it continues to **St Georgen**. From there it finally turns north to Schramberg.

Schramberg

Situated at the intersection of five valleys and guarded by three medieval castle ruins is the important clock manufacturing town of **Schramberg**. In 1861 the Junghans family established a clock factory here. By 1903 it was the largest in the world. Although some other Black Forest clock-makers have not survived the challenge of their Asian competitors the Junghans company is still flourishing. Always innovative, their company holds over 3,000 patents. In 1990 they developed the world's first radio-controlled wristwatch.

Appropriately enough one of the main attractions in the **Stadtmuseum** is a magnificently crafted Junghans clock. It is over 13ft (4m) high and was especially made for the Paris Exhibition in 1900. Apart from displaying antique clocks the museum also offers an insight into the town's economic and social history. Among other things one learns that before the manufacturing of clocks brought a measure of prosperity to Schramberg, the bitterly poor townsfolk had to eke out a living by weaving baskets and other products from straw.

The butchers' dog

It is big, powerfully built, has a reputation for aggression and is definitely not the kind of animal you want to have baring its teeth at you. The dog described is the Rottweiler and it gets its name from the town of its origin. They were originally bred by Rottweil's butchers in the Middle Ages to guard their herds of cattle or flocks of sheep – butchers in those days were also often livestock dealers.

Shrovetide

Highlight of the Shrovetide or carnival celebrations in Schramberg is the *Da-Bach-na* event on Rose Monday (the Monday before Lent). During this event around 40 wash-tubs, manned by costumed 'fools', are paddled down the icy-cold Schiltach. Before setting out each contestant downs a couple of glasses of schnapps, no doubt to steel his nerves against the prospect of capsizing – which is not uncommon but does earn extra points for the (un)fortunate.

Hornberg

Hornberg is quickly reached from Schramberg on the road via Lauterbach. It is quite picturesquely situated in the Gutach valley, on the route of the famous Black Forest Railway. The busy B33 also runs through Hornberg, which is a pity as it lessens the town's overall appeal.

Hornberg is known above all because of an event that took place in the sixteenth century and is remembered today as the *Hornberger Schiessen* (Hornberg Salute). In 1564 the Duke of Württemberg decided to pay Hornberg a visit. The townsfolk, well aware of what an honour this was, decided to greet the duke with a military salute. On the appointed day a lookout spied a cloud of dust from the castle tower. He sounded his horn and the canons and guns were discharged with a deafening roar. To everyone's disappointment it turned out that they had greeted a herdsman with his cattle. Again the horn sounded, again it was a false alarm. But then, just as the riflemen were considering lynching the watchman, he sounded his horn once more. At last, it really was the duke! As they started to reload their guns they realised, with a shock, that they had no gunpowder left. Not knowing what else to do they greeted the mighty duke by imitating the sound of canon as best they could. At first hardly amused by having 'boom! boom!, bang! bang!' shouted at him,

(cont'd on page 96)

Schwarzwaldbahn

Though the **Johannes-Täufer-Kirche** has some interesting old frescoes inside, the main attraction Hornberg has to offer is the Black Forest Railway. The most spectacular stretch of the **Schwarzwaldbahn** lies between Hornberg and St Georgen. The full journey actually begins in Offenburg, in the Rhine valley, and goes right through to Lake Constance (Bodensee) – the last major stop in the Black Forest is Villingen-Schwenningen. It is often claimed that the route follows one of the nicest stretches of mountain railway in Europe. During the summer months the Tourist Information in Triberg organises trips along this section of track. For details refer to 'Steam Trains' in the FactFile.

Cuckoo Clocks

S̲ome people would not be caught dead with one, others see in it a wonderful example of the inventiveness and skill of Black Forest craftsmen. Matters of taste aside, the fact remains that this wall clock has been a success story for what is now over 250 years. Even though they are by no means the only kind of clock manufactured in the Forest they have come to symbolise the region in much the same way as the traditional farmhouses and the red pompoms on the *Bollenhut* hat.

But was the cuckoo clock invented in the Black Forest? Nobody can answer that question for certain. However, it is fairly probable that the first cuckoo clocks in the Black Forest were made sometime between 1730 and 1750 by Franz Anton Ketterer, a clockmaker in the small village of Schönwald, near Triberg. Though some books claim he actually invented the cuckoo mechanism this is by no means proved. A number of experts point out that wooden clocks with mechanical figures were common in many regions of Europe and it is just as possible that the idea for a cuckoo clock was simply copied from elsewhere. Whatever, it was the Black Forest clockmaker who perfected this type of clock and made it famous throughout the world.

Cuckoo clocks have appeared in many different designs and shapes over the years but the classic form is that of the so-called '*Bahnhäusle*' clock. Designed by a professor of

Cuckoo clocks in all shapes and sizes can be admired along the Black Forest Clock Road, these examples are at Triberg

Josef Dold
Kuckucksuhren
Schonach
Schwarzwald

architecture in the 1850s, it was based on the small gate-keepers' houses once common at railway crossings in Baden in the 1840s. For the clock this plain little house was embellished with wooden carvings in the form of entwined grapevine leaves and hunting symbols. The cuckoo nests behind a door in the gable and metal weights hang below in the form of pine cones.

Even though the Bahnhäusle design remains the most popular to this day, there are of course cuckoos who are decidedly better off. Such cuckoos might live in palatial Black Forest houses complete with water mill, farm animals and mechanical figures dressed in traditional costumes. At the other end of the scale are the poor oriental cuckoos from Taiwan or Japan. They live in plastic houses, are powered by batteries and are sometimes so shy that they are neither seen nor heard.

Visitors to the Black Forest will have innumerable opportunities to buy cuckoo clocks in all shapes and sizes. But before buying it is definitely worthwhile visiting one of the several clock museums scattered around the Forest. The best ones are in Furtwangen, Schramberg, Triberg and Villingen-Schwenningen. Here collectors and the curious can learn much more about the history of the old cottage industry of clock-making and see some magnificent examples of the clockmakers' art at the same time. Books in English on the topic include *Black Forest Clock Makers and the Cuckoo Clock* by Karl Kochmann and *Black Forest Clocks* by R Mühe and H Kahlert, a publication available from the Deutsches Uhrenmuseum in Furtwangen.

the duke eventually calmed down when all was explained.

It almost goes without saying that this historic fiasco earned the townspeople much ridicule among their neighbours. However, they have made the best of a bad thing and now commemorate the event with an open-air re-enactment every summer.

Freilichtmuseum Vogtsbauernhof

Before returning to Triberg it is worth making an excursion north to the Freilichtmuseum Vogtsbauernhof, near Gutach. When this open-air museum was first opened in 1963 the only farmhouse on display was the **Vogtsbauernhof**. Built in 1570 this impressive building, with its huge thatched roof, is a superb example of a traditional farmhouse from the Gutach valley and has always stood at this site. The other five farmhouses that can now be seen were brought here from other areas of the central and southern Black Forest. Each comes complete with furnishings and ancillary buildings such as mill, storehouse and bakehouse.

Adding further interest to the museum is the fact that throughout the year there are demonstrations of old handicrafts and folk dancing. On weekends you can sometimes see one of the various mills in operation and on every first Saturday of the month you can taste examples of traditional cooking. All in all the museum offers a fascinating glimpse into a rural way of life which has long since ceased to exist.

Gutach, home of the *Bollenhut*

The village of Gutach would escape the attention of most were it not for the fact that the Vogtsbauernhof is near-by and that it is, along with **Kirnbach** and **Reichenbach**, the home of the famous *Bollenhut*. In spite of the fact that this hat is only worn by the women in these three villages it has become a symbol for the Black Forest as a whole. Covered with bright red woollen roses, or pompons, it decorates the covers of tourist brochures and travel guides, as well as being worn by the little costumed dolls that grace souvenir shops throughout the region. It is, without doubt, a particularly distinctive piece of headgear and perhaps this is one of the reasons it has been chosen from among the many other types of costume worn in the Forest.

The origins of the hat are uncertain. One theory contends that it developed in its present form when straw hats were introduced to the area from Italy or Switzerland in the eighteenth century. Eventually the brim of the hat was stiffened with a layer of plaster and the characteristic woollen 'roses' were added. Today the hat, which weighs a hefty 3lbs (1.4kg), is covered by a total of 14 balls – red ones for unmarried women, black ones for married women.

The hat, and the black costume that goes with it, is now only worn on certain religious holidays or at some village festivals. On such occasions it is also possible to see demonstrations of folk dancing. Among the best times to get a glimpse of the *Bollenhut* are during the *Sommerfest* (Summer Festival) in July and during the *Erntedankfest* (Harvest Festival) in October. Contact the local tourist office for other dates.

ACCOMMODATION

Freudenstadt

Campingplatz Langenwald
Strassburger Strasse 167
☎/Fax (07441) 2862
Camping ground with shop, restaurant, bike rentals and disposal facilities for chemical toilets.

Landhaus Endresenhof $
Freudenstadt-Igelsberg, Besenfelderweg 3
☎ (07442) 6926
Situated north of town at Igelsberg. Solarium, sauna, fitness room and reductions for children.

Pension Pfeifle $
Palmenwaldstrasse 20
☎ (07441) 2321
Quiet location, cot for children.

Gästehaus Schauinsland $$
Hartranftstrasse 56
☎ (07441) 2488, Fax (07441) 2478
Beautiful location at the edge of the Kienberg Nature Reserve, close to a cross-country ski trail. A solarium, a generous breakfast buffet and comfortable rooms make this place good value for money.

Hotel Palmenwald $$$
Lauterbadstrasse 56
☎ (07441) 8070,
Fax (07441) 807400
Lovely old hotel with all the comforts one could wish for. Reductions for children.

Gengenbach

Haus Schuler $
(Privatzimmer/ rooms in a private house)
Grünstrasse 35
☎ (07803) 2517
Not far from railway station, fridge for guests.

Gasthof Hirsch $$
Grabenstrasse 34
☎ (07803) 3387, Fax (07803) 7881
Central location.

Hotel Sonne $$
Hauptstrasse 23
☎ (07803) 93300,
Fax (07803) 40624
Central location in the old quarter of town.

Offenburg

Gasthaus Zauberflöte $$
Lindenplatz 12
☎ (0781) 24813, Fax (0781) 24812
Central location.

Rheinischer Hof $$
Hauptstrasse 52
☎ (0781) 24275, Fax (0781) 24285
Centrally located, reduction for children.

Hotel Sonne $$$
Hauptstrasse 94
☎ (0781) 71039, Fax (0781) 71033
Situated in the old part of town, reduction for children.

Rottweil

Hotel Lamm $$
Hauptstrasse 60
☎ (0741) 45015, Fax (0741) 44273

Haus zum Sternen $$$
Hauptstrasse 60
☎ (0741) 53300,
Fax (0741) 533030
Lovely old hotel with excellent food in the attached restaurant.

Triberg

Gasthaus Jägerhaus $
Wallfahrtstrasse 24
☎ (07722) 4495
Close to waterfall and town,
reduction for children.

Bergsee Stüble $$
Maria-Hofbauer-Strasse 19
☎ (07722) 96180,
Fax (07722) 961820
Next to a small lake,
10 minutes into town.

Parkhotel Wehrle $$$
Am Marktplatz/Gartenstrasse 24
☎ (07722) 86020,
Fax (07722) 860290
The best hotel in town has been
managed by the same family since
1707. Ernest Hemmingway was
once a guest here. Trout dishes
are a speciality of the attached
restaurant.

EATING OUT

Freudenstadt

Hotel-Gasthof Jägerstüble $$
Marktplatz 12
☎ (07441) 2387
Local specialities. Closed Sunday
evening and Monday.

Hotel-Weinstuben Bären $$
Lange Strasse 33
☎ (07441) 81129
Excellent food, including
vegetarian dishes. Closed Sunday
evening and Monday.

Gengenbach

Steinkellerhaus $
Hauptstrasse 33
☎ (07803) 2471, Fax (07803) 2114
Excellent wine and good food
(*Flammkuchen*) in idyllic
surroundings. Also offers holiday
flats. Closed Monday.

Pfeffermühle $$
Victor-Kreuz-Strasse 17
☎ (07803) 93350,
Fax (07803) 6628
Fish and wild game are specialities.
Also accommodation. Open: closed
Wednesday evening and Thursday.

Offenburg

Engel Brasserie $/$$
Hauptstrasse 58
☎ (0781) 25554
Attractive interior, good
selection of salads, beer garden.
Open: seven days a week.

Guglhupf $$
Metzgerstrasse 7
☎ (0781) 78155
Alsatian wine and food.
Closed Sunday.

Rottweil

Weinstube Grimm $
Oberamteigasse 5
☎ (0781) 6830
Closed Sunday
and Saturday evening.

Triberg

Restaurant Pfaff $$
Hauptstrasse 85
☎ (07722) 4479
Regional specialities, international fare.

PLACES TO VISIT

Alpirsbach

Alpirsbacher Brauereimuseum
Marktplatz 1
A chance to see how a good
German beer is brewed.
Open: daily by prior arrangement.
☎ (07444) 670 or 67117

Alpirsbacher Glasbläserei
Krähenbadstrasse 3
Glassblowing demonstrations.
Open: Monday to Friday 10am-
6pm, Saturday 10am-5pm. Shop
open on Monday only.

Souvenir shops offer a wide choice of hand-crafted goods

A mountain hut near Hausach

Klosterkirche/Kloster Alpirsbach
Romanesque basilica attached to the former monastery of Alpirsbach. Open: 15 March to 1 November, Monday to Saturday 9.30am-5.30pm, Sunday and public holidays 11am-5.30pm; 2 November to 14 March, Thursday and Saturday 1.30-3pm.

Bad Dürrheim

Narrenschopf
Am Kurpark
Germany's largest collection of carnival masks and costumes. Open: May to October, Monday to Saturday 2-6pm, Sunday 10am-6pm; November to April, Monday to Saturday 2-5pm, Sunday 10am-5pm.

Dornstetten

Barfuss-Park
Dornstetten-Hallwangen/ Reutesägmühle
Here the kids can run around in their bare feet. No entrance fee. Open: daily 9am-6pm.

Freudenstadt

Panorama-Bad
Ludwig-Jahn-Strasse 60
Beautiful pool complex with sauna, children's pools etc. Also suitable for disabled persons. Open: Monday to Friday 9am-10pm, Saturday, Sunday and public holidays 9am-8pm.

Stadtkirche
Marktplatz
Open: daily 10am-5pm. Guided tours at 2pm Wednesday and Friday.

Furtwangen

Deutsches Uhrenmuseum
Gerwigstrasse 11
The best clock museum in Germany. Open: 1 April to 31 October, daily 9am-6pm; 1 November to 31 March. daily 10am-5pm. Closed 24 to 26 December.

Gengenbach

Niggelturm
Hauptstrasse
Medieval tower now contains a carnival museum. Good views from top. Open: April to October, Saturday 2.30-5.30pm, Sunday 10am-12noon and 2.30-5.30pm.

Gutach

Vogtsbauernhof
On the B33
An open-air museum with original Black Forest farmhouses. Transport: train from Offenburg to Hausach, 30-minute walk from station. Open: 21 March to 7 November, daily 8.30am-6pm.

Haslach

Hansjakobmuseum Freihof
Hansjakobstrasse 17
Museum is dedicated to the life and work of this popular Black Forest author. Open: Wednesday 10am-12noon and 3-5pm, Friday 3-5pm.

Schwarzwälder Trachtenmuseum
In the old Kapuzinerkloster
This museum specialises in the region's beautiful traditional costumes. Open: 1 April to 31 October, Tuesday to Saturday 9am-5pm, Sunday and public holidays 10am-5pm; 1 November to 31 March, Tuesday to Friday 9am-12noon and 1-5pm.

Hexenloch

Hexenlochmühle
Lovely old Black Forest mill.
Open: mid-December to October,
daily from 9.30am-6.30pm.

Offenburg

Judenbad (Mikwe)
Glaserstrasse 8
A ritual bath once used by
Offenburg's Jewish citizens.
Can only be visited on a guided
tour through town. Inquire at
Tourist Office.

Rottweil

Dominikanermuseum
Am Kriegsdamm
Highlight of this museum is the
Roman Orpheus Mosaic. Open:
Tuesday to Sunday 10am-1pm and
2-5pm.

Römerbad
Corner Hölderstrasse/Königsstrasse
Ruins of a Roman bath.
Always open.

Stadtmuseum
Hauptstrasse 20
An interesting museum dealing with
local history and culture. Open:
Tuesday to Saturday 10am-12noon
and 2-5pm, Sunday 10am-12noon.

Rust

Europa-Park
Excellent amusement park. Reductions for children, senior citizens
(60 years and older) and disabled
persons. Entrance price includes all
attractions. Open: 27 March to 7
November, daily 9am-6pm;
extended hours in July/August.

Schiltach

Apothekenmuseum
Marktplatz 5
An old chemist's shop.
Open: 1 April to 31 October,
Tuesday to Friday and Sunday
10.30am-12noon and 2.30-5pm,
Saturday 2.30-5pm.

Hansgrohe Museum
Auestrasse 10
History of bathing and bathroom
design. Open: daily 11am-4pm.

Museum am Markt
Marktplatz 13
Exhibits on the town's eventful
history. Open: 1 April to 31
October, daily 11am-4pm.

Schüttesägemuseum
Hauptstrasse 1
Learn about how logs were floated
down the local rivers and about the
history of the local timber industry
in general. Open: 1 April to 31
October, Tuesday to Sunday 11am-
5pm. No entrance fee.

Schonach

World's Largest Cuckoo Clock
Untertalstrasse 28
Actually the world's second
largest. Open: daily 9am-12noon
and 1-6pm.

Schramberg

Stadtmuseum
Bahnhofstrasse 1
Interesting clock collection.
Open: Tuesday to Friday 2-6pm;
Saturday and Sunday throughout the
year, 10am-12noon and 2-5pm.
May to mid-September, Tuesday to
Friday 10am-12noon and 2-6pm;
mid-September to April,

Triberg

Schwarzwaldmuseum
Wallfahrtstrasse 4
One of the best museums in the region. Good collection of antique cuckoo clocks. Open: 1 May to 31 October, 9am-6pm daily; 1 November to 30 April, 10am-5pm daily; 15 November to 15 December, open only at weekends from 10am-5pm.

Triberg Waterfall
Open: daily. In summer there is an entrance charge for the walk along the falls.

Villingen-Schwenningen

Franziskaner Museum
Rietgasse 2, Villingen
Sacred art and folklore.
Open: Tuesday to Friday 10am-12noon, Tuesday, Thursday, Saturday 2-5pm, Wednesday 2-8pm, Sunday and public holidays 1-5pm.

Heimat- und Uhrenmuseum
Kronenstrasse 16, Schwenningen
Local history and a good collection of Black Forest clocks. Open: Tuesday to Sunday 10am-12noon and 2-6pm.

Internationales Luftfahrtmuseum
Schwenningen Flugplatz (aerodrome)
A collection of vintage airplanes. Open: daily 9am-7pm.

Kienzle Uhrenfabrik
Eichendorffstrasse 29, Schwenningen
Quality clocks and watches at reduced prices direct from the factory. Open: Monday and Wednesday 2-4pm, Tuesday and Thursday 2-4.30pm, Friday 8.30am-12.30pm.

Uhrenindustriemuseum
Bürkstrasse 39, Schwenningen
History of clock manufacturing industry. Open: Tuesday to Sunday 10am-12noon and 2-6pm.

Bread baked in the traditional fashion at the Vogtsbauernhof open-air museum

Triberg Waterfall,
Germany's highest

Wolfach

Dorotheenhütte
Glashüttenweg 4
Glassworks with demonstrations of glassblowing. Open: daily 9am-4.30pm.

Zell

Zeller Keramik
Hauptstrasse 2
Factory outlet for ceramics and stoneware. Some products up to 50 per cent cheaper. Open: May to December, Monday to Friday 9am-5pm, Saturday 9.30am-1.30pm.

TOURIST INFORMATION OFFICES

Alpirsbach

Tourist-Information Alpirsbach
Hauptstrasse 20
☎ (07444) 9516281,
Fax (07444) 9516283

Dornstetten

Tourist-Information Dornstetten
Marktplatz 2
☎ (07443) 962030,
Fax (07443) 962099

Durbach

Verkehrsverein Durbach
Talstrasse 36
☎ (0781) 42153, Fax (0781) 43989

Elzach

Verkehrsamt Elzach
In the Haus des Gastes
☎ (07682) 7990,
Fax (07682) 80472

Ettenheim

Tourist-Information Ettenheim
Kirchstrasse 4
☎ (07822) 43210,
Fax (07822) 43251

Freudenstadt

Gäste-Büro Freudenstadt
Am Promenadeplatz 1
☎ (07441) 864730,
Fax (07441) 85176
Open: Monday to Friday 10am-6pm, Saturday 10am-1pm.

Furtwangen

Tourist-Information Furtwangen
Marktplatz 4
☎ (07723) 939111,
Fax (07723) 939199
Open: Monday to Friday 8.30am-12noon, 2.30-6pm Monday only.

Gengenbach

Tourist-Information Gengenbach
Im Winzerhof
☎ (07803) 19433,
Fax (07803) 930142
Open: Weekdays all year, except 1 Sept to 31 May when closed between 1-2pm. Also open on Saturdays from 1 May to 31 Oct 10-12 noon

Gutach

Verkehrsamt Gutach
Hauptstrasse 38
☎ (07833) 938850,
Fax (07833) 938811

Haslach

Tourist-Information Haslach
Alten Kapuzinerkloster
☎ (07832) 8080 and 70670,
Fax (07832) 5909

Hornberg

**Städtisches Verkehrsamt
Hornberg**
Bahnhofstrasse 3
☎ (07833) 79333,
Fax (07833) 79329

Oberprechtal

Kurverwaltung Oberprechtal
☎ (07682) 1285, Fax (07682) 6296

Offenburg

Verkehrsverein Offenburg
Gärtnerstrasse 6
☎ (0781) 822253,
Fax (0781) 827251

Rottweil

**Städtisches Verkehrsbüro
Rottweil**
Hauptstrasse 21
☎ (0741) 494280,
Fax (0741) 494373

Rust

Fremdenverkehrsamt Rust
Fischerstrasse 51
☎ (07822) 61041,
Fax (07822) 61042

Schiltach

Tourist-Information Schiltach
Hauptstrasse 5
☎ (07836) 5850, Fax (07836) 5858
Open: 1 May to 30 September,
Monday to Friday 9am-12noon and

2-5pm, Saturday, 10am-12noon;
1 October to 30 April, Monday to
Thursday 9am-12noon and 2-5pm,
Friday 9am-12noon.

Schramberg

**Stadt- und Bürgerinformation
Schramberg**
☎ (07422) 29215,
Fax (07422) 29209

Triberg

Tourist-Information Triberg
Luisenstrasse 10
☎ (07722) 953230 or 953231
Fax (07722) 953236
Open: May to September, Monday
to Friday 9am-5pm, Saturday
10am-12noon.

Villingen-Schwenningen

**Verkehrsamt Bahnhof
Schwenningen**
☎ (07720) 821208,
Fax (07720) 821207

Verkehrsamt Villingen
Rietstrasse 8
☎ (07721) 822340,
Fax (07721) 822347

Wolfach

Kur- und Verkehrsamt Wolfach
Hauptstrasse 41
☎ (07834) 835353,
Fax (07834) 835359

Zell am Harmersbach

Kultur- und Verkehrsamt Zell
Alte Kanzlei
☎ (07835) 636947,
Fax (07835) 636950

3

Freiburg & Environs

F ocal point of this chapter is the lovely old university town
of Freiburg. Here the old mixes harmoniously with the
new to produce a lively, many facetted city that is neither too
big, nor too small – the population hovers at around 200,000.

Apart from having one of the best climates in Germany, the city has much to offer both within the bounds of its medieval streets and in the beautiful surroundings. Within easy reach is the summit of the Schauinsland, a mountain famed for its splendid views. At the top one can set off along any one of a dozen trails or, instead, explore the old silver mine that once filled the city's coffers. Back in town a big attraction is, of course, the magnificent cathedral, but it is also worth visiting the various museums and other

sights hidden away in the side streets. There you are bound to discover some delightful café (try looking around the Insel) or a photogenic house-front you can snap for the photo album back home. But what is perhaps most surprising is that even here, in the middle of the Altstadt, one can find peaceful nooks and crannies, where the bustle of the city seems worlds away and time stands still, if only for a moment.

Moving on from Freiburg the tour enters the Hell Valley, along a route

Opposite: Hotel Sternen at Höllsteig, in the Hell Valley

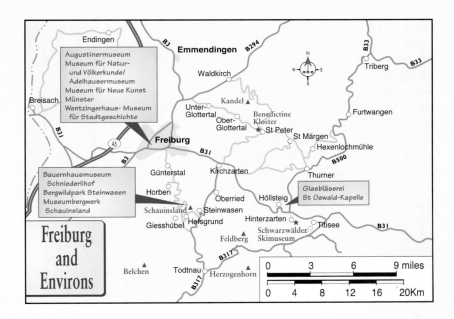

Freiburg and Environs

once travelled by Marie Antoinette. A stop is made to explore the lovely Ravenna Gorge, before continuing to Hinterzarten, a resort popular among outdoor enthusiasts. After Hinterzarten the Panorama Road is followed to the former monasteries at St Märgen and St Peter. Traditions are kept alive in these little mountain-top resorts and if one is lucky it is possible to see typical costumes being worn on Sundays at church, or on certain special occasions. From St Peter the road climbs to the Kandel, another mountain known for its views. Now it is not far back to Freiburg and a pleasant evening at one of the cafés on the cathedral square.

Freiburg im Breisgau

Freiburg is situated on the southwestern fringe of the Black Forest, with the cool heights of the Forest just to the east and the sun-soaked vineyards of the Kaiserstuhl to the west. Often referred to as the Black Forest capital it is a university town with pleasant parks and a lively cultural scene. Though heavily bombed in 1944 the old heart of the city has been beautifully restored and has preserved much of its medieval charm.

As attractive as Freiburg is, it is not a city that overwhelms visitors with its beauty at first sight. Its full charm can only be discovered in the course of a leisurely tour, not in a hurried appreciation of the town's medieval focal point; the Münsterplatz with its mighty Gothic cathedral. The old is very much mixed in with the new, but in the Altstadt (Old City) it is the old that sets the tone. A walk around the city's historic core reveals one lovely vista after the other; whether it be idyllic corners such as the Insel and Fisherau, or the impressive town gates with pointed turrets pointing skywards like exclamation marks of mortar and stone. As you weave your way through narrow cobbled streets, past inviting cafés, busy shops and along bustling thorough-fares, you will be able to form a much better impression of this vibrant city as it is today.

Altstadt walk

This walk starts at the **Freiburg-Information** office on Rotteckring – there are a number of places to park nearby. For those coming from the *Hauptbahnhof* (main railway station) it is only a short walk along Eisenbahnstrasse, past **Colombipark**, to the Information Office.

From the Information Office continue along Rathausgasse to the medieval **Rathausplatz** (Town Hall Square). Grouped together here is the **Altes Rathaus** (1555-59), **Neues Rathaus** (1896-1901) and the **Gothic Martinskirche**. In the middle of the square is a fountain dedicated to the monk Berthold Schwarz, who discovered gunpowder in the first half of the fourteenth century. Walk around the Martinskirche into

Franziskanerstrasse, where on the right-hand side, you can see the dark red façade of the sixteenth century **Haus zum Walfisch** (House of the Whale). For a couple of years it served as a home for the humanist Erasmus of Rotterdam, who sought refuge here after he was expelled from Basle in 1529. A particularly impressive aspect of the building is the late Gothic doorway.

Cross the busy Kaiser-Joseph-Strasse with its modern shops and enter the **Münsterplatz** via Münsterstrasse. The magnificent **Freiburg Münster** (cathedral), numerous cafés and a lively market on weekday mornings make this square Freiburg's most popular attraction. Apart from the cathedral other interesting buildings found here include the very medieval-looking **Kaufhaus**, with its exotically tiled roof, the **Kornhaus** where once grain was stored, and **Wentzingerhaus** which now houses the **Museum für Stadtgeschichte** (Municipal Museum). Here you can learn all about the history of Freiburg, from its beginnings up until the eighteenth century. The main attraction is a model of the cathedral as it was being built, complete with tin figures.

Münster

The **Münster Unserer Lieben Frau** is one of the greatest masterpieces of Gothic architecture in Germany. It has been modified at various times over a period of some three centuries, the oldest part of the cathedral dating back to the Romanesque period, around 1200. The Gothic west tower was completed around 1320, making it the first of its kind to be completed in the Middle Ages. Its delicate-looking open-work spire has induced one art historian to call

Gargoyles

The building's exterior is a kind of vast Gothic landscape of towers and spires, inhabited by a multitude of grotesquely shaped **gargoyles**. It is great fun just to stroll around the cathedral (it was only in 1827 that it received this status) in order to pick out some of the more bizarre figures that adorn the roof – a pair of binoculars is useful here. On the south side of the cathedral you are bound to discover a gargoyle in the shape of a man with his backside projecting out onto the square. One story has it that the stonemasons working on the minster carved it to show what they thought of the city fathers, who had not paid them for weeks.

it the 'most beautiful tower in Christendom'. However, despite its fragile appearance it was so skilfully constructed that it even withstood the otherwise devastating shock waves produced by exploding bombs in World War II.

Once your eyes have become accustomed to the gloom the full splendour of the church interior becomes apparent. There is no space to describe all the many fine works of art to be seen here, but at least a few of the more important deserve brief mention. In the Gothic choir is the **high altar**, painted between 1512 and 1516 by Hans Baldung Grien, who was a student of Albrecht Dürer. It depicts the Crowning of Mary with the wing pictures showing the apostles as on-lookers. In the chapels surrounding the choir there are also some out-standing altars including the **Oberriedaltar** (1521) by Hans Holbein the Younger and the so-called **Schnewlin-Altar** (1515).

Among the cathedral's greatest treasures are the medieval **stained glass windows**, which are even more impressive than those in Stras-bourg's famous minster. A large number of them were donated by the various trade guilds, as for in-stance the *Bäckerfenster* (Bakers' Window). It is identified by the guild's coat of arms, a white pretzel on a red shield. This window tells of the life and sufferings of St Katherina, who refused to marry a heathen and was therefore tortured – these scenes are depicted in all their gory detail. Also of note, and no less gory in content, is the *Märtyrerfenster* (Martyrs' Window). It shows the agonising ends of some of the early proponents of Christi-anity.

If you want a spectacular view over the roofs of Freiburg then you can conclude your exploration of the cathedral by climbing exactly 329 steps to the top of the 380ft (116m) high **West Tower**. On the way up you will pass the huge bell 'Hosanna', cast in 1258. From the

KEY

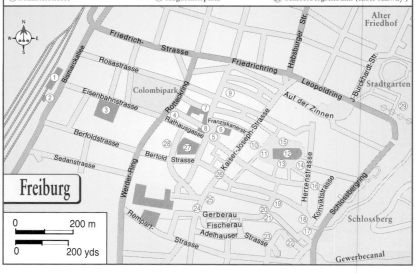

① Hauptbahnhof (main railway station)
② Busbahnhof (ZOB) (main bus station)
③ Hauptpost (main post office)
④ Freiburg-Information Office
⑤ Rathausplatz
⑥ Martinskirche
⑦ Neues Rathaus
⑧ Altes Rathaus
⑨ Haus zum Walfisch
⑩ Münsterstrasse

⑪ Münsterplatz
⑫ Münster Unserer Lieben Frau
⑬ Kaufhaus
⑭ Wentzingerhaus
⑮ Kornhaus
⑯ Münzgasse
⑰ Schwabentor
⑱ Hotel zum Roten Bären
⑲ Augustinermuseum
⑳ Augustinerplatz

㉑ Museum für Natur-
   und Völkerkunde
㉒ Insel
㉓ Museum für Neue Kunst
㉔ Martinstor
㉕ Markthalle
㉖ Bertoldsbrunnen
㉗ Alte Universität
㉘ Brunnenstrasse
㉙ Schlossbergseilbahn (cable railway)

Freiburg

0   200 m

0   200 yds

watchman's room (205 steps) there is still some distance to climb and those who do not have a head for heights should go no further! Be warned: on weekends it can get very crowded here (especially Saturday mornings) as the stairway is very narrow.

Near the south-eastern end of the cathedral is the **Haus der Badischen Weine**, a good place to stop if you wish to taste the local wine. Walk past it to reach Herrenstrasse. Turn right here and then enter Münzgasse, which brings you into the lovely **Konviktstrasse**. This street has been beautifully restored in recent years and there is a good choice of restaurants if it is time for a break. At

the end of Konviktstrasse is the **Schwabentor**, one of the city's two remaining town gates. Just to the north one could choose to dine at one of Germany's oldest inns; the **Hotel zum Roten Bären** has been in business since 1387.

Augustinerplatz and Augustinermuseum

From the Schwabentor go via Salzstrasse to the Augustinerplatz. Housed in the former church and monastery of the Augustinian Eremites is the Augustinermuseum. The old monastery provides a fitting background for the collection of medieval art that is the museum's main attraction. Here you can admire exquisitely carved wooden altars, precious tapestries and priceless objects of sacred art. Among the museums most valued treasures are paintings by Hans Baldung Grien, Lukas Cranach and Matthias Grünewald, the painter of the famous Isenheim Altar in nearby Colmar. Also on display are original sculptures and stained glass from the Freiburg Münster.

Above: Freiburg's Bächle is an irresistable attraction for small children
Opposite: No visitor should miss a stroll through Freiburg's lively market

Below: In Freiburg's Alstadt

111

Marriage of convenience

The picture gallery on one of the upper floors has a good collection of nineteenth century paintings by artists from the region. Particularly interesting are the Black Forest landscapes and the portraits of people in traditional costumes. A few of these pictures offer an insight into the social conditions of those times. In the painting *Vernunftsehe im Schwarzwald* (Marriage of Convenience in the Black Forest), the artist draws one's attention to the fact that practical reasons, rather than love, were paramount when it came to marrying in the nineteenth century. As the youngest son inherited the farm, and all that went with it, the other children could only hope to make a good match, if they did not want to end up as servants or poor farmworkers.

In the section dealing with applied arts there is a glass collection and displays of furniture from various historical periods. Another section of the museum has a fascinating display of portable sundials (*Reise-Sonnen-uhren*). This medieval version of the wristwatch reached the peak of its popularity between the fifteenth and eighteenth centuries. Just as today you have your Swatch and your Rolex watches, these old sundials came either in cheap versions, made of cardboard or wood, or luxury editions that might be made of ivory.

Unfortunately those who want to know more about the museum's many exhibits will have to be able to read either German or French. At the time of writing the museum had no English language leaflets describing the more important works. This is an unfortunate state of affairs that also exists at many other interesting museums in the region.

Natural History & Ethnological Museum

Also located in a former monastery is the Museum für Natur-und Völkerkunde (Natural History and Ethnological Museum) at Gerberau 32, near the south-western end of the Augustinerplatz. The department devoted to ethnology concerns itself with the ancient civilisations of East Asia and Egypt, as well as the tribal cultures of North and South America, Africa, the Pacific and Australia. In the natural history section the *Edelsteinkabinett* (collection of precious stones) is of especial interest. Lit by ultraviolet light the stones are shown at their aesthetic best.

The Bächle

Children notice the narrow, water-filled channels that curve their way through Augustinerplatz, and the rest of Altstadt immediately; Their parents, at the very latest, when they have accidentally stepped into one. The *Bächle*, as these channels are known, were designed in the Middle Ages to provide a handy source of water for combating the frequent fires and as a place for animals to drink. Today they are a place to cool the feet on a hot summer's day and, above all, an endless source of amusement for the kids.

From Augustinerplatz back to Rathausgasse

To the south-east of the Augustinerplatz is the *Insel*, a

picturesque ensemble of houses along the **Gerwerbecanal** (Industry Canal). The canal water was once used by tanneries and small workshops where precious stones were cut. Continue past the **Museum für Neue Kunst** (Museum of Modern Art), enter Adelhauser Strasse, turn right through the small square in front of the Adelhauser Neukloster church and then turn left into the **Fischerau**. This pretty street also lies along the Gewerbecanal and was once home to the local fishermen.

Freiburg's greener sights

If, after a tour of the cultural sights, you are yearning for a bit of greenery, then it might be worth heading for the **Stadtgarten** (City Park). It is only a few minutes walk from the Münsterplatz and once there you can take a ride on a cable railway to the top of the **Schlossberg**. There are good views over the city from here and numerous paths lead further into the woods.

The romantically inclined might be tempted to continue on from the Stadtgarten to the **Alter Friedhof** (Old Cemetery). For nearly 200 years it served as the city's main cemetery until a new cemetery was laid out in 1871. Today it is a peaceful spot, where the graves are shaded by majestic old trees. One of the most interesting of these graves is that of Caroline Walter, a young woman who died in 1867. The tradition, begun by her husband, of placing flowers on her stone effigy is continued to this day by the citizens of Freiburg.

The second of Freiburg's remaining town gates, the impressive **Martinstor**, is situated at the southern end of Kaiser-Joseph-Strasse, only a short distance from the Fischerau. Friends of fast food can dine in an adjoining building which houses a McDonald's restaurant. More original is the **Markthalle** across the road. Here one can try a whole array of exotic dishes from the various food stalls.

Continue up Kaiser-Joseph-Strasse to the **Bertoldsbrunnen**, a monument commemorating Duke Bertold III, one of the city's founding fathers. It marks the intersection of two old trade routes which existed before the town itself. Today the only vehicles that pass Duke Bertold are the city's tramcars, as a large area of the Altstadt is now a pedestrian zone. Bertoldstrasse leads past the **Alte Universität** (Old University) building, from where you enter Brunnenstrasse, which in turn leads to Rathausgasse near the start of this walk.

Excursion to Schauinsland

A popular excursion from Freiburg is to the 4,211ft (1284m high) Schauinsland, a mountain to the south. Literally translated the mountain's name means 'look into the countryside' and it is more than appropriate. In clear weather (best times are autumn and winter) the view can be breathtaking, as it encompasses Freiburg, the Rhine lowlands, the Vosges mountains in France and even the Swiss Alps.

It is possible to get to Schauinsland with public transport from the middle of Freiburg, or you can drive – the route is well signposted from the city. Those who prefer to leave their car behind can take tram-line 4 to

walks on Schauinsland

There are dozens of interesting trails that start from the Schauinsland summit – maps can be bought at the top of the cable railway. A walk around the summit (*Gipfelrundweg*) takes about 50 minutes. Another possibility is to walk all the way back to Freiburg (3 hours). From the cable car station first walk in the direction of

Giesshübel, then follow the *Dreiländerweg* ('Three Countries' long-distance walk) down to Freiburg. The trail is marked by a blue diamond and a D. There are some fine views along this route and refreshments are available at a number of places along the way.

Apart from some great walking (and skiing in winter) there are also a few things to see

Dozens of walking trails start from the Schauinsland summit

Günterstal, from where bus no 21 departs for the lower terminus of the *Seilbahn* (cable railway) near **Horben**. The trip with the *Seilbahn* takes about 20 minutes. From the restaurant at the top it is another 20 minutes on foot to a lookout tower on the summit.

Bergwildpark Steinwasen

For those who have come by car the return drive via **Hofsgrund**, Oberried

On the Schauinsland, near Freiburg

in the vicinity of the upper cable car terminus and summit. An interesting walk downhill from the summit lookout tower leads past a large stone monument known as the **Engländer Denkmal**. It is dedicated to the memory of a group of English schoolchildren who died here in a snowstorm in the 1930s. Those who continue on downhill will eventually come to the **Bauernhausmuseum Schniederlihof**. This lovely old farmhouse was built in 1593 and is now a museum illustrating rural life in the area.

Only a 10-minute stroll from the upper terminus is the **Museumsbergwerk Schauinsland**. The museum documents 800 years of mining history on the Schauinsland. Mining for silver, lead and zinc began in the twelfth century and operations only ceased in 1954. It was, in fact, the silver that was mined here that greatly contributed to Freiburg's wealth in the Middle Ages. Without this wealth the construction of the Freiburg Münster would never have been possible.

and Kirchzarten is very scenic. Near Hofsgrund is the Bergwildpark Steinwasen, a wildlife park that specialises in mountain animals such as chamois, moufflon and lynx. It covers an area of 99 acres (40ha) and a 2-mile (3.3km) long circular walk takes visitors past the animal enclosures. Kids, especially, will love it here as additional attractions include a 2,625ft (800m) long summer toboggan-run and roller-coaster rides.

Route 8 THROUGH THE HELL VALLEY TO THE KANDEL

The Höllental

The Höllental (Hell Valley) is entered shortly after **Kirchzarten**, a pleasant little town that is a popular base for mountain bikers and for those who prefer the quiet of the countryside to the bustle of Freiburg. The origin of the valley's name is uncertain but it may be a reference to the fact that passage through the deep, narrow gorge was once a difficult undertaking. Flash floods, falling rocks, treacherously narrow paths and, in the fourteenth century, robber barons were all very real dangers for any person who ventured into it. It was not until 1755 that a road was finally built that was suitable for stagecoaches and the transportation of goods. A few years later this road was further improved for Marie Antoinette, who passed through on her way to marry the Dauphin, who later became Louis XVI of France.

Because the Höllental is so narrow there are only a few places where motorists can stop and take in the scenery. The first such place is at a spot known as **Hirschsprung**, where the valley is no more than 65ft (20m) wide. A bronze statue of a stag, on a rocky outcrop above the road, recalls the story of how this animal accomplished a mighty leap over the chasm in order to escape pursuing hunters. It would be easy to relegate this tale to the realm of legend, were it not for the fact that before the road was built the valley was even narrower here.

At the end of the valley it is worth pausing to visit the small **Glasbläserei** (glassworks) next to Hotel Sternen in **Höllsteig**. Here one can watch demonstrations of the traditional craft of glassblowing and in the attached shop some may find an original souvenir. A chance to stretch the legs afterwards is offered by a picturesque trail that leads through the nearby Ravennaschlucht (Ravenna Gorge) – see also Hinterzarten below. Those who want to spend the night at the hotel

---

Touring tip

It is of course possible to drive through the scenic Höllental along the busy B31, but it is even more enjoyable to do this section of the tour by train – those reliant on public transport should note that the section of this route between Hinterzarten and St Peter is only accessible by bus. The **Höllentalbahn** (Hell Valley Line) starts at Freiburg and ends in Donaueschingen, though the valley itself only extends for a distance of 5½ miles (9km) between **Himmelreich** and **Höllsteig**. With this in mind a shorter alternative would be to get off at Hinterzarten or Titisee. Those who do want to get out at one of the smaller stations en route should make sure that they catch one of the local trains (*Nahverkehrszug*), as they stop everywhere.

might be interested to know that both Marie Antoinette and Goethe were once guests here.

Only a five-minute walk from Hotel Sternen is the **St Oswald-Kapelle**, the oldest church in this part of the Black Forest. Named after Oswald (about 605-641), the Christian King of Northumbria, it was built in 1140 and consecrated in 1148. Inside is a copy of the original sixteenth century winged altar. Ask at Hotel Sternen for the key to the church.

Hinterzarten

A popular health and winter sports resort **Hinterzarten** lures its visitors with the promise of clean mountain air and the great outdoors. In the summer months people flock here to go cycling or walking in what must be one of the loveliest parts of the Black Forest. But the real high season is in winter, when the town becomes a Mecca for cross-country and downhill skiers. Catering for the holiday crowds are some fine restaurants and a wide spectrum of accommodation ranging from the modest *Gästehaus* to 'Parkhotel Adler', a five-star hotel that has been run by the same family since 1446.

Prior to the advent of tourism in the nineteenth century the town's inhabitants were mainly poor farming folk, doing their best to make a meagre living from the land. In those days a long-distance walk was not something one did for fun, it was just hard work. For instance many people supplemented their incomes by transporting glassware on their backs over the mountain passes. From the seventeenth century onwards clock-making provided another source of income then, in the nineteenth century, the

Löffelindustrie (spoon-making industry) also provided much needed jobs. If you walk along a trail known as the *Heimatpfad Hochschwarzwald* (*see* overleaf) you will pass through a couple of valleys that once resounded to the hammering of the *Löffelschmiede*, as the water-powered smithies that produced spoons were known.

The town's only place of historic interest is the Catholic **Pfarrkirche** (parish church), which is easily recognisable by the onion-shaped dome that tops the church tower. The main objects of interest in the modern interior are the Baroque high altar and a sixteenth century pietà that was found in 1955 in the attic of an old farmhouse. Outside the church the so-called *Sonntagsläden* (Sunday shops) are also of note. These small stalls are relics of an old tradition; in days gone by the farmers only came into town once a week, on Sundays, to visit church and then do their shopping.

The Panoramastrasse between Hinterzarten & Waldkirch

From Hinterzarten leave the B31 and continue along the B500 (Panoramic Road) to the road junction at **Gasthaus Thurner**. From here follow a scenic country road in the direction of St Märgen and St Peter. After driving only a short distance further on from Gasthaus Thurner a detour can be made to the Hexenlochmühle, already mentioned in Chapter 2.

St Märgen

St Märgen is a tranquil health resort situated at an altitude ranging from 2,950 to 3,600ft (990 to 1,100m). The first *(cont'd on page 120)*

—— Along the Heimatpfad Hochschwarzwald to the Ravenna Gorge ——

This 7-mile (11.5km) circular trail requires around three hours and leads through some lovely countryside into valleys that were once lined by dozens of water-mills and water-powered smithies. A highlight is the descent through the romantic **Ravennaschlucht** (Ravenna Gorge) near Höllsteig. The path is fairly easy to follow as signposts bearing its name appear at regular intervals. Maps and a detailed booklet in German describing places of interest along the walk are available from the Hinterzarten Tourist Information on Freiburger Strasse.

Start from the large car park near the railway station – the trail is signposted. Walk a short distance along an asphalt road, then enter an area of upland moor that is part of the **Naturschutzgebiet Hinterzarten** – a nature reserve. After passing the 300 year-old **Königsfichte** (a large fir tree) turn left in the direction of Heiligenbrunnen/Weisstannenhöhe – follow red dot and purple diamond. Continue through meadows just below the B500 and eventually come to a fork. Take the right-hand fork towards the road and after passing a group of buildings near the Földi-Klinik, cross under the road via a pedestrian subway. A short distance further on another subway takes you under the B500 once again, from where a paved path is followed to the point where a trail dips down into the woods in the direction of the Ravennaschlucht.

Not long after passing a house covered by wooden shingles (also identified by a large collection of garden gnomes), the trail enters the Ravenna Gorge. At what was once the site of an old *Löffelschmiede* (smithy) is now a pleasantly situated self-service restaurant next to the stream. Further down the restored **Grossjochenmühle** is situated in the prettiest part of the gorge. Built in 1883 this old water-mill was used to grind grain and was in operation until 1956. Nearby is the 47ft (15m) high **Ravenna Waterfall**. From here it is no longer far to **Hotel Sternen,** where there is another self-service restaurant and a glassworks that can be visited.

From the hotel follow the sign in the direction of the **Löffeltal**. As the name suggests this valley was once the location of several *Löffelschmieden*. Though none of the smithies remain today one can still view a restored water-driven sawmill known as the **Kingenhofsäge**. It can sometimes be seen in action on weekends and dates from the eighteenth century. On reaching the edge of town turn left under the railway bridge and then follow Freiburger Strasse back towards the railway station.

In the Ravenna Gorge

things one notices on approaching the village are the attractive twin towers of the **Klosterkirche**. In spite of its Baroque exterior the present church is not all that old, as it had to be rebuilt after a fire destroyed it in 1907. The church and attached monastery have actually been burnt down five times since the monastery was first established in the twelfth century. The abbots that once lived here did not fare all that much better: in the fifteenth century three of them were murdered within a period of only 55 years. Though not as impressive as the church at St Peter, the restored Baroque interior is still worth a look.

But, in the end, St Märgen's real attractions are the superb panoramic views that its location offers and, of course, the lovely surroundings. Activities here include walking and cycling in summer and skiing in winter. One interesting circular walk is the so-called **Pfisterwaldrundweg**.

Genuine
Black Forest Cake

No visit to the Black Forest is complete without visiting a local *Konditorei* (cake shop) for a slice of *Schwarzwälder Kirschtorte* (Black Forest cherry cake) with a cup of coffee. According to some sources the man who 'invented' this world famous cake came from Bad Godesberg. His name was Josef Keller and he baked the world's first *Kirschtorte* in 1915. Since then this delicious gateau has entered more mouths than any statistician might care to record.

But more important than who made it first is who makes it now. Any local will tell you that the most important thing about a Black Forest cake is not the cherries, it's the real *Kirschwasser* that goes into it! Not every pastry cook sticks to the genuine ingredients. When you bite into a good slice of cake you should be able to taste the schnapps. If not, and if the cream is not freshly whipped, then you have picked the wrong place – something that can happen even in the Black Forest.

A tip

One of the very best *Kirschtorten* that the authors have eaten in the Forest came from the Café am Rathaus in Todtnau. But if you want to try baking it yourself here is the recipe:

Ingredients for the cake

4oz (100g) butter, 4oz (100g) sugar, pinch of salt, 2 level teaspoons of vanilla sugar, 4 egg yolks, 3oz (70g) blanched and ground almonds, 4oz (100g) ground semi-sweet chocolate, 4 egg whites, 2oz (50g) flour, 2oz (50g) cornstarch/cornflour, 2 level teaspoons baking powder, butter for greasing the tin.

The 2$\frac{1}{2}$-mile (4km) trail is marked by a green dot and leads past the **Rankmühle**, a picturesque old water-mill. Starting point for this, and other walks in the area, is the *Postamt* (post office) or Hotel Hirschen.

St Peter

That monks in the Middle Ages had a talent for picking the loveliest spots to build was already evident in St Märgen and is now confirmed by the former **Benedictine Kloster** in **St Peter**. Beautifully set in the landscape, the monastery looks back on a long history that began in 1093, when it was founded by Duke Bertold II, a member of the then powerful Zähringen family – the same family that founded Freiburg.

Like its counterpart in St Märgen, this monastery too was destroyed a number of times by fire. The present church, however,

---

Ingredients for the filling and decoration

7 dessertspoons *Kirschwasser* (kirsch or cherry brandy), 26fl oz ($\frac{3}{4}$l) heavy (double) cream, 1 dessertspoon sugar, $\frac{1}{2}$ teaspoon vanilla essence, 30oz (750g) sour cherries, drained and pitted (from a jar), 2oz (50g) semi-sweet chocolate for making shavings, eventually 16 cocktail (drained) or maraschino cherries with stems for decorating the top.

Preparation

In a bowl cream butter, slowly adding sugar with salt and vanilla sugar. Mix in one egg yolk after the other. Add the ground almonds and the ground chocolate. In a separate bowl beat the egg whites until stiff, then scrape onto the butter and sugar mixture. Mix the flour with the cornstarch and baking powder. Add to the top of the beaten egg whites and fold in carefully. Grease a round cake tin and then pour in the batter. Put the cake tin on the middle rung of a preheated 350°F (180°C) oven. Bake for 30 minutes. After baking let the tin cool 5 minutes, then put the cake on a wire rack to cool for an hour. Once cooled, cut the cake twice horizontally.

Filling and topping

Sprinkle the bottom layer of cake with the kirsch. Beat the cream with the sugar and vanilla sugar until it is very stiff. Spread a third of the cream over the bottom layer. Cover that with half of the sour cherries. Leave 16 of the best cherries aside (maraschino or cocktail cherries could be used instead), to decorate the cake later. Cover with the second layer of cake, pressing it down gently. Sprinkle once again with kirsch, cover with another third of the cream and the rest of the cherries. Place the final layer on top and press it lightly down. Now cover the entire cake with cream, spreading it smoothly. Pipe sixteen rosettes of whipped cream around the top edge. Place a cherry on top of each rosette. Decorate the sides and top middle of cake with chocolate flakes – use a vegetable peeler to get thin shavings from a chocolate bar. Chill in fridge until ready to serve.

Rural landscape near Kirchzarten

Hinterzarten has a good selection of comfortable hotels for its guests

has survived unscathed from the eighteenth century. Executed in Baroque style by the master-architect Peter Thumb (1681-1766), the church has a lavishly decorated interior. But the absolute highlight of the monastery complex is the splendid **Rococo Library**, which can only be visited in the course of a guided tour.

Like St Märgen, which is only 5 miles (8km) distant, St Peter also has much to offer in the form of outdoor activities such as walking and cycling. A special treat for the kids in winter would be a ride through the snow-covered landscape on a horse-drawn sleigh – there are also coach rides offered in summer. A good place to dine at the end of the day is Hotel Zur Sonne. The emphasis here is on traditional cooking and they have been awarded a *Michelin* star for their efforts. Another tip is Restaurant-Café Schuler, which serves a delicious Black Forest cake – you can taste the schnapps!

Continuing from St Peter motorists can choose the low road through the lovely **Glottertal**, or the equally pretty high road along the Panoramastrasse to the summit of the **Kandel**. At 4,075 feet (1,242m) the Kandel is the highest mountain in this part of the Forest and is famed for its views. In the Middle Ages the area of the summit was better known as a place where witches gathered, though these days the only people likely to be seen flying about are hang-glider pilots.

From the Kandel the picturesque road snakes its way slowly down to **Waldkirch**, then it is a quick drive along the B294 back to Freiburg.

Monastery church at St Peter

Schäppele

On certain special occasions, such as religious holidays, it is still possible to see traditional costumes being worn in St Peter. The most interesting feature of the costumes worn by young women is the *Schäppele*. Though not as famous as the *Bollenhut* hat worn in the Gutachtal, this head-dress is just as distinctive with its many glass beads and tiny metal discs that glitter in the sunlight. Shaped to resemble the crown of the Virgin Mary, it is also worn by unmarried women in the Glottertal and around St Georgen.

ACCOMMODATION

Freiburg

Campingplatz Hirzberg
Kartäuserstrasse 99
☎ (0761) 35054,
Fax (0761) 289212
Camping ground with shop and restaurant on the edge of town. Open throughout the year.

Hotel-Gasthof Schützen $/$$
Schützenallee 12
☎ (0761) 720210,
Fax (0761) 7202133
On the edge of town, near Hirzberg camping ground. Breakfast buffet, attached restaurant.

Weinstube & Hotel Sichelschmiede $$
Insel 1
☎ (0761) 35096, Fax (0761) 31250
Rooms in a fifteenth-century house right in the middle of the Altstadt.

Colombi-Hotel $$$
Rotteckring 16
☎ (0761) 21060, Fax (0761) 31410
Top hotel with three outstanding restaurants.

Hotel zum Roten Bären $$$
Oberlinden 12
☎ (0761) 387870,
Fax (0761) 3878717
One of the oldest hotels in Germany with a gourmet restaurant, reduction for children.

Hinterzarten

Altevogtshof $
Oberzartener Weg 1
☎ (07652) 1631
Holiday on a farm, great for families. Kitchen for guests, pony rides.

Gäste- und Ferienhaus Berne $/$$
Sonnenbühlweg 7
☎ (07652) 225
Quiet location, kitchen for guests, generous breakfast. Also holiday flats.

Hotel Pension Waldheim $$
Windeckweg 9
☎ (07652) 286, Fax (07652) 451
Situated in a small park, non-smoking.

Parkhotel Adler $$$
Adlerplatz 3
☎ (07652) 1270,
Fax (07652) 127717
Owned by the same family since 1446 this hotel offers luxurious rooms, several restaurants, a park with children's playground and much more besides.

Höllsteig

Hofgut Sternen $$/$$$
Höllsteig 76
☎ (07652) 9010, Fax (07652) 1031
Next to the Ravenna Gorge, mountain bike hire.

Kirchzarten

Campingplatz Kirchzarten
☎ (07661) 3939 and 39375
One of the best camping grounds in the region. Open throughout the year.

Rombach $
(Privatzimmer/
rooms in a private house)
Zartener Strasse 25a
☎/Fax (07661) 5965
Sink and fridge in room, shared bathroom. Also offers holiday flats.

Martha Willmann $
(Privatzimmer/
rooms in a private house)
Eschenweg 17
☎ (07661) 5552, Fax (07661) 6421
Fridge for guests, solarium,
children's cot provided.

Gasthof-Hotel Sonne $$
Hauptstrasse 28
☎ (07661) 62015,
Fax (07661) 7535
Reduction for children, breakfast
buffet, rooms for non-smokers.

St Peter

Campingplatz Steingrubenhof
Camping ground is also
open in winter.
☎ (07660) 210, Fax (07660) 1604

Gaststätte Bürgerstüble $/$$
Bürgerschaft 11
☎ (07660) 272, Fax (07660) 489

Hotel Sonne $$/$$$
Zähringer Strasse 2
☎ (07660) 94010,
Fax (07660) 940166
Comfortable accommodation and a
gourmet restaurant.

EATING OUT

Freiburg

Markthalle $
*Kaiser-Joseph-Strasse 237/
Grünwälderstrasse 4*
From the various snack stalls one
can try delicious food from around
the world. Those who prefer to sit
while eating can try the nearby
Martin's Bräu restaurant, where
they also brew their own beer.
Next door the Kolben-Kaffee-
Akademie serves good coffee and
tasty snacks. Open: during normal
business hours.

Weinstube Sichelschmiede $/$$
Insel 1
☎ (0761) 35037
An idyllic spot right in the middle
of the Altstadt. Here one can try
typical local fare and sip wine from
the region. Open: from 12noon.

Zille-Stube $/$$
Kartäuserstrasse 54
☎ (0761) 37440
Romantic surroundings and a
varied menu. On Sunday and

Monday Japanese delicacies are
served. Open: seven days a week
from 5.30pm.

Schlossbergrestaurant Dattler $$
Am Schlossberg 1
☎ (0761) 31729
Regional specialities and great views
over town. Closed Tuesday.

Hinterzarten

**Hotel Restaurant-Café
Alemannenhof $/$$**
Bruderhalde 21/am Titisee
☎ (07652) 91180, Fax (07652) 705
Located at the southern end of
Titisee at Hinterzarten-Bruderhalde,
also accommodation. Great views
over lake from restaurant terrace,
Black Forest specialities served.
Open: seven days a week.

Hotel Schwarzwaldhof $$
Freiburger Strasse 2
☎ (07652) 12030, Fax (07652) 120322
Local specialities, also
accommodation.
Open: closed Tuesday.

Kirchzarten

Weinstube Trotte $
Hauptstrasse 43
☎ (07661) 7906
Flammkuchen and local wine are the specialities here. Open: from 6pm, closed Sunday and Monday.

Café und Pilgergaststätte St Laurentius $$
On the Giersberg
☎ (07661) 5398
Wonderful views over the Dreisam valley, original vegetarian dishes. Closed Tuesday until 6pm, Thursday until 3pm.

Landgasthof zum Rössle $$
Kirchzarten-Dietenbach, Dietenbach 1
☎ (07661) 2240,
Fax (07661) 98022
Lovely situation, local specialities, also accommodation. Closed Monday, Tuesday until 5pm.

St Peter

Restaurant-Café Schuler $/$$
Sägendobel 14
☎ (07660) 221, Fax (07660) 1615
The Black Forest cake is delicious, also offers accommodation. Closed Thursday.

FREIBURG CITY INFORMATION

Area Code: ☎ (0761)

Important Telephone Numbers

Automobile Breakdown Service ☎ (01802) 222222
German Automobile Association (ADAC) ☎ 36880
Emergency Medical ☎ 8099800
Taxi ☎ 41464 or 83333
Taxi for women only: ☎ 24040

Freiburg's Münster (cathedral)

The countryside around Freiburg offers plenty of scope for mountain bike tours

Airlines

Crossair, Oberlinden 21 ☎ 207780
Lufthansa, Citycenter, Herrenstrasse 50-52 ☎ 388040
Swissair, Münsterplatz 15 ☎ 3860611

Guided Tours and Excursions

Organised tours in and around Freiburg are arranged by **Freiburg Kultour** (☎ 2907447, Fax 2907449), at the Tourist Information on Rotteckring. Very informative is their $1^1/_2$ to 2 hour tour (in English) of the town and cathedral. Other tours (only German speaking guides) include outings to Strasbourg and Colmar in France and Luzern, Montreux and Zürich in Switzerland.

Post Office

The **Hauptpost** (main post office) is located on Eisenbahnstrasse, not far from the main railway station. It is open Monday to Saturday during normal business hours.

Trains and Buses

The **Hauptbahnhof** (main railway station) and the **Busbahnhof** (bus station) are situated next door to each other on Bismarckallee. Information counters are located at both stations.

The **Tourist Office** at Rotteckring 14, and the **VAG-pluspunk**t shop at Salzstrasse 3, can also help visitors with information on the various forms of transport in and around the city. The *pluspunkt* shop also sells tickets

for the Schauinsland cable railway and for other destinations throughout the region.

Useful for those who plan to make use of the local trains, buses and trams is the **Regio24** ticket. It is valid for 24 hours for up to 2 adults, accompanied by as many as 4 children up to 14 years old (the children travel for free). It can be purchased from automatic ticket machines or from the *pluspunkt* shop.

Airport transport to the international **EuroAirport** near Basle (it serves both Basle and Freiburg) is provided by the SBG-AirBus. The bus runs on a roughly hourly basis from the ZOB bus station next to Freiburg's main railway station. Timetables are available from the SBG-Verkaufsbüro (sales counter) at the bus station, or any travel agent.

PLACES TO VISIT

Freiburg

Augustinermuseum
Am Augustinerplatz
Fascinating collection of medieval art. Open: Tuesday to Sunday 10am-5pm. Entrance fee includes entrance to Wentzingerhaus.

Museum für Natur- und Völkerkunde/Adelhausermuseum
Gerberau 32
Interesting natural history and ethnological museum. Open: Tuesday to Sunday 10am-5pm. No entrance fee.

Museum für Neue Kunst
Marienstrasse 10a
Modern art. Open: Tuesday to Sunday 10am-5pm. No entrance fee.

Münster
Münsterplatz
Open: Monday to Sunday 7am-7pm. West Tower (*Turm*) is open Monday to Saturday 10am-5pm, Sunday 1-5pm.

Wentzingerhaus – Museum für Stadtgeschichte
Münsterplatz 30
Exhibits on Freiburg's history. Open: Tuesday to Friday 9.30am-5pm, Saturday and Sunday 10.30am-5pm.

Zinnfigurenklause
In the Schwabentor
Dioramas with tin figures. Open: Tuesday to Thursday 2.30-5pm, Saturday and Sunday 12noon-2pm.

Hinterzarten

Schwarzwälder Skimuseum
Hugenhofweg
History of skiing in the Black Forest. Open: Wednesday and Friday 3-6pm, Saturday, Sunday and public holidays 12noon-6pm.

Höllsteig

Glasbläserei
At Hofgut Sternen
Glass-blowing demonstrations. Open: Monday, Tuesday and Friday 10am-12noon and 2-4pm, Wednesday 10am-12noon.

St Oswald-Kapelle
Near Hofgut Sternen
Open: key from reception at Hofgut Sternen.

St Peter

Benedictine Kloster
Beautiful Baroque church and library.
Open: guided tours through the
rococo library at 11am Tuesday,
2.30pm Thursday, 11.30am Sunday
and public holidays.

Schauinsland

Bauernhausmuseum Schniederlihof
Oberried-Hofsgrund
Traditional Black Forest farmhouse.
Open: May to October, Saturday
and Sunday 10am-6pm.

Bergwildpark Steinwasen
Oberried
Wildlife park specialising in
mountain dwelling animals.
Open: during summer, daily 9am-
6pm, in winter, daily 10am-5pm.

Museumsbergwerk Schauinsland
Historic silver mine.
Open: guided tours 11 April to 31
October, Saturday from 11am-5pm;
during summer, Wednesday and
Sunday 2-5pm.

TOURIST INFORMATION OFFICES

Freiburg

Tourist-Information Freiburg
Rotteckring 14
☎ (0761) 3881880,
Fax (0761) 37003
Open: 1 May to 31 October,
Monday to Friday 9.30am-8pm,
Saturday 9.30am-5pm, Sunday and
public holidays 10am-12noon;
1 November to 30 April, Monday
to Friday 9.30am-6pm, Saturday
9.30am-2pm, Sunday and public
holidays 10am-12noon.

Hinterzarten

Tourist-Information Hinterzarten
In Kurhaus, Freiburgerstrasse
☎ (07652) 120642,
Fax (07652) 120649
Open: Monday to Friday 8am-
12noon and 2-6pm, Saturday
10am-12noon, Sunday 10.30am-
12noon.

Kirchzarten

Verkehrsamt Kirchzarten
Hauptstrasse 24
☎ (07661) 3939,
Fax (07661) 39345

St Märgen

Tourist Information St Märgen
Rathausplatz 1
☎ (07669) 911817,
Fax (07669) 911840

St Peter

Kurverwaltung St Peter
Klosterhof 11
☎ (07660) 910224,
Fax (07660) 910244

4

Vineyards of the South Kaiserstuhl & Markgräflerland

Beginning in Breisach, on the Kaiserstuhl, this chapter explores the southern reaches of the Baden Wine Road, as it moves south through Markgräflerland to its end station in Lörrach, near the Swiss border. A huge fortress-like church looming over the Rhine in Breisach, a cycle tour through the vineyards, an idyllic valley and wonderful mountain views; all this and more is waiting to be discovered in the land of vines and wines.

Around 16 million years ago the Upper Rhine valley was convulsed by volcanic eruptions. Vast quantities of magma were spewed forth from the bowels of the earth. After the volcanic activity finally subsided, it left behind hills of volcanic rock that rose like islands from the Rhine plains. One of these hilly massifs is the **Kaiserstuhl** and though not particularly high, it dominates the otherwise flat landscape around it.

The contrast between the hills of the Kaiserstuhl and the Black Forest mountains to the east could hardly be greater. When spring has already arrived on the slopes of the Kaiserstuhl, the nearby mountain tops might still be sprinkled with the remains of snow. Whereas the one was already settled in Roman times, can boast fertile soils and has a climate reminiscent of the Mediterranean, the other was not settled before the Middle Ages, has a raw climate and poor soils. While the mountains attract hikers with their expansive forests and cool heights,

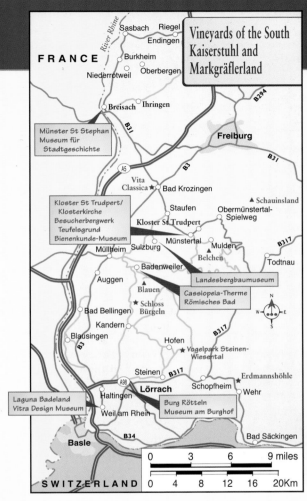

Vineyards of the South Kaiserstuhl and Markgräflerland

FRANCE

River Rhine

Sasbach   Riegel
Endingen
Burkheim
Niederrotweil   Oberbergen

Breisach   Ihringen

B294

Münster St Stephan
Museum für
Stadtgeschichte

B31

Freiburg

B31

A5

Vita
Classica ★   Bad Krozingen

▲ Schauinsland

Kloster St Trudpert/
Klosterkirche
Besucherbergwerk
Teufelsgrund
Bienenkunde-Museum

Staufen   Obermünstertal-
Spielweg

Kloster St Trudpert

B3

Müllheim   Sulzburg   Münstertal   Mulden
Belchen ▲

B317

Todtnau

Badenweiler

Auggen

Blauen

★ Schloss
Bürgeln

Landesbergbaumuseum

Cassiopeia-Therme
Römisches Bad

Bad Bellingen

Kandern

Blausingen

B3

Hofen

B317

★ Vogelpark Steinen-
Wiesental

N
W ● E
S

Steinen   B317

A98   Lörrach   Schopfheim

Laguna Badeland
Vitra Design Museum

Haltingen

Weil am Rhein

Burg Rötteln
Museum am Burghof

Erdmannshöhle

Wehr

Basle

B34

Bad Säckingen

0   3   6   9 miles
0   4   8   12   16   20Km

SWITZERLAND

Opposite: Münster St Stephan, Breisach am Rhein

the warm Kaiserstuhl lures connoisseurs of wine, who visit its lovely wine-growing villages. Here they can sample excellent vintages made from Müller-Thurgau, Silvaner or Grauburgunder grapes. Those who come in summer, however, should note that it can be stiflingly hot in the vineyards; soil temperatures of up to 154°F (68°C) have been measured on the slopes!

Markgräflerland is often titled the 'Tuscany of Germany' and, like the Italian, it lavishes its guests with a mild, sunny climate, fine food and good wines. This is the home of the Gutedel grape, which produces a light, white wine that is otherwise grown mainly in Switzerland, as Fendant, and in France, as Chasselas. In recent years a hybrid grape, known as 'Nobling', has also become quite popular. It is a cross between Silvaner and Gutedel grapes and produces a fruity, full-bodied wine with a delicate bouquet.

The exact boundaries of Markgräflerland are rather vague, but it is generally assumed to be that region of foothills, between the Rhine and the Black Forest Mountains, stretching south from Freiburg to Basle. It gets its name, incidentally, from the margraves of Baden, who once ruled here.

Route 9 ALONG THE BADEN WINE ROAD FROM THE KAISERSTUHL INTO MARKGRÄFLERLAND

Breisach am Rhein

Separated from France by the Rhine the small town of Breisach, on the edge of the Kaiserstuhl, is dominated by the huge, fortress-like **Münster St Stephan**. Work began on the minster in the twelfth century and was completed in the late fifteenth century, so the present building is mainly a mixture of Romanesque and Gothic styles. Though the church had survived the wars and political upheavals of previous centuries relatively unscathed, it was reduced to rubble in 1945 and had to be completely rebuilt.

Church interior

Among the minster's many treasures one of the most outstanding is the wooden **high altar**. It was carved between 1523 and 1526 by a master who was long known only by the initials H L. Though not proved beyond any doubt it is now believed that 'H L' stood for Hans Loi. Whatever the artist's true identity there is no doubt that the altar is one of the finest achievements of late Gothic German sculpture. The exquisitely carved central shrine portrays the Coronation of Mary and was almost certainly inspired by Hans Baldung Grien's altar painting in Freiburg's cathedral.

A masterpiece of late Gothic stonemasonry is the fifteenth century **choir screen**. In medieval churches these screens served to separate the clergy from the congregation. Also of note is the *Last Judgement* by Martin Schongauer. The artist worked on this monumental wall fresco from 1488 until his death in 1491. On three walls it depicts Hell (north wall), Paradise (south wall) and Christ Pronouncing Judgement (west wall). In spite of the fact that they are somewhat worn by the passage of time the paintings are still quite impressive.

Though the Münster is the main attraction the town has a few picturesque corners waiting to be discovered in the course of a stroll. One such corner is the **Gutgesellentorplatz** with its pleasant cafés and medieval town gate. There were once 30 gates and defensive towers surrounding Breisach, though now only 6 remain. The **Rheintor** (1675), another town gate to the north of the Münster, is an impressive reminder of the days when Breisach was one of the largest and most important fortresses in Europe. It now serves as a museum with interesting exhibits relating to the town's long and often violent past.

The Kaiserstuhl-Radwanderweg

This 40-mile (65km) circular cycle tour takes you around the Kaiserstuhl and past the neighbouring Tuniberg. Marked by the letters Ka it goes through vineyards, orchards, the woods bordering the Rhine and also through pretty wine-growing villages like Burkheim, Sasbach, Endingen and Ihringen. The best time of the year to do this tour is either in spring, when the fruit trees are in blossom, or in autumn. In summer it can be excruciatingly hot around the Kaiserstuhl.

Starting point for the tour is the railway station in Breisach – bicycles can be hired from the Firma Schweizer at Neutorstrasse 31. The route is shown quite clearly on the following map: *Schwarzwaldvereins-Karte Blatt 6*. On this map the cycling routes are marked by green lines, walking routes are marked by red ones. The Tourist Information in Breisach will also have more information.

Places of interest around the Kaiserstuhl

Of course, a tour of the small villages and towns scattered around the slopes of the Kaiserstuhl will provide plenty of opportunities for buying and trying the local wine. However, in the quest for a good vintage many visitors will discover that some of these small wine-growing communities have more to offer than just *Weinproben* (wine-tastings) and *Kellereibesichtigungen* (tours of the wine cellars). In some cases it might be an ancient church with medieval frescoes, in others an idyllic townscape of half-timbered houses. What follows are suggestions for just a few places that might justify a longer stop.

Niederrotweil awaits visitors with one of the most important examples of religious art that the Kaiserstuhl has to offer. In the Catholic church of **St Michael** is a beautiful late Gothic **high altar** that was possibly carved by the master H L. He was also responsible for the altar in Breisach's Münster (see above) and once again it deals with the Coronation of Mary. Also of interest are some frescoes from the fourteenth century.

Just to the north of Niederrotweil is the small wine-growing town of **Burkheim**. A Baroque town gate, a ruined castle, cobblestone streets and fine old half-timbered buildings are the ingredients that make this town one of the loveliest on the Kaiserstuhl. Of interest inside the **St Pankratius-Kirche** are the sixteenth-century wall and ceiling **frescoes**.

Endingen is situated on the north-eastern edge of the Kaiserstuhl. The nicest part of town is the Marktplatz with its picturesque ensemble of buildings. Of note here is the late Gothic **Kornhaus** (1617), the old **Rathaus** (1527) and the new **Rathaus** (1775). Also on the Marktplatz is the pilgrimage church of **St Martin**. The annual pilgrimage to view the miraculous image of the Weeping Mother of God has taken place since 1615.

The Kaiserstuhl vineyards produce some excellent wine

Vineyards versus nature

Viewed from certain angles the terraced, vineyard-covered slopes of the Kaiserstuhl have the appearance of a vast eroded Mayan pyramid, somehow stranded on the Rhine plains. The huge 'steps' or terraces cut into the slopes are the result of major re-landscaping activities in the 1970s. The aim of this landscaping was to remove the small vineyards and to replace them with larger, more productive ones that could be easily worked with agricultural machinery.

The result, at first, was an ecological disaster. The fragile, for Germany unique, ecosystem of the Kaiserstuhl was altered drastically. Plants and animals that are normally found at more southerly latitudes lost their habitat. However, in the last few years some of that flora and fauna has started to return. Biologists have counted some 2,700 species of butterfly, 700 species of beetle and have discovered insect rarities like the praying mantis (*mantis religiosa*). There are also many rare plants growing on the slopes, but the biggest botanical attractions are the 33 varieties of orchid that grow wild here – they flower in May and June. Those interested in seeing a bit of this natural world for themselves will find **Oberbergen**, to the north of Breisach, a good place to start.

Moving on

No longer on the Kaiserstuhl but still in wine-growing country, on the fringes of Markgräflerland, is the spa town of **Bad Krozingen** – from Breisach follow the B31 south. The town's hopes of getting rich with oil were dashed in 1911 when instead of oil they struck water. Fortunately this water was not just wet, it also had health-giving properties. The thermal waters enabled the town to achieve its status as a spa and have proved useful in the treatment of various ailments, including heart diseases and rheumatism. If your own limbs are aching (or even if they are not) then a plunge in the thermal waters at the bath complex **Vita Classica** might be just the thing. They were reopened in 1996 in the style of an antique bathing temple.

Staufen

Just to the south-east of Bad Krozingen is the small town of Staufen. Idyllically situated along the banks of the Neumagen river, Staufen has one of the loveliest historic townscapes in the Black Forest. Especially photogenic are the houses lining Hauptstrasse and the Marktplatz with its impressive Renaissance **Rathaus**. Crowning a vineyard-covered hill on the edge of town are the ruins of a medieval **Burg** (castle) destroyed in the Thirty Years' War. For those with the energy a comfortable path leads up to the ruins, from where there are good views over town and beyond.

Staufen would be a wonderful base for people who want to get away from it all. It is quiet, there is good accommodation and of course there is plenty of good walking in the vicinity; for instance up to the Belchen, one of the highest mountains in this part of the Forest. But if time is short it would still be worth stopping at least for a lunch-break, as it would be hard to find more

Strausswirtschaften

Few foreigners ever find their way to a *Strausswirtschaft* (a place where home-grown wine is served), as they are often tucked away in side streets and the significance of the wreath or broom that usually hangs outside these establishments is lost on most. This is a pity, as they offer an excellent opportunity to sip the local wine at prices much lower than in normal wine bars or restaurants. The tasty home-made snacks that go with the wine are also quite cheap and on top of all this the cosy atmosphere inside a wine-grower's house makes it easy to meet the locals.

The tradition of the Strausswirtschaft or *Besenwirtschaft* began with the Emperor Charlemagne in the year 800. In that year he decreed that wine growers were allowed to sell some of their wine directly. Among other things this medieval law stipulated that wine could only be served when the 'wine bell' rang after the day's work was over or on Sundays after mass. Furthermore, the wine growers were only allowed to sell wine they had harvested themselves and then only for a limited period of time during the year.

To this day Strausswirtschaften may only sell home-grown wine and can only stay open for a total of 4 months in the year. German law also requires that only simple meals may be served and that a Strausswirtschaft may provide seating for no more than forty guests. Being Germany these restrictions are very strictly controlled! Whether these establishments are called a *Strauss*wirtschaft or *Besen*wirtschaft depends on whether a *Strauss* (wreath) or *Besen* (broom) is hung outside – something that varies from region to region and even within a region. Once again this is a custom that goes back to the time of Charlemagne.

In the Black Forest Strausswirtschaften are found in the wine-growing regions along the Rhine: the Ortenau in the north, the area around Freiburg and the Kaiserstuhl and along the southern reaches of the Baden Wine Road in Markgräflerland. They are mostly open in spring and autumn but a number of places are also open in June and July. Normally it is not possible to reserve places at tables; you simply turn up and join other guests at the same table or, if there is no room, wait with glass in hand until somebody has left. Specialities served include *Zwiebelkuchen* (onion tart) and *Flammenkuchen*, a kind of Germanic pizza!

Boat trips on the Rhine start from Breisach

Endingen has a picturesque Marktplatz

pleasant surroundings than in Staufen's traffic-free Altstadt. There are several restaurants and cafés along Hauptstrasse and on the Marktplatz, including **Gasthaus Löwen**, where the legendary Dr Faustus came to a sticky end (see below).

Excursion into the Münstertal

A pleasant detour from Staufen leads east through the lovely Münstertal to **Kloster St Trudpert**. This former monastery is named after the Irish missionary Trudpert, who arrived in this then isolated valley in the seventh century. After he died a martyr's death a small chapel was erected which, about a hundred years later, was followed by a monastery complex. It was from here that the settlement of not only the Münstertal but also much of this region of the Black Forest began.

The present complex dates from the eighteenth century and it is only the church that can be visited – in any case the Kloster is most impressive from the outside. The interior is rather subdued for a Baroque church and some find it a

Doctor Faustus in Staufen

A terrific explosion shook the room, it quickly filled with smoke and the stench of sulphur. Doctor Johannes Faustus, alchemist by profession, lay sprawled on the floor, his face blackened, his neck broken. It happened one day in 1539, in room no 5 on the third floor of Gasthaus zum Löwen in Staufen. Had Doctor Faustus paid the ultimate price for his pact with the Devil? Was it Mephistopheles himself who broke his neck and claimed his soul for eternal damnation?

The legend of Faustus and his 24-year pact with the Devil has inspired many great literary figures over the centuries, including Christopher Marlowe and Goethe. However, even if some of the circumstances of his death belong to the realm of fiction, Dr Faustus himself did in fact exist and did live for a while in Staufen. According to an old chronicle he was invited to town by Baron von Staufen, who had money problems and hoped that the alchemist could make gold for him. It was probably while conducting experiments in his room at the Löwen that an explosion occurred which killed him.

This mural on the Gasthaus zum Löwen recounts the legend of Dr Faustus

bit disappointing. Of note is the fine stucco and some frescoes depicting, among other things, scenes from the life of St Trudpert.

At the southern end of the valley, near **Mulden**, is a former silver mine which is now a museum. Mining operations at the **Besucherbergwerk Teufelsgrund** began at least as early as the eleventh century. Though silver mining brought the valley considerable prosperity in the Middle Ages, yields from the Teufelsgrund mine were already dwindling by the sixteenth century. Fluorspar (fluorite) was mined briefly between 1942 and 1956, after which the mine was finally closed.

In **Obermünstertal-Spielweg** the **Bienenkunde-Museum** claims to be the biggest bee museum in Europe. Be that as it may, visitors need not fear a huge collection of lifeless insects pinned under glass; the place is literally buzzing with activity! Using models, videos and live honeybees the museum attempts to shed light on bee keeping and life in the beehive.

Sulzburg

From Staufen the Wine Road heads south to Sulzburg. Of interest in this pleasant little town is the Romanesque church of St **Cyriak**, a mining museum on the Marktplatz and an ancient **Jewish cemetery** near the local camp site. This cemetery, together with a restored synagogue, is all that remains as a reminder of Sulzburg's once flourishing Jewish community – in 1864 around 30 per cent of the population were Jewish.

Badenweiler

Badenweiler lies just off the Wine Road, to the east of Müllheim. Situated on sunny slopes at the foot of the Blauen, this distinguished spa town enjoys one of the warmest climates in the Black Forest. No doubt impressed by the surrounding vineyards and orchards, a nineteenth century German poet once claimed that Badenweiler *'was a piece of Italy on German soil'*. If that statement had been made around 2,000 years earlier it would have been quite true: Badenweiler was firmly in the hands of the Roman Empire during the first century AD.

Close to the Roman bath (see opposite) is the **Cassiopeia-Therme**, a modern bath complex that is housed within the confines of the old Markgrafenbad building. Appropriately enough the design of the luxurious interior was inspired by its antique predecessor. Also in the park is a castle ruin (good views over the

---

Burefastnet in Sulzburg and the Sulzbachtal

Those who are lucky enough to be in Sulzburg in January can witness the so-called **Burefastnet** (Farmers' Carnival). It commences about a week after carnival festivities have finished elsewhere in the Black Forest (the Sunday after Ash Wednesday) and begins with a parade in traditional carnival costumes. Once night falls the festivities are concluded by rolling flaming wooden wheels down a nearby hill – an event known as the *Schübefier*.

Roman bath house

Located in the lovely **Kurpark** (Spa Park), with its stands of exotic trees, are the ruins of a **Römisches Bad** (Roman bathing complex). Like the more well-known spa town of Baden-Baden in the northern Black Forest, Badenweiler also had its beginnings as a Roman thermal spa. The baths were erected during the reign of the Emperor Vespasian in 75 AD and were dedicated to the Black Forest goddess Diana Abnoba. An interesting feature of the ruin, which is considered to be the best preserved Roman bath in Germany, is that it is divided into two completely symmetrical halves. Archaeologists therefore assume that men and women bathed separately.

Rhine plain from here) and below that an architecturally interesting **Kurhaus**, where concerts often take place.

Though Badenweiler did not attract nobility in the way that Baden-Baden did, it nevertheless had its share of distinguished personages. A memorial tablet in the Kurpark is dedicated to the Russian dramatist and short story writer Anton Chekhov, who died here in 1904. A few years earlier the American novelist Stephen Crane also spent the last few weeks of his life here, before he finally died of tuberculosis.

Only 5 miles (8km) to the southeast of Badenweiler is the 3,823ft (1,165m) high **Blauen**. The mountain summit is accessible by road and it is worth the drive because of the fantastic views. From the lookout tower it is possible to see as far as the Alps to the south and across to France in the west. In autumn the summit is often free of cloud, while the Rhine valley, far below, is shrouded in mist. There are also good views from **Gasthaus Hochblauen** (restaurant and accommodation), just below the summit.

On to Lörrach

From Badenweiler there are a few possibilities for the continued journey to Lörrach, at the end of the Baden Wine Road. The scenically most attractive, and most direct, is to continue directly south via **Kandern**. Shortly before reaching Kandern there is a turn-off to **Schloss Bürgeln**, an eighteenth century residence with an interesting Rococo interior. Kandern itself is mainly interesting as the starting point for a trip by steam train (Kandertalbahn Museum Railway) to **Haltingen**, near the Swiss border.

Those who want to keep to the Wine Road can go via the wine-growing towns of **Müllheim** and **Auggen** (both are good places for wine tasting) to **Bad Bellingen**. The town owes its status as a spa, like Bad Krozingen, to the quest for oil. During drilling operations in 1956 they discovered the thermal springs and the town has now developed into a pleasant health resort.

A bit further south, the village of **Blansingen** has one of the most interesting churches in Markgräflerland. Though unassuming from the outside the parish church of **St Peter** contains some magnificent fifteenth century frescoes of St Peter. The wall paintings depict, among other things, the Last Judgement and scenes from the life of St Peter.

Staufen is one of the prettiest towns in this part of the Black Forest

There are plenty of opportunities to buy wine on the Baden Wine Road

Lörrach

Lörrach is a rather nondescript modern town, though it does make a useful base for trips to France and nearby Basle in Switzerland – accommodation is cheaper here than in Basle itself and the Swiss city is quickly reached by suburban train. Ravaged by numerous wars in the past there is not much of historical interest to be seen in town. On the outskirts, however, it is worth visiting the imposing ruins of **Burg Rötteln**. These castle ruins belong to the largest in southern Germany and date from the twelfth century. There are great views over the Wiesental from here and some good walking in the surrounding woods.

Back in town visitors can learn more about the history of Burg Rötteln at the **Museum am Burghof**. Also to be seen here are exhibits on the early and pre-history of the region, folklore, natural history and an extensive art collection devoted to artists from the Markgräflerland region.

Moving on

Those who want to extend this tour can follow the B317 north to Todtnau, at the start of Route 10. On the way it might be worth pausing in **Schopfheim**. Located in the attractive Altstadt is the Gothic church of **St Michael**, where there are remnants of wall paintings from the fifteenth century. About 4 miles (6.5km) to the east of town, near **Wehr**, one can explore the fascinating underground world of the Erdmannshöhle – see Route 10, Chapter 5.

Trips from Lörrach

Weil am Rhein is virtually next door to Lörrach, so if the weather is bad and the kids are grumbling the solution might be to head straight for **Laguna Badeland**. They claim that spring never ends at this swimming pool and sauna complex with its (fake) tropical landscape, 213ft (65m) long water chute and a pool with waves that crash on an artificial shore. Less physical, but a lot more edifying, would be a visit to the **Vitra Design Museum**. Designed by the Californian architect Frank O Gehry the museum building itself is already a work of art; a giant cubist sculpture set amidst green pastures. Inside some 3,000 exhibits not only document the history of industrial furniture design but also show current trends. Popular souvenirs are miniature models of chairs designed by such famous architects as Le Corbusier and Henry van der Velde.

Another outing for families would be to visit the **Vogelpark Steinen-Wiesental**, north-east of Lörrach. Covering an area of 25sq acres (100,000sq m) this bird park is home to 300 different species of birds from various parts of the world. A highlight of the complex is one of Europe's loveliest tropical houses, where the birds are free to fly around you. On top of this there is the inevitable restaurant and a large adventure playground for the children.

ACCOMMODATION

Badenweiler

Campingplatz Badenweiler
Weilertalstrasse 73
☎ (07632) 1550, Fax (07632) 5268
Camping ground with a quiet location, shop, playground.

Gästehaus Friedrich $
Weilertalstrasse 21a
☎ (07632) 6654, Fax (07632) 6658
On edge of town, fridge for guests, generous breakfast, reduction for children.

Hotel Siegle $$
Römerstrasse 4
☎ (07632) 82240,
Fax (07632) 822450
Central location, large garden, reduction for children.

Hotel Eckerlin $$$
Römerstrasse 2
☎ (07632) 8320,
Fax (07632) 832299
Indoor swimming pool, sauna, solarium, close to park.

Hotel Römerbad $$$
Schlossplatz 1
☎ (07632) 700, Fax (07632) 70200
Famous guests at this luxury hotel have included Friedrich Nietzsche, Thomas Mann and Andy Warhol.

Breisach am Rhein

Gästehaus Schillinger $
Harelungenweg 3
☎/Fax (07667) 6991
Facilities for children, cycle hire. Also holiday flat available.

Hotel Bären $$
Kupfertorplatz 7
☎ (07667) 281, Fax (07667) 7055
In the middle of town, facilities for children, buffet breakfast.

Pension Schlossberg $$
Kapuzinergasse 29
☎ (07767) 93770,
Fax (07767) 937711
Facilities for children, mini-bar in room.

Hotel-Restaurant Kapuzinergarten $$$
Kapuzinergasse 26
☎ (07667) 93000,
Fax (07667) 930093
Great views over the Kaiserstuhl, facilities for children, cycle hire and one room suitable for disabled persons.

Lörrach

Campingplatz Lörrach
Grüttweg 8
☎ (07621) 82588,
Fax (07621) 165034
Restaurant, toilet and shower for disabled persons.

Landgasthaus Krone $$
Dorfstrasse 36
☎ (07621) 2795,
Fax (07621) 164067

Hotel Villa Elben $$/$$$
Hünerbergweg 26
☎ (07621) 2066,
Fax (07621) 43280
Art Nouveau villa in a park.

Inzlinger Wasserschloss $$$
Inzlingen
☎ (07621) 47057
Situated in the small town of Inzlingen, near Lörrach, this moated palace offers noble surroundings and gourmet cuisine in the attached restaurant.

Staufen

Campingplatz Belchenblick
Münstertäler Strasse
☎ (07633) 7045, Fax (07633) 7908
Nicely situated camping ground
with excellent facilities.

Hotel Sonne $$
Albert-Hugard-Strasse 1
☎ (07633) 95300,
Fax (07633) 953014
Quiet location, middle of town.

Hotel-Gasthof zum Löwen $$$
Hauptstrasse 47
☎ (07633) 6017,
Fax (07633) 500121
Faust was a guest at the Löwen
(room no 5) in 1539.

EATING OUT

Badenweiler

Markgräfler Winzerstube $
Luisenstrasse 6
☎ (07632) 254
Markgräfler wine and *Vesper* dishes.
Open: every day from 5pm.
Closed mid-December to 1 March

Uli's Schlemmerstuben $$
In Club-Hotel Eberhardt-Burghardt,
Waldweg 2-4
☎ (07632) 8110
Varied menu with good salads,
steaks, pancakes and trout dishes.
Open: seven days a week from
11am.

Restaurant Schwarzmatt $$$
In Hotel Schwarzmatt,
Schwarzmattstrasse 6a
☎ (07632) 82010
One of the best restaurants in
town. Open: seven days a week.

Breisach

Jack Daniel's $/$$
Hafenstrasse 11
☎ (07667) 1023
Steaks, Flammkuchen and snacks.
Like many other restaurants in the
Kaiserstuhl region they also serve

the *Burgunderteller;* a glass of
Burgunder wine and a local speciality that costs no more than 15 to
30 marks. Open: daily 10am-3pm.

Kappadokien $/$$$
Gutgesellenplatz 2
☎ (07667) 940272
Excellent Turkish restaurant.

Restaurant Bären $$
Kupfertorplatz 7
☎ (07667) 281
Local and international dishes, also
Burgunderteller. Closed Monday.

Lörrach

Restaurant zum Meyerhof $/$$
Basler Strasse 162
☎ (07621) 46012
In the middle of town, wild game a
speciality. Closed Sunday.

Zum Kranz $$$
Basler Strasse 90
☎ (07621) 89083
Recommended by *Gault Millau.*
Closed Sunday and Monday.

Staufen

Café Decker $
Am Neumagen
☎ (07633) 5316
Next to the river, great place for a snack on a sunny day, delicious cakes and chocolates.
Closed Monday.

Restaurant-Weinstube Kornhaus Staufen $/$$
Marktplatz
☎ (07633) 5401
Local specialities, good selection of local wines. Open: seven days a week.

PLACES TO VISIT

Bad Krozingen

Vita Classica
Herbert-Hellmann-Allee 12
Thermal pools designed like an antique Roman spa. Open: Monday to Friday 9am-11pm, Saturday and Sunday 9am-10pm.

Badenweiler

Cassiopeia-Therme
In the Kurpark
Luxurious themal bathing complex. Open: Monday to Friday 8am-9pm, Saturday, Sunday and public holidays 9am-7pm.

Römisches Bad
In the Kurpark
Ruins of a Roman bathing complex. Open: can be viewed at any time or on a guided tour. Inquire at Tourist Office for details.

Below: Many restaurants and country inns publicise themselves with attractive wrought Iron signs

Opposite: The castle ruins of Burg Rötteln belong to the largest in southern Germany

Breisach am Rhein

Münster St Stephan
Magnificent medieval church.
Open: outside church services.

Museum für Stadtgeschichte
In the Rheintor, Rheintorplatz
Open: Tuesday to Friday 2-5pm,
Saturday 11.30am-5pm, Sunday
and public holidays 11.30am-6pm.

Kandern

Schloss Bürgeln
North of Kandern
Rococo palace, nice views from
restaurant terrace. Open: guided
tours daily, except Tuesday, at
11am, 2pm, 3pm, 4pm and 5pm.

Lörrach

Burg Rötteln
One of the largest ruined castles
in southern Germany.
Open: 10am-6pm daily.

Museum am Burghof
Basler Strasse 143
Prehistory of the region, folklore
and a collection of regional art.
Open: Wednesday to Saturday 2-
5pm, Sunday 11am-1pm and 2-
5.30pm.

Vogelpark Steinen-Wiesental
*North-east of Lörrach
at Steinen-Hofen*
Large bird park with everything
from kookaburras to hornbills.
Open: 15 March to 1 November
9am-6pm daily; November and
February, Sunday 11am-5pm (only
if weather is fine).

Münstertal

Kloster St Trudpert/Klosterkirche
Baroque monastery church is also a
venue for concerts of classical
music. Open: 8am-6pm daily.

Besucherbergwerk Teufelsgrund
Old silver mine. Open: 15 June to 15
September, Tuesday to Sunday 2-
5pm; 1 April to 14 June and 16
September to 31 October, Tuesday,
Thursday, Saturday and Sunday 2-
5pm; 1 to 30 November, Saturday
and Sunday 2-5pm. Last tour at 5pm.

Bienenkunde-Museum
Obermünstertal-Spielweg
A museum devoted to bees
and the making of honey.
Open: Wednesday, Saturday,
Sunday and public holidays 2-5pm.

Sulzburg

Landesbergbaumuseum
Marktplatz
History of mining in the region.
Open: Monday to Friday 2-4.30pm,
Saturday and Sunday 2-5pm.

Weil am Rhein

Laguna Badeland
Sportplatz 1
Impressive swimming pool complex
with a touch of the Caribbean.
Open: Monday 2-10pm, Tuesday to
Thursday 10am-10pm, Friday 10am-
11pm, Saturday and Sunday 9am-
10pm.

Vitra Design Museum
Charles-Eames-Strasse 1
One of the most important
museums in the region, with
exhibitions on themes related to
design and architecture.
Open: Tuesday to Sunday and
public holidays 11am-6pm.

TOURIST INFORMATION OFFICES

Bad Bellingen

Bade- und Kurverwaltung Bad Bellingen
☎ (07635) 808220,
Fax (07635) 808290

Bad Krozingen

Kur- und Bäderverwaltung Bad Krozingen
Herbert-Hellmann-Allee 12
☎ (07633) 400863,
Fax (07633) 150105

Badenweiler

Kur- und Touristik GmbH Badenweiler
Ernst-Eisenlohr-Strasse 4
☎ (07632) 72110,
Fax (07632) 72170
Open: Monday to Friday 8.30am-12noon and 3-5pm, Saturday 8.30am-12noon, closed Saturday from November to February.

Breisach am Rhein

Breisach-Touristik
Marktplatz 16
☎ (07667) 940155,
Fax (07667) 940158
Open: Monday to Friday 9am-6pm, Saturday 10-1pm, Sunday 1-4pm.

Kandern

Fremdenverkehrsamt Kandern
Hauptstrasse 18
☎/Fax (07626) 89960

Lörrach

Touristinformation Kartenhaus Lörrach
In the Burghof, Herrenstrasse 5
☎ (07621) 9408911,
Fax (07621) 9408914

Open: Monday to Friday 10am-6pm, Saturday 10am-4pm.

Münstertal

Kurverwaltung Münstertal
Wasen 47
☎ (07636) 70730,
Fax (07636) 70748

Schopfheim

Städtisches Verkehrsbüro Schopfheim
Am Marktplatz
☎ (07622) 396116,
Fax (07622) 396178

Staufen

Touristik-Information Staufen
Hauptstrasse 53
☎ (07633) 80536,
Fax (07633) 50593
Open: 15 May to 31 October, Monday 7.30am-12.30pm and 1.30-6pm, Tuesday to Thursday 7.30am-12.30pm and 1.30-4.30pm, Friday 7.30am-12.30pm and 1.30-4pm, Saturday 9.30am-12.30pm.

Sulzburg

Verkehrsamt Sulzburg
Marktplatz
☎ (07634) 560040,
Fax (07634) 560034

Weil am Rhein

Tourist- und Stadtinformation Weil am Rhein
Rathausplatz 3
☎ (07621) 9567771,
Fax (07621) 9567779

I n terms of natural scenery this is perhaps the loveliest part of the Forest. Here one finds one of Germany's most spectacular gorges (the Wutach Gorge), two of the region's largest lakes and its highest mountains. True, the Black Forest peaks rise to no spectacular heights, but the views they offer from their bald, rounded summits are nonetheless spectacular.

In winter the whole region is transformed into a snow-covered paradise, drawing cross-country and even downhill skiers from far and wide. This is in fact a region for outdoor enthusiasts, as in summer it is just as attractive for mountain biking and walking. Except for a few larger resorts like Todtnau, Titisee and Bad Säckingen, the area is thinly populated, with the towns few and far between. The only cultural monument of greater significance is the huge monastery church at St Blasien; otherwise the real attraction here is simply the landscape itself.

As a region within a region the **Hotzenwald**, which is explored on Route 10, is especially attractive for those who are drawn to lonely, austerely beautiful landscapes. Situated between the river valleys of the Wehra, Rhine and Schlücht, the Hotzenwald plateau is cut by numerous gorges formed by streams that twist their way south to the Rhine

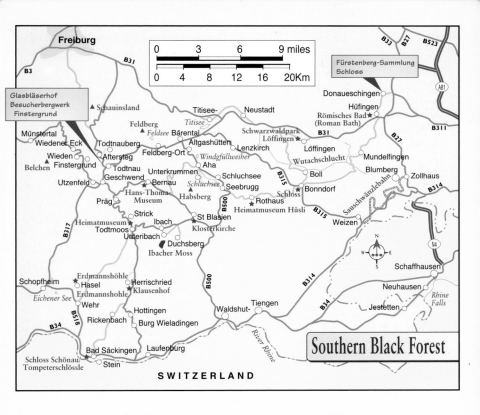

Freiburg

0   3   6   9 miles
0   4   8   12   16   20Km

Fürstenberg-Sammlung Schloss

B3

B31

B33 B27 B523

A81

Glasbläserhof
Besucherbergwerk
Finstergrund

Donaueschingen

Hüfingen

Römisches Bad ★
(Roman Bath)

▲ Schauinsland   Titisee-   Neustadt

B31

B311

Titisee

Feldberg

Schwarzwaldpark

B27

Münstertal

▲ Feldsee Bärental

Löffingen ★

Wiedener Eck   Feldberg-Ort

Altgashütten

Lenzkirch

Löffingen

Mundelfingen

Todtnauberg

Windfüllweiher

Wutachschlucht

Wieden   Aftersteg

Aha

Boll

Blumberg

Finstergrund

Todtnau

Unterkrummen

Zollhaus

Belchen

Geschwend

Schluchsee

B315

Boll

Bonndorf

Utzenfeld   Bernau

Schluchsee

Seebrugg

B314

Hans-Thoma-

Schloss

Präg   Museum   Habsberg

Rothaus

Sauschwänzlebahn

Strick

Heimatmuseum Hüsli

Weizen

Heimatmuseum   Ibach   St Blasien

B315

N4

Todtmoos   Klosterkirche

B317

Unteribach

Duchsberg

Ibacher Moss

Schaffhausen

B500

Schopfheim   Erdmannshöhle

Herrischried

Neuhausen

Hasel   Klausenhof

Rhine

Eichener See   Erdmannshohle

Falls

B514

Wehr   Hottingen

Tiengen

Jestetten

Rickenbach   Burg Wieladingen

Waldshut-

B34

B518

B34

B500

Bad Säckingen   Laufenburg

River Rhine

Schloss Schönau/
Tompeterschlössle   Stein

Southern Black Forest

SWITZERLAND

below. There are no towns here, only solitary farms or small villages, some of which consist of no more than a few houses clustered loosely together. In the past the people who lived in these settlements had a hard life, eking out a meagre living from the poor soils of the forest they had cleared. They had, however, an independent nature which led to a series of uprisings known as the Saltpetre Wars. In these conflicts they fought, in the end unsuccessfully, against repression on the part

of the monastery at St Blasien, the region's most powerful landowner.

Those who visit the Hotzenwald in early spring or late autumn are often rewarded with fantastic views over the mist-filled Rhine valley below. In fact the Hotzenwald is one of the sunniest regions in south-west Germany. On clear winter days too, the views towards the Alps can be breathtaking. At times like this, whether on foot or on skis, the Hotzenwald is surely an unforgettable experience.

Route 10 FROM TODTNAU TO THE HOTZENWALD PLATEAU (circular route)

Todtnau

Todtnau can be reached from Freiburg by bus. They depart from the *Hauptbahnhof* (main railway station) several times a day. Those with a car can either follow the route via Kirchzarten (also the bus route), or go via the Schauinsland. Both roads are scenically attractive, though the one via Kirchzarten is a bit faster to drive because it is not so curvy – for a description of the Schauinsland route see Chapter 3.

Todtnau is, like Hinterzarten, mainly interesting because of the possibilities for outdoor recreation that the surrounding mountains and forests offer. There is nothing much to see in the town itself, as it was destroyed by fire in 1876. One picturesque corner is, however, the area around the **Stadtkirche** (town church). With its twin towers and a dramatic backdrop of forested slopes it is definitely in the 'picture postcard' category.

Walking and cycling

In summer, of course, Todtnau and its outlying villages (Todtnauberg, Aftersteg, Brandenberg-Pfahl and a few other villages now belong to Todtnau for administrative purposes) are firmly in the grip of hikers and mountain bikers. From Todtnau a chair-lift transports cyclists to the **Mountain Bike Fun Park** on the 3,799ft (1,158m) high Hasenhorn. The main feature of this park is a 2-mile (3.25km) downhill run that can be managed by all

Winter sport

Situated on the south-west flank of the Feldberg the small town of Todtnau is not only a popular base for hiking holidays but also for winter sports. In 1891 Germany's first ski club was founded here and together with the mountain resort of Feldberg it is now in the middle of the most popular ski region in the Black Forest. Over twenty ski-lifts take downhill skiers to the mountain tops, whereas for cross-country skiers there are around 37 miles (60km) of prepared trails. Those who want to be at the hub of winter activities can base themselves at **Todtnauberg** (3,350ft/ 1,021m), a ski village only a short drive from Todtnau itself.

In the vicinity of Todtnau are 3 cross-country trails that belong to the most interesting that Germany has to offer. Starting point for the **Schauinslandspur** (11 miles/ 18km) and the **Stübenwasenspur** (15 miles/ 24km) is **Notschrei**, to the north of Todtnau. The **Haldenspur** (3½ miles/5.6km) is the easiest of the three and is flood-lit during the week from 6.30pm to 8.30pm. Starting point is the car park at the Haldenköpfle lifts, north-west of Notschrei.

cyclists, insofar as they match their speed to their abilities. For walkers some 186 miles (300km) of waymarked hiking trails ensure that one never has to follow the same path twice.

The walk from Todtnau to the 318ft (97m) high **Todtnau Waterfall** (signposted as Todtnauer Wasserfall) takes about 30 minutes. From the *Busbahnhof* (bus station) continue in an easterly direction to the Marktplatz. Pass the Stadtkirche (church) and follow the trail marked by a blue diamond to the waterfall. Those who continue from the waterfall in a westerly direction could also visit the **Glasbläserhof** (glassworks) in **Aftersteg**. Here you can watch the glassblower at work, browse through the shop and afterwards dine in the rustic interior of the attached restaurant.

Feldberg

At 4,898ft (1,493m) the Feldberg is the Black Forest's highest mountain.

Ease of access, panoramic views and excellent ski facilities have made it one of the most popular destinations in the Black Forest. From near the Feldberger Hof (hotel), in **Feldberg-Ort**, the summit of the **Seebuck** (4,751ft/1,448m) can be reached by chair-lift or in the course of a steep uphill climb. The rest of the way to the actual Feldberg summit has to be done on foot.

In spite of attempts to reduce the detrimental effects of tourism in recent years, the treeless summit area remains one of the least attractive in the whole region. This impression is especially strong in the summer months, when no snow hides the flattened vegetation along the downhill runs and the ski-lifts only seem to scar the slopes. In spite of this the climb (or ride) to the top is still worth it for the magnificent views in clear weather – usually best in autumn or in winter.

Although ugly buildings and ski-lifts have spoiled the summits of the

Feldberg walk

This 9-mile (14.5km) walk around the Feldberg massif is well signposted and requires about 6 hours. There are plenty of opportunities for refreshments at huts along the way. A useful map for this and other walks in the area is the *Wanderkarte Todtnauer Ferienland*, available from the Tourist Office in Todtnau. Walking maps can also be obtained in Feldberg-Ort and are recommended because the sheer number of trails up here can make orientation difficult.

From **Feldberger Hof**, where there is a large car park, continue in the direction of **Todtnauer Hütte**. After passing the hut the track climbs slightly on its way to **Wilhelmer Hütte** (closed Friday, children will enjoy the mini-zoo with its farm animals). From here it levels out before dropping down to **Zastler Hütte** (closed Thursday), directly below the meteorological station (*Wetterwarte*) on the Feldberg summit. North of the hut turn right, in the direction of the Naturfreundehaus and **Baldenweger Hütte** (closed Monday). A narrow road now leads down to **Rinken** and from there to **Raimartihof** (closed Tuesday). The trail continues past a lovely mountain lake known as the **Feldsee** and then follows the steep Karl-Egon-Weg back to Feldberger Hof.

Stadkirche, Todtnau

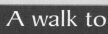

Seebuck and Feldberg (the Feldberg massif is, in fact, made up of several peaks) there is still some good walking in the vicinity. Those who avoid busy summer weekends will even find that once the various tracks move on from the viewpoints they are by no means crowded.

Belchen

Many claim that the Black Forest's third highest peak, the Belchen (4,636ft/1,414m), offers even better views than the Feldberg. In clear weather the view extends south to the Swiss Alps, to the north as far as Freiburg and west as far as the Vosges mountains in France. As is the case with the Feldberg the views are at their most spectacular on cool autumnal days, when the surrounding peaks rise like islands

M any paths lead up to the Belchen, for instance the 9-mile (14.5km) circular trail from **Gasthof Haldenhof**. To get to the start of this 4-hour walk drive south from Schönau on the B317, turn right at Wembach and then follow a winding road in the direction of Badenweiler.

Across from Gasthof Haldenhof (closed Tuesday) enter the woods and follow the clearly waymarked trail (red diamond of the Westweg long-distance walk) to the **Hohe Kelch** (4,147ft/1,264m). There are nice views down into the valley from here and in the mornings there is a good chance of seeing chamois on the surrounding rocks. From the Hohe Kelch it is no longer far to the bare summit of the Belchen.

From the summit descend to Belchenhaus. The descent to Neuenweg begins at the crash barrier on the road that leads up to the summit from the settlement of Multen – waymark is a blue diamond. The path goes steeply downhill, passing weather-

through the sea of mist covering the plains and valleys below. At such times it can even be a few degrees warmer on the tops than down in the valley.

Just below the Belchen's bare, grassy summit is the Belchenhaus

The Belchen

beaten trees and curious rock formations on the way, until it reaches the small settlement of **Neuenweg** in the valley below. A signpost near the Aral filling station points out the rest of the way: to Nonnenmattweiher $1\frac{1}{2}$ miles (2.5km), to Haldenhof 3 miles (4.75km).

A little used farm road continues uphill from Neuenweg to the road from Wembach, which is crossed. After walking through forest the **Nonnenmattweiher** is eventually reached. This idyllic little lake with its tiny island is part of a nature reserve. It is possible to bathe here, though the water is a bit cool. The final climb back to Gasthof Haldenhof begins on the lake's western shore.

Other starting points for walks to the Belchen summit include Schönau (follow the blue diamond) and **Hotel Wiedener Eck** (follow the red diamond), which can be reached on the road from Schönau – continue past the turn-off to the Belchen summit at Multen. The up-market Hotel Wiedener Eck enjoys a good reputation for its cooking, though when the authors visited they were a little disappointed.

One of several **Bergvesperstuben** *(serve snacks and light meals) on the Feldberg*

restaurant (closed Monday) and a large car park. As the presence of a restaurant suggests, the Belchen also attracts its fair share of day-trippers with consequent problems for the environment. Erosion caused by people leaving the marked trails, littering, and the stinking exhaust fumes of countless motor vehicles have all become serious problems. In an attempt to counteract these negative effects, the road up to the summit is now closed for motorists on Sundays and holidays from July through to December – weekends are anyway best avoided at such destinations. The only way up is on a bus from Todtnau or Schönau, or on foot.

Besucherbergwerk Finstergrund (Mining Museum)

An outing from Todtnau to the Belchen could also include a visit to this old mine on the itinerary. From Todtnau follow the B317 to **Utzenfeld**, then the country road in the direction of **Wieden**. The turn-off to the mine is signposted.

Before the advent of brush and broom manufacturing in the eighteenth century (still important in the Todtnau area today) and tourism in the nineteenth century, Todtnau was an important mining town. From the eleventh century until the late Middle Ages silver and lead was mined in the hills and valleys surrounding town. Today the only relic of those times in the Todtnau region is the former silver mine **Finstergrund**.

Though originally a silver mine interest in the twentieth century switched to the extraction of fluorspar (also known as fluorite), which was mined until the galleries were finally closed in 1972. The men who guide visitors through the mine once worked here as miners themselves. In a single shift they were able to extract 200 tons of fluorspar. Those who join one of the guided tours underground should bring warm clothes as the temperature in the mine scarcely rises above 43°F (6°C).

From Todtnau into the Hotzenwald

From Todtnau a scenic stretch of road winds its way via **Geschwend**

and **Präg** to **Todtmoos**. Todtmoos has all the hallmarks of a popular tourist village; attractive location, plenty of souvenir shops, lots of hotels and no fewer restaurants. Worth a look in town is the **Wallfahrtskirche** (pilgrimage church) and the small **Heimatmuseum**, which is housed in an old Black Forest farmhouse that is typical for the area. In **Strick**, a small settlement that is a comfortable stroll north of town, there are some more old farmhouses to be seen. Also of interest here is the pretty **Josephskapelle**.

Just east of Todtmoos, near **Ibach**, is an interesting area of upland moor known as the **Ibacher Moos**. There are in fact several moors around here, some of which are up to 26ft (8m) deep. Typical for the moor vegetation are the stunted trees and bushes, cotton grasses and the rare insect-eating sundew. Fringing the moors are attractive woods

Excursion to

A bit further south of Todtmoos motorists have the choice of following the Wehra valley down to Wehr, to visit the Erdmannshöhle (caves), instead of continuing directly south to Bad Säckingen.

According to legend the Erdmannshöhle at **Hasel**, near Wehr, gets its name from the little *Erdmännchen* or dwarfs that lived in its caverns. These industrious little beings used to do all the work in the fields and around the house, while the villagers were busy praying in church. One day, however, the local youths spread ash on the ground to find out whether or not the dwarfs really

characterised by old stands of pine. Compared to the upland moors in the northern Black Forest these Hotzenwald moors are relatively little visited. Starting point for circular walks (waymarked) is the village of **Unteribach**, just south of Ibach. The walking trail between Todtmoos and St Blasien also goes through this area of moor. Waymark is a blue diamond and white oval. In winter a cross-country ski trail goes past the **Naturschutzgebiet Moos** (Moos Nature Reserve).

Another interesting natural feature between Hasel and Schopfheim is the **Eichener See**. This lake only appears periodically but when it does it can cover an area of 4 acres (1½ha) and is up to 10ft (3m) deep. Its appearance is due to the accumulation of ground water in a circular depression in the terrain known as a doline. After winters with heavy snowfall, or after periods of very heavy rain, the water carried by underground rivers rises through the layers of limestone to the surface. Once the lake actually appears it can rise at a rate of between 3 to 5½ inches (8-14cm) per day.

Todtmoos to Bad Säckingen

Those who continued directly south from Todtmoos to Bad Säckingen will find the first place of interest at **Herrischried**. Of note in this tiny health and winter sports resort is what is probably the oldest farmhouse that is still standing in the Black Forest. Built in 1424 the **Klausenhof** in Herrischried-Großherrischwand (just north of the main village) was meant to have been transferred to the open-air museum Vogtsbauernhof, near Hornberg. Plans were changed, however, and it remained where it always was, in its new function as Heimatmuseum.

With cross-country ski trails at altitudes of between 2,800 and 3,450ft (850m and 1,050m) Herrischried can be reasonably certain of snow in most winters. The main starting point for the various ski circuits is at Herrischried-Großherrischwand, not far from the Klausenhof. Those who want to gain altitude quickly can take advantage of the Ödland ski tow, which whisks skiers up to the start of the 6-mile (9.6km) **Ödlandspur** (Ödland ski circuit) at an altitude of 3,396ft (1,035m). Close to the ski-lift is a toboggan-run.

Further south in **Rickenbach** the **Dorfkirche** (village church) is worth visiting because of its surprising and highly original interior. Dissatisfied with a church that had all the charm

the Erdmannshöhle

had webbed feet. The observant dwarfs discovered the trick and were less than pleased. Since that day the unfortunate citizens of Hasel have had to do their own work.

The spectacular caverns were first discovered in 1753 but it is only in recent times that they have been made accessible. Formed by an underground river the caverns have an estimated length of around 9 miles (14.5km). In the course of a guided tour it is possible to penetrate some 1,837ft (560m) into the depths of the earth. A feature of the caves are the magnificent stalactite and stalagmite formations.

of a railway waiting-room, the locals gave Emil Wachter, an artist from Karlsruhe, the job of redecorating it. Instead of drawing upon the usual vocabulary of religious art he contrasted scenes from the Bible with scenes from modern life. The results include stained glass windows depicting subway trains and a camping ground, a nuclear power plant behind the altar and an interesting rendering of the Tower of Babel.

Murg Valley

The narrow Murg Valley, to the south-east of Rickenbach, is one of the loveliest, least spoiled valleys in the Black Forest. From **Hottingen**, just east of Rickenbach, it is possible to follow a narrow, unsealed road along its entire length. This trip would be best done on bicycle and after passing through several tunnels one could visit the ruins of **Burg Wieladingen** (thirteenth century). From the castle keep there is a grand view towards the Swiss Alps.

Bad Säckingen

At Bad Säckingen one has reached the Rhine, which is straddled here by the longest **Holzbrücke** (covered wooden bridge) in Europe. The bridge dates from the sixteenth century and is closed to motor vehicles. A walk over the bridge leads to the town of **Stein** in Switzerland – though one is not normally controlled by customs here, it is advisable to have a passport just in case. From Stein you have the best views over the old town of Bad Säckingen.

Situated in the Altstadt, or old part of town, which spreads out behind the bridge, is the imposing **Fridolinsmünster**. Named after an Irish monk who came here in the sixth century to christianise the heathens, the minster presents itself today as a mainly Baroque church. The elaborate interior decoration is the work of Johann Michael Feuchtmayr and Franz Joseph Spiegler. Both artists were counted among the *crème de la crème* of the German art world in the eighteenth century. The ceiling frescoes by Spiegler depict scenes from the life of St Fridolin.

Schloss Schönau is located in a lovely park that borders the Rhine, not far from the minster. Also known as the *Trompeterschlössle* ('Trumpeter' palace), it is associated with a poem by Viktor von Scheffel known as the *Trumpeter of Säckingen* (1854). This verse epic tells the true love-story of the poor trumpeter, Franz Werner Kirchhofer (1633-90), and the noble Maria Ursula von Schönau (1632-91), who lived in the Schloss. With its happy ending (despite class barriers the couple were able to marry) the poem was something of a best-seller in the nineteenth century and even today it helps attract visitors to town.

Appropriately enough the Schloss now houses a **Trompetermuseum** (Trumpet Museum) with what is supposed to be the largest collection of trumpets in Europe. Also of interest here is the **Schwarzwälder Uhrensammlung** (Black Forest Clock Collection) and, occupying the upper floors, the **Hochrhein-Museum** (Upper Rhine Museum). Here visitors can examine exhibits concerning the region's pre- and early history.

The Hüsli Museum at Rothaus

The longest covered wooden bridge in Europe at Bad Säckingen

Waldshut-Tiengen

After passing through the picturesque little town of **Laufenburg**, the B34 continues north-east along the Rhine to Waldshut. Until 1973 a separate town, it has now been joined with nearby Tiengen.

Waldshut has not always enjoyed the friendly relations with the now so neutral Swiss, on the opposite bank of the Rhine, that it has today. In 1468 a Swiss army consisting of 16,000 soldiers laid siege to the fortified town, which could only muster some 800 armed men in its defence. For five weeks the Swiss bombarded the town walls with heavy catapults (the medieval equivalent of heavy artillery) and it seemed certain that the town would soon be stormed. Although the defenders, weakened by hunger, awaited the final attack at any moment, nothing occurred. Indecisiveness on the part of the Swiss? Did they not realise that the town was theirs for the taking? Questions that remain unanswered. In any case the bishop of Basle had time to intervene before the situation could turn to the disadvantage of Waldshut's defenders and a peace treaty was signed.

In gratitude, and to commemorate, this lucky escape the locals have since celebrated the event with their most important festival, the so-called **Chilbi Festival** in August. It is celebrated with dances, concerts, a parade and folklore evenings. Even the former Swiss enemy is more than welcome to join in the festivities – not all that surprising when one considers that many of the locals actually work in Switzerland today.

The loveliest part of Waldshut's Altstadt is **Kaiserstrasse**. Now a pleasant pedestrian zone it is lined with unbroken rows of beautiful old houses, some of which have been built in a style that is more characteristic of nearby Switzerland than the Black Forest. Among the most impressive are **Zum Wilden Mann**, **Rebstock** and the eighteenth century **Rathaus**. The impressive **town gates** at both ends of this long street serve as reminders of Waldshut's often turbulent history as a border town.

Tiengen lies about 5 miles (8km) to the north-east of Waldshut. Here too it is possible to wander through medieval streets and alleyways, dotted here and there by historic old buildings – for instance along the **Hauptstrasse**. Perhaps the most significant of these buildings is the parish church of **St Maria** (1753-1755). Like a number of other important churches in southern Germany it is the work of the Baroque architect Peter Thumb.

As was the case with Waldshut, the citizens of Tiengen also had their problems with the Swiss in days gone by. However, the Swiss army that attacked the town in 1415 was successfully repelled by the defenders and this event is also commemorated as a local festival. The **Schwyzertag** in July is celebrated with a parade in traditional costumes, brass band music and Swiss flag-throwers. The Swiss also take the chance to demonstrate their skills with the $6\frac{1}{2}$ft (2m) long alphorn. Made of wood these horns were once used to summon cattle in the mountains.

Moving on

From Waldshut the B500 leaves the Rhine and heads back north into the Hotzenwald, in the direction of St Blasien. Those who are tantalised by the fact that Switzerland is just across the border could get a taste of this alpine country by visiting the **Rhine Falls** (*Rheinfall*), near Schaffhausen – see Chapter 6. From Tiengen follow the road to **Jestetten**, shortly after which the border is crossed. The Falls are signposted on the Swiss side.

St Blasien

The most significant feature of the small town of St Blasien is the mighty dome of the former **Klosterkirche** (monastery church). After St Peter's in Rome and St Paul's in London it is the third largest dome in Europe. Vast as it is, the church dominates the town as it does the valley. Already from afar one can see the light green of the dome in dramatic contrast with the dark green conifers that cloak the surrounding slopes.

Apart from the monastery church the main interest in St Blasien lies in the surrounding countryside. There are plenty of possibilities for walking in the area, whether it be to nearby villages like **Dachsberg** and Bernau or to a lake further north known as Schluchsee – see Route 11 below.

Back to Todtnau

An attractive stretch of road goes north-west from St Blasien, via **Bernau**, back to Todtnau. One of the Black Forest's best known artists, the landscape painter Hans Thoma, was born in Bernau in 1839. An exhibition of some of his works can be seen at the **Hans-Thoma-Museum** in Bernau-Innerlehen.

St Blasien's monastery church

The history of the monastery stretches back to the ninth century and the Benedictine monks who once lived here played a vital role in the later settlement and economic development of the region. Today, however, nothing is left of the original abbey buildings; fire and other disasters meant that the monastery had to be rebuilt several times over the ensuing centuries. The present neo-Classical church was erected between 1772 and 1781. It was designed by the French architect Michel d'Ixnard, who let himself be inspired by the Pantheon in Rome.

Secularisation in 1803 brought many centuries of monastic life to an end. With the departure of the monks (they took themselves and a large amount of the monastery's treasures with them to Austria) the monastery buildings were variously used as a machine factory, a small-arms factory and a cotton spinning-mill – until 1931. A more appropriate use was found for the buildings when the Jesuits opened a school here in 1934.

Route 11

FROM TODTNAU TO THE LAKES AND TOWNS OF THE SOUTH-EAST (circular tour)

Schluchsee

From Todtnau follow the B317 northeast in the direction of Titisee, then follow the B500 past **Altglashütten** to the resort of **Schluchsee**, on the lake of the same name.

Dreiseenbahn (Three Lakes Railway)

Visitors reliant on public transport will find that this branch line from Titisee is one of the most pleasant ways of getting to the walking country around the Feldberg and the Schluchsee. The three lakes it passes on its way are the Titisee, the relatively untouched **Windgfällweiher** and of course Schluchsee. Stops en route are at **Bärental**, Altglashütten, **Aha**, Schluchsee resort and the terminus at **Seebrugg**. Apart from being very scenic the line also has the distinction of serving Germany's highest railway station at Bärental (3,172ft/967m).

What is today the largest lake in the Black Forest was once much smaller. Prior to the building of a dam between 1929 and 1932 the lake was only 2 miles (3.25km) long and had a maximum width of 448 yards (410m). After the building of the dam (its purpose is to provide enough water to supply a series of hydro-electric power stations) its

size more than doubled and it is now 4½ miles (7.25km) long and has a maximum width of 1 mile (1.6km). With the increase in size came, without doubt, a decrease in charm, though the Schluchsee has not been commercialised to quite the same extent as the nearby Titisee.

In the summer months the holiday crowds flock to the lake to go yachting, windsurfing and of course swimming. There are also row boats for hire and the possibility of a relaxing cruise around the lake on one of the small passenger launches. As the crowds (and the busy B500) are confined to the eastern side of the lake, the quiet western shore is the preferred domain of anglers, hikers and cyclists – though it is possible

Altglashütten is a popular resort in both summer and winter

Wutach Gorge

Opposite: The local cheeses are a tasty addition to the picnic hamper

to walk around the entire lake it is probably more interesting to do this by bicycle.

In winter the larger crowds are absent and the lake's environs are now populated by cross-country ski enthusiasts. An interesting ski trail starts near the dam at **Seebrugg** and follows the western shore as far as **Unterkrummen**. For those in need of refreshments there is a rustic *Gasthaus* at this spot known as the Unterkrummenhof (closed Mondays). From here it is a steep climb up to the $6\frac{1}{2}$-mile ($10\frac{1}{2}$km) long Habsberg circuit, followed by a fast descent back to Unterkrummen – watch out for people climbing! Details of other trails are available from the *Kurverwaltung* at the resort of Schluchsee.

The road to Bonndorf

From Schluchsee continue along the B500 past Seebrugg. Shortly after passing the village turn left along a country road towards Rothaus and Bonndorf.

At **Rothaus** the main point of interest is the **Heimatmuseum Hüsli** – the museum is signposted from the main road. Though the *Hüsli* (it means 'little house') appears to be a particularly attractive example of a typical old Black Forest farmhouse it is, in fact, nothing of the sort. It was never used as a farmhouse but was built according to an ideal conception of what such a house should look like.

Though there is a shop where it is possible to buy snacks and refreshments near the museum, it is probably nicer to sit in the beer garden at the **Rothaus Brauerei** (brewery), next to the main road. If the weather is not suitable for dining outside (only self-service and light meals in the beer garden) then one can dine in the attached restaurant.

Bonndorf is mainly interesting as a base for an exploration of the nearby Wutachschlucht (Wutach Gorge, see opposite). In the town's sixteenth century **Schloss** there is a display of 400 miniature figures in traditional carnival costumes. At various times of the year the Schloss is also a popular venue for concerts.

The Hüsli

The Berlin opera singer Helene Siegfried had the 'Hüsli' built for herself in 1911 as a holiday home and eventual place of retirement. Long a great fan of the Black Forest and its traditions, she spent a lot of her free time going around the villages on collecting expeditions. The poor farmers she met were usually only too delighted to part with an old cupboard, or antique stove, as Frau Siegfried would often offer a modern, more practical replacement. In the course of time she had an impressive collection of antique furnishings from farmhouses in the region. Thus, after she died at the venerable age of 100, her house had all the prerequisites necessary for the local history museum it later became.

On foot to Wutachmühle

Another alternative for Wutach hikers is the 8-mile (13km) trail from Bonndorf to Wutachmühle. This 4-hour walk follows the

The Wutachschlucht

The Wutachschlucht is one of the Black Forest's most spectacular natural features. Situated between **Titisee-Neustadt** and **Mundelfingen** the 18½-mile (29.75km) long gorge has been protected as a nature reserve since 1939. Made accessible by a well-maintained hiking trail the *Schlucht* offers not only magnificent, canyon-like scenery but also one of those rare chances to experience the region as it may have been before human settlement. Of special interest is the richly varied flora and fauna, which include rare native orchids and hundreds of different species of butterflies among its highlights.

There are numerous points of entry for those who want to walk through the Wutachschlucht. Close to Bonndorf there are car parks near **Schattenmühle** and **Boll**. From Schattenmühle car park a short walk (about 40 minutes return) leads up the very romantic **Lotenbachklamm**. This narrow little gorge would be a good alternative to the trail along the River Wutach for those with limited time.

The entire walk through the Wutachschlucht would require about 10 hours and could be divided as follows: Kappel/Gutachbrücke to Schattenmühle, 7 miles/11.25km (3 hours), Schattenmühle to Wutachmühle, 8 miles/13km (4 hours) and Wutachmühle to Grimmelshofen, 7 miles/11.25km (3 hours). There is accommodation at Gasthof Schattenmühle and a few other points along the route.

Ludwig-Neumann-Weg through some of the gorge's most dramatic scenery. It requires good boots and a head for heights, as in some places the narrow track edges its way along cliff faces up to 131ft (40m) above the river.

The walk from Bonndorf begins near Gasthof zum Kranz at Martinstrasse 6, which also happens to be on the route of the B315 through town. From here walk up Brunnenstrasse, continue briefly to the right and then follow the trail out of town – the waymark along this section from Bonndorf to the Wutachschlucht is a blue diamond with a vertical white line in the middle. Eventually the trail reaches the village of Boll, from where there is a steep descent down into the gorge, passing on the way a castle ruin.

In the Wutach gorge itself hikers will notice a small, crumbling chapel. This is all that remains of the former spa resort of Bad Boll. In the nineteenth century the Wutach was renowned for the best trout fishing in Europe, which was a good enough reason for the exclusive English Fishing Club to set up shop here. Apart from catching lots of fish, the gentlemen of the club were also responsible for opening up the gorge for hikers. However, after World War I the spa fell into decline and only the chapel remains as a poignant reminder of bygone days.

For the rest of the walk through the gorge it is just a matter of following what is now a red and white diamond in an easterly direction to Wutachmühle. Here it is possible to get refreshments and a bus back to Bonndorf.

A steam train Trip along the Pig's Tail

The excursion from Bonndorf to **Blumberg** is only worth it for those who want to ride the **Sauschwänzlebahn** (Pig's Tail Museum Railway). However, as this is one of the most interesting museum railways in the Black Forest railway fans will not want to miss it.

The Sauschwänzlebahn or Wutachtalbahn runs close to the Swiss border between Blumberg and **Weizen**. It was built between 1887 and 1890 for strategic reasons; the military needed a transportation route that would not cross into neutral Swiss territory and could therefore stay open in times of war. To accomplish this the line had to climb 757ft (231m) within a distance of only 6 miles (9.6km), as the crow flies. This was only made possible by a considerable engineering feat that required 6 tunnels and 4 viaducts along a winding route that now had a total length of 16 miles (25.75km). The nickname 'Sauschwänzle' comes from the **Stockhalde-Kreiskehrtunnel** (Germany's only spiral tunnel), which on a map resembles a curly pig's tail.

Because the route was not considered profitable the *Deutsche Bundesbahn* (German Federal Railways) closed it down in 1976. Fortunately the town of Blumberg thought otherwise and reopened it in 1977 as a steam railway. The trains are equipped with historic carriages, including a buffet car, and the trip takes about an hour in one direction. Prospective passengers should bear in mind that trains only operate in the summer months and then mostly only on weekends.

A beautiful summer's morning at Titisee

Other possibilities for walking in the vicinity of the Wutachschlucht include the four circular walks that start from Boll and the interesting excursion into the **Gauchach-schlucht**, near Wutachmühle. The Tourist Office in Bonndorf, or a good map, will provide even more options.

Donaueschingen

To reach Donaueschingen from Bonndorf continue north-east on a pleasant country road via Mundelfingen and Hüfingen. Coming from Blumberg simply follow the B27 north.

In Donaueschingen the main attraction is the **Schloss** and park. Located in the palace courtyard is the so-called **Donauquelle** (Danube Spring), though it is not in fact the source of the Danube, but rather a romantic conception of what it should be like. The real sources of the Danube are the Breg and Brigach rivers, which join to form the Danube near Donaueschingen, but have their sources further west in the Black Forest.

Those who want to see how the counts of Fürstenberg lived in days gone by, can visit the Schloss as part of a guided tour. The nearby **Karlsbau** contains the **Fürstenberg-Sammlung**, an important collection of paintings from the fifteenth and sixteenth centuries. Of particular note are works by Lucas Cranach, Hans Holbein the Elder and Matthias Grünewald. In **Moltkestrasse**, not far from the Schloss complex, are a number of impressive buildings in Art Nouveau style. Note the peacock and swan motifs on some of the houses.

On to Titisee

On the trip via Titisee back to Todtnau the archaeologically interested might consider pausing in **Hüfingen**, just 2 miles (3.25km) south of Donaueschingen. On the outskirts of this attractive little town are the remains of a **Roman bath**. The town of **Löffingen**, further along the B31, is an old market town characterised by the stepped gables of its houses. Like Bonndorf further south it can also serve as a starting point for a detour to the Wutachschlucht. Of interest in Löffingen for those visitors with children is the **Schwarzwaldpark**, a kind of combined zoo and amusement park.

Titisee

Roughly 1 mile (1.6km) long and 875 yards (800m) wide the Titisee is the largest naturally formed lake in the Black Forest and, along with the resort of the same name on its shores, one of the most visited. Anyone who arrives on a busy summer afternoon might be surprised to learn that tourism did not really start to develop here until the 1920s and that early in the nineteenth century there was nothing but a lonely farmhouse near the lake. Today, however, the lakeshore gives the impression of an enlarged souvenir stall. Everywhere it is possible to buy cuckoo clocks, vacuum-packed *Schwarzwälder Schinken* (Black Forest ham) and dozens of other articles of a more, or less, 'genuine'

nature. Edging one's way past bus loads of elderly tourists from Dortmund or, perhaps, a group of boy scouts from nearby France, one has the feeling that Titisee has long since become the victim of its own beauty.

Having said all this, it has to be admitted that the lake and resort do have a few positive points. Those who can manage to avoid weekends, or who arrive early in the morning, will find that even the lakeshore near the resort can be quite pleasant, almost idyllic. This is where the passenger launches depart for cruises around the lake and where visitors can hire boats if they want to paddle about themselves. There are also several cafés and restaurants along here, which make nice places to sit and just gaze out over the lake with its lovely backdrop of forested mountains.

Visitors who want it more tranquil can go for a stroll along the lake's eastern shore to the camp ground at **Seehäusle**. There is a nicely situated restaurant here and the stroll there and back takes about an hour. Otherwise there is plenty of scope for cycling and walking in the general surroundings. In winter there is some good cross-country skiing close to the resort and around nearby **Neustadt** – Titisee and Neustadt have been combined to form the town of **Titisee-Neustadt**.

From Titisee the B317 returns to the start of this route at Todtnau, or one can follow the B31 through the Höllental to Freiburg at the start of Route 3.

ACCOMMODATION

Bad Säckingen

Haus am Kurpark $
(Privatzimmer/
rooms in a private house)
Meisenhardtweg 12
☎/Fax (07761) 53364
Quiet location, reductions for
children, non-smoking.

Hotel Kater Hiddigeigei $$
Tanzplatz 1
☎ (07761) 405556, Fax (07761) 1066
Central, quiet location, restaurant
attached.

Hotel Goldener Knopf $$$
Rathausplatz 9
☎ (07761) 5650, Fax (07761) 565444
Rooms with views over the Rhine,
good restaurant attached.

St Blasien

Haus Bernhardt-Fromm $
Hasenmatt 3
☎ (07672) 2132, Fax (07672) 9464
Sauna, solarium, reductions for
children and holiday flat available.

Dom Hotel $$
Hauptstrasse 4
☎ (07672) 4686, Fax (07672) 4655
Central location, attached restaurant.

Schluchsee

Gästehaus Staub $
Hinterer Giersbühlweg 2
☎ (07656) 663, Fax (07656) 1733
Quiet location, reductions for
children, holiday flat available.

Seehotel Hubertus $$/$$$
Schluchsee-Seebrugg
☎ (07656) 524 and 525,
Fax (07656) 261
Former hunting lodge, most
rooms have a view over the lake.

Titisee-Neustadt

Campingplatz Bühlhof
☎ (07651) 1606
Good facilities, open in winter.

Terrassencamping Sandbank
☎ (07651) 8243 and 8166
Camping ground on lake shore at
southern end of lake.

Gasthaus Rehwinkel $/$$
Neustädter Strasse 7
☎ (07651) 8341,
Fax (07651) 88322
Close to lake, arrangements for
children, attached restaurant.

**Treschers Schwarzwaldhotel
am See $$$**
Seestrasse 10
☎ (07651) 8050, Fax (07651) 8116
On lake shore, indoor pool.

Todtnau

Campingplatz Hochschwarzwald
Todtnau-Muggenbrunn
☎ (07671) 1288,
Fax (07671) 95190
Good facilities, open in winter.

Gästehaus Silberdistel $
*Paßstrasse 33,
Todtnau-Brandenberg*
☎ (07671) 661
Rooms in a Black Forest house,
reductions for children, generous
breakfast, holiday flats available.
Guests can arrange to be picked up
from bus station.

Gasthof-Pension Bären $
*Feldbergstrasse 2,
Todtnau*
☎ (07671) 273, Fax (07671) 9366
Central location, reductions for
children.

Landhaus Sonnenhof $$
Hochkopfstrasse 1,
Todtnau-Präg
☎ (07671) 538, Fax (07671) 1765
All rooms equipped with
traditional hand-painted farmhouse
furniture, reductions for children,
breakfast buffet.

Landhaus Herrihof $$
Kurhausstrasse 21,
Todtnau-Todtnauberg
☎ (07671) 918180,
Fax (07671) 9181850
Sauna, solarium, indoor pool and
attached restaurant. Guests can
arrange to be picked up by the
hotel's bus at the end of a day's
walking.

EATING OUT

Bad Säckingen

Café-Restaurant Bergsee $
Bergseestrasse 93
☎ (07761) 7575
Next to a small lake a short drive
north of town, local specialities.
Closed Tuesday and in winter.

Schlosspark-Café $/$$
In the Schlosspark
☎ (07761) 4861
Lovely situation above the Rhine.
Open: seven days a week.

Fuchshöhle $$$
Münsterplatz 24
☎ (07761) 7313
Regional specialities in the middle
Closed Sunday and Monday.

Schluchsee

Vesperstüble Wiesengrund $
Im Wiesengrund 6
☎ (07656) 1488
Black Forest specialities in the
rustic restaurant.
Closed Wednesday.

Restaurant-Hotel

Glassblower at the Glasbläserhof
(glassworks) in Afterstag

Auerhahn $/$$$
On B500, Schluchsee-Aha
☎ (07656) 542,
Fax (07656) 9270
Black Forest and
international specialities.
Open: seven days a week.

Todtnau

Café am Rathaus $
Thoma-Strasse, Todtnau
Best Black Forest cake in the area.
Open: seven days a week.

**Restaurant
Schwarzwald-Bähnle $/$$**
Next to bus station, Todtnau
☎ (07671) 8355
Regional and international dishes.
Closed Thursday.

PLACES OF INTEREST

Bad Säckingen

**Schloss Schönau/
Tompeterschlössle**
In the Schlosspark
The Schloss houses a trumpet
museum and a collection of Black
Forest clocks. Open: Tuesday,
Thursday and Sunday 2-5pm.

Bernau

Hans-Thoma-Museum
*Rathaus Strasse 18,
Bernau-Innerlehen*
Collection of paintings by the
nineteenth century artist Hans
Thoma. Open: Tuesday to Friday
10am-12noon and 2-5pm,
Saturday, Sunday and public
holidays 10.30am-12noon and
2-5pm. Closed from 15 November
to 10 December.

Bonndorf

Schloss
The *Narren-Stuben* contains a
display of beautifully carved
miniature figures in carnival
costumes. Open: Wednesday to
Saturday 10am-12noon and 2-
3pm, Sunday 2-5pm; 1 November
to 31 December, Wednesday and
Sunday 2-5pm.

Donaueschingen

Fürstenberg-Sammlung
In the Karlsbau
Important collection of old masters.
Open: Tuesday to Sunday 9am-
12noon and 1.30-5pm, closed in
November.

Schloss
Open: Easter to September, guided
tours Wednesday to Monday from
9am-12noon and 2-5pm.

Hasel

Erdmannshöhle
Spectacular caverns with stalactites
and stalagmites. Open: June, July
and August, daily 9am-12 and 1-
5pm; April, May, September and
October, Monday to Friday 1-5pm.

Herrischried

Klausenhof
One of the oldest farmhouses in
the Black Forest. Open: Tuesday,
Wednesday and Saturday 2-5pm,
Sunday 1-6pm.

Hüfingen

Roman Bath (Römisches Bad)
At the southern edge of town
Open: Sunday 2-5pm.

Löffingen

Schwarzwaldpark Löffingen
On the B31
Interesting zoo with a summer
toboggan run and other activities.
Open: Easter to 1 November,
daily 9am-6pm.

Rothaus

Heimatmuseum Hüsli
Charming local history museum
in a picturesque house.
Open: Tuesday to Saturday 9.30-
12noon and 1.30-5.30pm, Sunday
and public holidays 1.30-5.30pm.

St Blasien

Klosterkirche
Impressive monastery church with
a huge dome. Open: 1 October to
30 April, daily 8am-5.30pm; 1 May
to 30 September, daily 8am-
6.30pm. Closed for sight-seeing
during church services and
concerts.

Todtnau

Glasbläserhof
Tal 6, Todtnau-Aftersteg
Glassblowing demonstrations,
attached restaurant.
Open: daily 9am-6pm.

Besucherbergwerk Finstergrund
West of Todtnau, near Wieden
Old silver mine.
Open: Wednesday, Saturday
and Sunday 10am-4pm.
Last tour at 4pm.

Todtmoos

Heimatmuseum
Murgtalstrasse
Old Black Forest house, now a
museum. Open: Wednesday, Friday
and Sunday 2.30-5pm, also
Tuesday and Thursday in summer.

TOURIST INFORMATION OFFICES

Bad Säckingen

Kurverwaltung Bad Säckingen
Waldshuter Strasse 20
☎ (07761) 56830,
Fax (07761) 568317
Open: Monday to Friday 8am-
12noon and 2-5pm, Saturday
9am-12noon.

Bernau

Tourist-Information Bernau
Rathausstrasse 18, Innerlehen
☎ (07675) 160030,
Fax (07675) 160090

Blumberg

Verkehrsamt Blumberg
Hauptstrasse 97
☎ (07702) 5128,
Fax (07702) 5155

Bonndorf

**Tourist-Informations-
Zentrum Bonndorf**
Schloßstrasse 1
☎ (07703) 7607,
Fax (07703) 7507

Donaueschingen

Fremdenverkehrs- und Kulturamt Donaueschingen
Karlstrasse 58
☎ (0771) 857221,
Fax (0771) 857228

Feldberg-Ort

Tourist-Information Feldberg
Kirchgasse 1
☎ (07655) 8019,
Fax (07655) 80143
Open: Monday, Tuesday, Thursday and Friday 10am-12noon and 3-5pm, Wednesday and Saturday 10am-12noon.

Herrischried

Kurverwaltung Herrischried
Hauptstrasse 28
☎ (07764) 920040,
Fax (07764) 920049
Also information about other towns in the Hotzenwald.

Löffingen

Kurverwaltung
Rathausplatz 14
☎ (07654) 400, Fax (07654) 77250

St Blasien

Tourist-Information St Blasien
Am Kurgarten 1-3
☎ (07672) 41430,
Fax (07672) 41438
Open: Monday to Friday 9am-12noon and 2-5pm, Saturday 10am-12noon.

Schluchsee

Kurverwaltung Schluchsee
Fischbacher Strasse 7
☎ (07656) 773233,
Fax (07656) 7759

Open: Monday to Friday 8am-6pm, Saturday and Sunday 10am-12noon.

Schönau

Belchenland Tourist-Information
Gertnerstrasse 2
☎ (07673) 918130,
Fax (07673) 9181329
Information about the towns and villages in the vicinity of the Belchen.

Titisee-Neustadt

Tourist-Information Titisee
Strandbadstrasse 4
☎ (07651) 98040,
Fax (07651) 980440,
Hotel bookings ☎ (07651) 980423
Open: Monday to Friday 8am-6pm, Saturday and Sunday 10am-12noon and 3-5pm.

Todtmoos

Tourist-Information Todtmoos
Wehratal-Strasse 19
☎ (07674) 90600,
Fax (07674) 906025

Todtnau

Tourist-Information Todtnau
Meinrad-Thoma-Strasse 21
☎ (07671) 375, Fax (07671) 99634
Open: Monday to Friday 9am-12.30pm and 1.30-5pm, Saturday 10.30am-12.30pm.

Waldshut-Tiengen

Bürgerservice Rathaus Tiengen
Hauptstrasse 34
☎ (07741) 833440,
Fax (07741) 833469

Tourist-Information Waldshut
Wallstrasse 26
☎ (07751) 833198,
Fax (07751) 833126

6 Out and About

Old Heidelberg as seen from the Philosophers' Path

The Black Forest's location on the national boundaries of Switzerland and France makes it easy for visitors to indulge in a little border hopping. Many places of interest like Basle and Strasbourg are less than an hour's drive from towns on the Forest's western fringes. This, in itself, would be justification enough to include a few sights outside the book's 'proper' boundaries, but in many ways their insertion is no more than a logical consequence of the region's shared history (the Alsace region of France was for many years German), culture and modern political developments.

There is in fact much that binds rather than separates the regions along the River Rhine. Variations of the Alemannic dialect are spoken not only in the western section of the Black Forest, but also in Switzerland and the Alsace region of France. Indeed, in Alsace the locals are as happy to speak German as they are French. Cross-cultural influences have not stopped at language either; the so-called *Badische Küche* (Baden cuisine) is a happy amalgam of Swiss, Swabian and Alsatian cooking. Beyond this happy cohabitation of tongues and palates it might also be pointed out that cultural traditions have much in common as well: artists in the Middle Ages developed a style that was in many ways unique to the Upper Rhine and, at a more down-to-earth level, carnival in Switzerland (Basle) has a lot in common with *Fastnet* celebrations in the Forest.

Of course it has not always been 'love and harmony' between the nations, and wars have probably been more typical than handshakes but that, in modern Europe, will hopefully be a thing of the past. These days there are virtually no customs checks when crossing between France and Germany (take your passport anyway!) and Freiburg, Strasbourg and Basle even share the 'EuroAirport' at Mulhouse, in France. On top of this the local authorities in the border regions have got together and formed what they call the 'Regio', that is the region on the Upper Rhine between Basle, Freiburg and Strasbourg. Among other things this means that there is much cooperation in terms of cultural activities and tourist offices like the one in Freiburg regularly organise tours to Strasbourg and Colmar.

On the eastern borders of the Black Forest a few places have been selected from Swabia, a region which belongs to the German state of Baden-Württemberg, like the Black Forest. The inclusion of Heidelberg, in the north, is due to the fact that it lies roughly in the path of those who are coming down to the Forest from Frankfurt International Airport.

FRANCE

Strasbourg

Soaked in the cultures of both France and Germany and with the cosmopolitan outlook of an important European metropolis, it is perhaps fitting that Strasbourg was chosen as the seat of the European Council and the European Parliament. But these administrative functions should in no way lead people to believe that the city is a dull place, populated by dark-suited hordes of European bureaucrats; the city pulses with life and offers culinary and cultural pleasures that bear all the very best hallmarks of French *joie de vivre*.

Getting there

Strasbourg is quickly reached from any of the towns in the north-west area of the Black Forest. From Offenburg on Route 5 (Chapter2) there are also good train connections. Those travelling by car will find it most convenient to park at the large car park at the Place de l'Étoile. There is a Park and Ride (P & R) system here and the parking ticket includes a tram ride into the middle of the city and back.

Strasbourg Cathedral

At the heart of the city Strasbourg's mighty **Cathédrale Notre-Dame** draws visitors like an irresistible magnet. With a **tower** that rises to a height of 456ft (142m) it is one of Europe's largest cathedrals and even today it dominates the city silhouette. Begun as a Romanesque church it was completed in the Gothic style in the fourteenth century. Those who approach it from the Rue Mercier will be particularly impressed by the massive proportions of the Gothic **west façade**. In the light of late afternoon the sandstone seems to glow red with a life of its own, further underlining the grandeur of this masterpiece of church architecture.

The west façade with its single tower, elaborately decorated portals and the huge rose window deserves a closer look. On nearing the **main portal** it is hard not to be impressed by the wealth of sculptural detail. In fact the exquisitely carved figures here, together with those on the left and right portals, had a seminal influence on German sculpture after 1300. They depict nothing less than a summary of biblical history from the Creation to the Last Judgement. Note the expressive features of the

Angels' Pillar

One of the most interesting features of the cathedral interior is the so-called Angels' Pillar, which is situated in the south transept, near the astronomical clock. It is decorated with stone reliefs that depict the Last Judgement and ranks among the great masterpieces of Gothic sculpture. The lower reliefs show the Evangelists Mark, John, Matthew and Luke (their respective symbols are the lion, eagle, angel and ox), the middle reliefs show trumpet blowing angels and at the top Christ sits in judgement, surrounded by more angels.

Prophets on the main portal and the story of the Clever and Foolish Virgins on the right portal – judging from the very lively rendering of the Foolish Virgins it is not hard to guess where the sympathy of the artists lay. Above the main portal is the beautiful **rose window**. It has a circumference of 49ft (15m) and though a work of the fourteenth century it is now filled with stained glass from the nineteenth century. After examining the fascinating details on the cathedral doorways those with sufficient energy can climb the tower for a magnificent view over Strasbourg.

The **astronomical clock** is a mechanical masterpiece that will interest the kids as well as the parents. Originally constructed in 1547 it received its present clockwork mechanism in the nineteenth century. Every day at 12.30pm it attracts hordes of tourists who come to watch the procession of animated figures. First the Twelve Apostles file past Jesus, who raises a hand in blessing. At that moment a cock crows thrice and flaps its wings. Once the Apostles have disappeared the figure of Christ blesses the camera-clicking onlookers.

Other sights

Thus blessed, visitors can devote themselves to the many other sights that Strasbourg has to offer. Close to the cathedral is the magnificently decorated **Maison Kammerzell**, one of the loveliest of the many medieval buildings that surround the Place de la Cathédrale (Cathedral Square). This half-timbered house was built in 1549 by a rich merchant. It is covered by wooden carvings depicting heroes of antiquity, allegorical motifs and signs of the Zodiac. Today it houses a noble hotel and a much-visited restaurant.

There are dozens of museums to visit in Strasbourg, but those who are only spending a few hours in the city are better off confining themselves to a few within easy walking distance of the cathedral. The imposing **Palais Rohan** houses a **Musée des Arts Décoratifs** (Museum of Applied Art), a **Musée Archéologique** (Archaeological Museum) and a **Musée des Beaux Arts** (Museum of Fine Art). Next door the **Musée de l'Oeuvre Notre Dame** (Our Lady's Museum) contains the most important collection of medieval art in the Upper Rhine region.

Winstuben

Wine bars are as typical of Alsace as pubs are of London and bistros of Paris. Often decorated in a rustic fashion they serve not only fine Alsatian wines but also traditional Alsatian cuisine. Specialities worth trying include *choucroute* (sauerkraut), *baeckeoeffe* (a kind of stew) or perhaps a *filet de sandre* (pike-perch fillet). These dishes might be washed down with a good local Riesling or Gewürztraminer – the latter wine is nice as an aperitif and goes well with cheese or dessert. Those who like a fruity red wine should try a Pinot Noir, which is an excellent accompaniment to (red) meat dishes.

In Strasbourg there are a number of good *Winstuben* (also known as *Wistub*) in the area of the cathedral and in the alleyways of **La Petite France**.

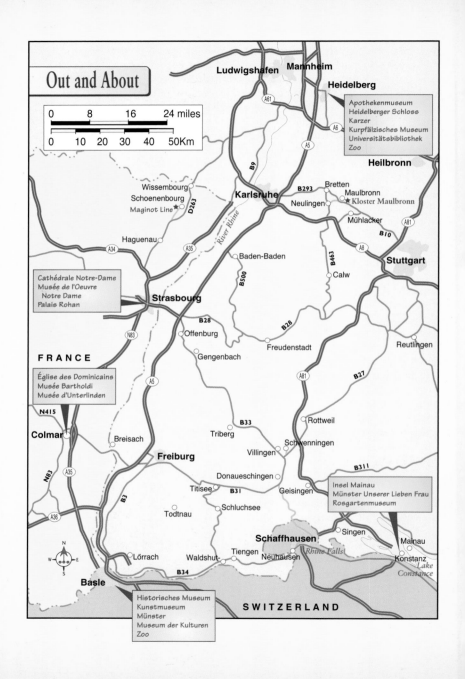

Out and About

0	8	16	24 miles

0	10	20	30	40	50Km

Ludwigshafen **Mannheim**

Heidelberg

Apothekenmuseum
Heidelberger Schloss
Karzer
Kurpfälzisches Museum
Universitätsbibliothek
Zoo

Heilbronn

Wissembourg
Schoenenbourg
Maginot Line ★ D263

Karlsruhe B293 Bretten
Neulingen Maulbronn
★ Kloster Maulbronn

Mühlacker
B10

Haguenau

River Rhine

Baden-Baden B463 A8 **Stuttgart**
B500 Calw

Cathédrale Notre-Dame
Musée de l'Oeuvre
Notre Dame
Palais Rohan

Strasbourg

B28

Offenburg B28
Freudenstadt Reutlingen

Gengenbach

FRANCE

Église des Dominicains
Musée Bartholdi
Musée d'Unterlinden

A81 B27

N415

B33 Rottweil
Triberg
Colmar
Breisach Schwenningen
Villingen
Freiburg
B311
Donaueschingen
Titisee B31 Geisingen
Insel Mainau
Münster Unserer Lieben Frau
Rosgartenmuseum
Todtnau Schluchsee

Singen
Schaffhausen Mainau
Tiengen Rhine Falls
Lörrach Waldshut Neuhausen Konstanz
B34 Lake
Constance

Basle

Historisches Museum
Kunstmuseum
Münster
Museum der Kulturen
Zoo

SWITZERLAND

Above: Exploring La Petite Venice by boat

Right: Street musician, Colmar

Below: The lovely old town of Colmar

La Petite France

Perhaps the most idyllic area of Strasbourg is La Petite France, to the west of the cathedral. Much of the charm of this former tanners' quarter comes from the canals that run through it, many of which are lined with lovely old half-timbered buildings. It is a place to wander about at leisure, but those with tired feet will find that a canal trip (boats depart from the landing-stage near the Palais Rohan) is an excellent alternative. Last but not least it is also a great place to go for lunch, as there are dozens of inviting cafés and restaurants scattered around the crooked little streets and alleyways.

Excursion to the Maginot Line

Remnants of the defensive system known as the Maginot Line (*Ligne Maginot*, 1928-32) are situated to the north of Strasbourg at **Schoenenbourg**, between **Haguenau** and **Wissembourg**. Built to defend France's eastern border against a German attack, it was outflanked by the Germans in World War II, when they invaded from the north via neutral Belgium.

A tour of the fortifications at Schoenenbourg takes around 2 hours. During the course of a visit it is possible to explore the underground galleries and view the command quarters and gun emplacements. The site is quickly reached from both Baden-Baden and Karlsruhe in Germany.

Colmar

To say that Colmar is one of the loveliest and most interesting towns in Alsace is an assertion that few will care to dispute. Throughout the summer bus-loads of tourists pour into the town to walk its medieval streets, many of which are so beautifully preserved that one almost has the impression of visiting an open-air museum. That this is not the case is clearly evident to those who arrive on one of the lively market days. If it happens to be a Saturday morning the market held on the **Place St Joseph** is worth a look. Among other things shoppers can choose from a mouth-watering variety of delicious French cheeses – nothing tastes better on a fresh *baguette*!

Getting there

Colmar is easily reached from both Freiburg and Breisach. There are no direct train connections but there is an SBG bus service between Freiburg, Breisach and Colmar. Bus tours can also be organised from Freiburg.

From the Place d' Unterlinden to La Petite Venise

Colmar's other sights can all be discovered in the course of a leisurely stroll. Only a short walk from the Unterlinden Museum and the Tourist Office is the **Église des Dominicains** (Dominican Church). The church contains some lovely medieval stained glass windows but it is above all Martin Schongauer's exquisite *La vierge au buisson de roses* (Madonna in the Rose Garden) that attracts most attention. The same artist also executed the

Unterlinden Museum

Though the old part of town is a major attraction in itself many visitors also come to view the famous **Issenheim Altar** in the **Musée d'Unterlinden** (Unterlinden Museum). This huge, winged altar was completed by Matthias Grünewald in 1515 and is ranked not only as his masterpiece, but as one of the great works of an entire period. Especially remarkable is the Crucifixion scene, which is scarcely to be equalled in the intensity with which it portrays suffering.

There is of course much more to the museum than Grünewald's altar. Along with archaeological exhibits and decorative art, the collection of Rhenish sculpture and painting from the late medieval period is quite outstanding. Artists represented include Hans Holbein, Lucas Cranach and Martin Schongauer. One painting with an intriguing title that visitors should look out for is *Le miracle de la résurrection des poulets rôtis* ('The Miracle of the Resurrection of the Grilled Chickens', around 1480). Those who are curious can learn more about it at the museum. A tip: it has nothing to do with divine intervention at a Kentucky Fried restaurant.

impressive Last Judgement fresco in the minster in Breisach – see Route 9 (Chapter 4).

Between the Place d' Unterlinden and the **Quartier des Tanneurs** (Tanners' Quarter) there are many fine old Renaissance houses. A few places to look out for are the **Maison des Têtes** (Rue des Têtes), **Maison Pfister** (corner Rue des Marchands/ Rue Mercière) and **Maison Adolphe** (1350), Colmar's oldest house in the Place de la Cathédrale, near the imposing-looking church of **St Martin**. Also nearby is the **Musée Bartholdi**. The museum is located in the house where the sculptor Frédéric-Auguste Bartholdi was born in 1834. He was the man who created, among other things, New York's Statue of Liberty

in 1886. In the museum there is a model of the statue, as well as other works by the artist.

From the **Koïfhus**, or *Ancienne Douane* (Old Customs House) as it is also known, at the Place du Marché aux Fruits, it is well worth continuing through the picturesque Quartier des Tanneurs to **La Petite Venise** (Little Venice). Here visitors will find dozens of beautifully renovated half-timbered houses lined along the River Lauch. Not a few of these houses are now restaurants and it is hard to imagine a more idyllic setting for lunch. Those who wish can also depart on a tour of La Petite Venise by boat, for instance from *Winstub* 'La Krutenau', in the Rue de la Poissonnerie.

GERMANY

Heidelberg

'Romantic Heidelberg'; the name is virtually synonymous with 'Romantic Germany' and must never fail on any crammed itinerary covering the country's major attractions. The oldest university on German soil is to be found here and today it is still very much a student, as well as a tourist town. Heidelberg's history goes a back a long way but settlement in the general area goes back even further, as is proved by the well preserved jawbone of *Homo erectus heidelbergensis* (Heidelberg Man), which is over 500,000 years old. The city was lucky to escape destruction in World War II and there is still more than enough left of old Heidelberg to fully justify the epithet 'romantic'.

Arriving by car and train

Many Black Forest visitors will find it most convenient to visit Heidelberg on their way to or from the international airport at Frankfurt. However, as it is only 36 miles (58km) from Karlsruhe on the fast A5 motorway, it would also be an interesting day trip from that city.

On arriving it is best to try and find a car park as soon as possible; look for the P & R (Park and Ride) signs which will direct you to free car parks, from where a bus or tram will take you to the Altstadt. Those who venture into the old city district will find the car parks expensive. Note also that the many one-way streets and pedestrian zones make traffic a bit confusing.

The narrow streets of the Altstadt, Heidelberg, are generally thronged with tourists

For those arriving by train it is a good idea to get a map from the Tourist Information at the *Hauptbahnhof*. It will not only be useful for picking out sights around the Altstadt, but also for finding those places, like the **Heidelberger Zoo**, which lie on the outskirts of town. Buses going to the Altstadt from the railway station are bus 33 (in the direction of Ziegelhausen) to Bismarckplatz, or bus 11 (in the direction of Karlstor) to the *Bergbahn* (cable railway).

Exploring the Altstadt

A good place to begin a tour of Heidelberg is in the Marktplatz which is dominated by the Gothic **Heiliggeistkirche** (1400-63). It is worthwhile entering the church if only to climb the tower for a splendid view over the inner city. Across from the church is the **Haus zum Ritter** (1592) with its beautiful Renaissance front. To get to the castle from the Marktplatz it is either a steep 15-minute walk or a comfortable ride on the *Bergbahn* (cable railway), which starts from the Kornmarkt just behind the Marktplatz.

Heidelberg Castle

A ruin since the French destroyed it at the end of the seventeenth century the **Heidelberger Schloss**

(Heidelberg Castle) is majestically situated high above the River Neckar. The various buildings of the castle complex are mainly Renaissance in style, the most important of which are the **Ottheinrichsbau** (1556-59) and the **Friedrichsbau** (1601-07). There are regular guided tours through the **Friedrichsbaukapelle** (Chapel), the **Königssaal** (Royal Hall) and the **Kaisersaal** (Imperial Hall). Situated in the Ottheinrichsbau is the **Apothekenmuseum** (Apothecary Museum) with its unique exhibits from the past to the present day. Another attraction is the huge wine barrel in the cellar. It could hold 48,802 gallons (221,726 l) of wine!

Back at the Marktplatz it is a short walk down to the river to the picturesque **Alte Brücke** (Old Bridge) with its Baroque gates. Cross over the bridge to be presented with a classic view of old Heidelberg and the castle. Photos are best made in the late afternoon. Those who wish to get the nicest overall view of town and Schloss should walk along the **Philosophenweg** (Philosophers' Path) on this side of the river – follow the zig-zagging Schlangenweg uphill.

A few of Heidelberg's other sights can be seen by going from the Marktplatz into the busy Hauptstrasse. The **Karzer** (Detention Room) at the back of the **Altes Universitätsgebäude** (Old University Building, 1713) is where students who took university life a bit too lightly were once locked up. The walls are decorated with amusing graffiti. Opposite the **Neue Universität** (New University, 1929-32) is the **Universitätsbibliothek** (University Library) with its famous collection of Old German hand-written documents. A bit further along

Authors' tip

The famous old student taverns **Zum Sepp'l** and **Roter Ochsen** are located in the vicinity of the Marktplatz. Here generations of students have met to relax after exams, discuss matters of great intellectual import or simply get drunk. Those who were caught drunk in the streets (up to about 1914) invariably ended up in the Karzer (Detention Room) – see also main text.

Hauptstrasse is the **Kurpfälzisches Museum** (Palatinate Museum). The jawbone of Heidelberg Man can be seen here, as well as a masterpiece by Tilman Riemenschneider known as the *Zwölfbotenaltar* (Twelve Apostles' Altar).

Konstanz on Lake Constance

Most of Lake Constance (Bodensee) is divided between Germany and Switzerland, with Austria controlling a small portion of its south-eastern shore. It is sometimes given the rather exaggerated title of *Schwäbisches Meer* (Swabian Sea). A total area of 335sq miles (538sq km) is, however, big by German standards, even though North Americans might smile when they compare it to their Great Lakes. Unique to the lake are some excellent wines (in the area of Meersburg and Hagnau) and tasty fish dishes of *Blaufelchen* (powan) or *Kretzer* (perch).

Close to the Swiss border Konstanz is the largest town on the lake. In the Middle Ages the town grew rich through trade as its geographical situation was ideal and even today there is still much to give evidence of this early prosperity. An interesting fact on the side is that one of the town's most famous sons was Count (*Graf*) Ferdinand von Zeppelin. It was he who designed the famous airships later named after him.

Getting there

Konstanz can be reached by train from Freiburg or Donaueschingen. From Freiburg motorists can follow the B31 to **Geisingen**, from where the A81 motorway is taken as far as **Singen**. Exit the motorway on the B33 to Konstanz. The distance from Freiburg to Konstanz is roughly 81 miles (130km).

The Altstadt

The port in Konstanz is not, perhaps, as picturesque as that in **Lindau**, at the lake's other end, but it is still a good place to form first impressions – especially for those coming by train as it is near the station. On the lake front is the old **Kaufhaus** or *Konzil* (1388), a large building that was formerly used as a storage house. Boats doing excursions on the lake leave from near here. To get to the Altstadt go through the subway passage next to the station, at the end of which is a Tourist Office.

The **Münster Unserer Lieben Frau** is the town's most important church. Parts of the basilica date back to the tenth century but the overall impression is that of a medieval church. Of particular interest are some finely carved doors (1470) and the **Heiliges Grab** (Holy Sepulchre) in the **Mauritiuskapelle** which dates from around 1280. A small charge is made for the climb up the tower, but clear views over the lake make it worthwhile.

Mainau and Reichenau

There are a number of places outside Konstanz that are worth visiting and **Insel Mainau** is one of the most interesting. It is also called the *Blumeninsel* (Island of Flowers) because it was turned into one large flower garden by Grand Duke Friedrich I of Baden, in the nineteenth century. Apart from a multitude of exotic flowers there is also a Schloss and church to be seen. A fee is charged for entering the gardens and the island is reached over a footbridge, near the large car park on the mainland. There are also boat connections from Konstanz.

The island of **Reichenau** can be driven to over a tree-lined causeway and is famed for its vegetables rather than its flowers. The main interest here lies in the island's three Romanesque churches: in **Oberzell** the **Stiftskirche St Georg** (Collegiate Church) has outstanding frescoes from the tenth century; in **Mittelzell** the **Münster** has a valuable collection of reliquary shrines and in **Niederzell** the former **Stiftskirche St Peter und Paul** contains Romanesque frescoes that were discovered in 1900.

Lake Constance

Most of the other places of interest in Konstanz lie within or near the pedestrian zone and can be reached in the course of a pleasant stroll. The **Dreifaltigkeitskirche**, in Rosengasse, is a Gothic basilica famous for its cycle of wall frescoes (fourteenth century). Nearby in the **Rosgartenmuseum** are collections dealing with pre-history and medieval art. Some of the town's most attractive buildings include the **Wohnturm zum Goldenen Löwen** (1450), in Hohenhausgasse, and the **Rathaus** (1594), in Kanzleistrasse. Concerts take place in the pretty Rathaus courtyard during summer.

Just west of Konstanz is an area of marshy land known as the **Wollmatinger Ried**. It is the habitat of many species of birds and rare plants. As the *Ried* stands under strict protection it is only possible to visit it as part of a guided tour. Inquire at the Tourist Information in Konstanz for more details.

Kloster Maulbronn

This former Cistercian monastery was founded in 1147 and has survived the passage of time since the Middle Ages virtually unchanged. In recognition of the fact that it is the most perfectly preserved monastery complex north of the Alps it was declared a World Heritage Site by UNESCO in 1993.

Getting there

Maulbronn is conveniently reached from Karlsruhe on the B293 via **Bretten,** or follow the B294 north from Pforzheim, then turn right at **Neulingen.** Those using public transport can reach the Kloster using a combination of train and bus – change to bus at **Mühlacker**. From both Karlsruhe and Pforzheim the trip takes a little over an hour, depending on connections.

The Cistercians
of Maulbronn

Ora et labora (pray and work) was the strict motto of the Cistercian monks who came to this swampy, isolated part of the Salzach valley in 1147. Shunning all outward show of luxury the essentially Romanesque church they built was originally quite simple in design and devoid of superfluous decoration. In this the monks were faithfully adhering to the ascetic principles laid down by Bernard of Clairvaux, the spiritual leader of the order. He had already founded a Cistercian monastery in the Aube valley of north-eastern France in 1115 and it remained the most influential Cistercian house until its suppression in 1790, during the French Revolution.

Of course the ideals of monastery life were not only reflected in the architecture. The rules of the order forbade the consumption of meat, conversation and heated rooms. In the entire monastery complex there was only one room where the monks could warm themselves in the bitter cold of winter, the so-called **Calefaktorium**. Those monks who could not express themselves with a simple gesture had to shuffle off to the **Parlatorium**, a room specially set aside for conversation. Furthermore, even though they grew wine they were not supposed to drink it – although according to some sources the monks did manage to find a way around that one.

Interior of Romanesque church at Oberzell, Reichenau

Growing affluence

During the 390 years that the Cistercians lived at Maulbronn they were nothing if not industrious. Forests were cleared, vines were cultivated, rivers were dammed, irrigation canals were introduced and fish were farmed in a total of nineteen fish ponds. In sticking to their motto of 'all work and no play' they not only transformed the landscape (the vineyards and fish ponds are still visible to this day), they also amassed great wealth. And that, naturally, was rather nice but it did not exactly fit in with their ascetic ideals.

Increased wealth enabled the monks to embellish their church, even though that led to an adulteration of the original, spartan style. The once simple basilica received painted net-vaulting in the choir to replace the plain wooden roof. At an earlier date a Gothic atrium, or narthex (or 'paradise'), was added. Together with the **refectory** this **Paradies** is considered to be an outstanding example of early Gothic architecture.

From secularisation to the present day

In the course of the Reformation the monastery was secularised and in 1556 a Protestant monastery school was established within its walls. In 1806 this became a Protestant seminary, which still exists today. Famous students who attended the strict seminary include the astronomer Johannes Kepler, who was an excellent student but did not like it there; the poet Friedrich Hölderlin, who fell in love with the daughter of the

A monastery for the blind

Architecture students at the University of Karlsruhe have built a unique model of Kloster Maulbronn for the blind. Made of birch, the model has been constructed in such a way that there is neither too much, nor too little detail for the fingers that will glide over it. The various buildings of the monastery complex can also be identified by descriptions in Braille. The model can be found in the Frühmesserhaus.

principal, and the novelist Hermann Hesse, who hated the school and described his experiences in the novella *Unterm Rad* (Under the Wheel).

Today a number of buildings in the monastery complex serve quite different purposes from those for which they were originally intended. The Renaissance **Jagdschloss** (Hunting Lodge), built by Duke Ludwig of Württemberg after secularisation, now houses the seminary school. In the **Klostermühle** (Mill) there is now a youth hostel and the old **Marstall** (Stables) has become a town hall. However, other monastery buildings and the church can be visited on a guided tour or independently. Of particular interest is the already mentioned 'Paradies', the **Kreuzgang** (Cloister), the late Gothic **Brunnenkapelle** (Well Chapel) and the elaborate carvings on the choir stalls in the so-called **Mönchschor** (Monks' Choir).

SWITZERLAND

Basle

Basle, the second largest city in Switzerland, is situated on the River Rhine at the point where the Swiss, German and French borders meet. Located in the heart of Europe it lies at the junction of international transportation routes (France and Germany each have their own railway stations in Basle), is Switzerland's chief river-port as well as being the headquarters of major pharmaceutical companies and banks. Apart from being an important commercial and industrial city it is also the home of Switzerland's oldest university (founded 1460), a place which has seen such great scholars as Erasmus of Rotterdam, Paracelsus, Friedrich Nietzsche and the psychologist Carl Gustav Jung, to name but a few.

Getting there

From Freiburg to the Swiss border near Basle it is around 37 miles (60km) on the A5 motorway. There are also good train connections. Those who want to spend more time in Basle could base themselves in Lörrach. From here it is only a relatively short trip on one of the regular local trains to **Basel Badischer Bahnhof**. It is even possible to cycle or walk into Basle from Lörrach.

Münster

Basle can look back on over 2,000 years of history and the **Altstadt**, or old part of the city, while not as picturesque as those of Strasbourg or Colmar, is still well worth a look. Here the most notable historic building is the Romanesque-Gothic **Münster** (Cathedral), which is situated on a hill above the Rhine. In terms of grandeur it cannot compete with the cathedrals in Freiburg or Strasbourg, but it is still quite imposing with its red sandstone walls, twin towers and the brightly patterned tiles that decorate its roof. The most outstanding feature of the cathedral exterior is the so-called **Galluspforte**, a richly decorated portal that dates from the twelfth century. Inside the church is the red marble tomb of the humanist scholar Erasmus, who died in Basle in 1536.

After exploring the cathedral it is worth strolling around it to the terrace overlooking the Rhine. From here there are wonderful views over the river to the industrial quarter of Kleinbasel (Lower Basle) and towards the mountain ranges of the Vosges and Black Forest. Steps lead down from the terrace to the banks of the Rhine, where one of Basle's famous little ferries departs for the opposite bank. The **Münsterfähre** (Münster Ferry) is attached to a cable strung across the river and is propelled by nothing more than the strong current. The trip is not only fun (and relatively cheap) but rewards you with a wonderful view back towards the Münster.

Around the Altstadt

To the north-west of the Münster (descend the hill along a narrow street known as Münsterberg, then turn right into Freie Strasse) is Basle's attractive **Marktplatz**. It is dominated by the magnificent medieval **Rathaus** (Town Hall), a bright red building decorated with frescoes and flanked by a tower added in the

nineteenth century. Interesting to stroll through are the streets climbing the hill to the west of the Marktplatz. They go through a very picturesque part of the city and eventually lead to the area of the university and the famous Spalentor – from the Marktplatz walk up Hutgasse to Spalenberg, then follow the street known as Spalenvorstadt.

The fourteenth century **Spalentor** is reputed to be one of the loveliest town gates in Switzerland. It is, in fact, quite imposing with two massive round towers flanking the actual gate-tower itself. Somewhat detracting from the overall impression, however, is the busy road which runs right past the front of the gate. Here the contrast between modern and old is a bit too crass and when viewed from what should be the most impressive angle it seems rather out of place, even forlorn.

By returning the same way along Spalenvorstadt, and then walking downhill along Heuberg, you eventually reach the Barfüsserplatz. This square is named after the barefooted Franciscan friars who once attended the former Barfüsserkirche (Franciscan Church). Erected in the fourteenth century the church now houses the **Historisches Museum**. With its extensive collections of art and cultural artefacts from the Middle Ages and the Renaissance, it is one of the most important museums of its kind in Switzerland.

Other museums

In a city which can boast over 30 museums the visitor will have no trouble finding something to do on a rainy day. One of the most outstanding is the **Kunstmuseum** (Fine Arts Museum). It contains the largest and most significant collection of art in Switzerland and ranks as one of the world's great art museums. Beginning with paintings and sketches by masters of the medieval period, the visitor can follow the development of European art right through to the twentieth century. Highlights of the museum include 11 from a total of 20 known works by Konrad Witz, works by Hans Baldung Grien, Lucas Cranach the Elder, Rembrandt and Hans Holbein. The nineteenth and twentieth century collections contain

Authors' tips

1 A shopping spree in Switzerland is unlikely to produce much in the way of cheap bargains. Switzerland is simply expensive. However, if you have a sweet tooth you are in luck! *Schweizer Schokolade* (Swiss chocolate) not only tastes great, it is also relatively cheap. The best (cheapest) place to buy it is of course in the supermarket. One of the best brands to look out for is Lindt, but the authors have discovered other, lesser-known brands, that tasted just as good. More exclusive, and more expensive, are the chocolates and cakes made in a specialist *Confiserie* or *Konditorei*.

2 Those who are not keen on hearing Bruce Willis speak German can breath a sigh of relief. In Basle English language films are shown in the original.

works by Arnold Böcklin, Hodler, Cézanne, Picasso and Braque. Those who have visited other museums and churches along the Upper Rhine will by now appreciate just how productive this region once was in terms of (especially medieval) art and just how much of cultural significance is shared by the border regions, despite present boundaries.

Another superlative, the **Museum der Kulturen**, is the largest ethnological museum in Switzerland. Here the accent is on the environment, art and religion of Oceania, but the collections also include fascinating masks and sculptures from Zaïre (or the Congo, as it is presently named),

along with handicrafts from India, Indonesia and America (native Indian peoples). A big attraction is a 52ft (16m) high ceremonial house from Papua New Guinea. All in all the museum offers a fascinating insight into the lives and ways of thinking of non-European cultures.

The Zoo

Culture is not, of course, everything and those with children will probably find a visit to Basle's excellent zoo just as rewarding. The *Zolli*, as the locals call it, lies on the edge of the inner city area and is quickly reached with public transport. Opened in 1874 with a total of 510

The boat trip to the foot of the Rhine Falls is short but dramatic

animals the zoo now holds around 4,000 and covers an area of 32 acres (13ha). The many successes that the zoo has had in breeding animals is indicative of just how 'at home' they feel here. Among the rarest that can be seen are okapis, snow leopards, gorillas and the primeval-looking Indian rhinoceros. Those who pause to look at the bears might be interested to know that brown bears once roamed the hills surrounding Basle. One of the zoo's highlights is the **Vivarium** with fish, reptiles and a penguin colony. Children will not want to miss the **Kinderzolli** (Children's Zoo), where they can pat and feed the animals – cuddly little goats and ponies, no lions or crocodiles!

Rhine Falls near Schaffhausen

Getting there

The falls are a relatively short drive from Waldshut-Tiengen (Route 10, Chapter 5) but they also make a pleasant day's outing from Todtnau, at the start of the same route. There are train connections from the stations at Waldshut and Tiengen to Schaffhausen in Switzerland. From there catch a suburban train (SBB) to the Falls at Neuhausen.

Formed in the last Ice Age around 15,000 years ago the **Rheinfall** (Rhine Falls) is, in terms of the volume of water, the largest waterfall in Europe. At a bend in the river the water roars through a gap of 492ft (150m), to drop 75ft (23m) over the rocks at a rate of 24,700 cubic feet per second (700cbm per second). It is an awe-inspiring spectacle (especially in June and July when the river carries the most water) and if one could somehow imagine away the huge car park, restaurants and souvenir booths and conjure up a pristine landscape, it would no doubt assume an even more spectacular aspect.

Still, the car park is convenient (but not free) and from the busy Rhine promenade it is possible to go for an exciting boat trip to a large rock in the middle of the torrent. The rock can be climbed along a stairway and offers a fantastic view over the raging waters. Another good place to view the falls is the 'Känzle' platform on the Zurich side of the river. It juts so far out into the waterfall that the onlookers standing on it appear to be in imminent danger of being swept away by the water frothing around them.

Schaffhausen

It is common knowledge that Switzerland was a neutral country during World War II; however that did not prevent Schaffhausen from getting bombed by the Americans in 1944. But this bombing was, in fact, an honest mistake. The real target for the bombs was nearby Singen, in Germany. Due to the complicated twistings of the border here, the pilots thought they were flying over German territory, with the result that numerous buildings were destroyed in Schaffhausen and 40 people died.

Schaffhausen is only 2 miles (3.25km) from the waterfall and if time allows it might be worth exploring the town's lovely medieval **Altstadt**. Among its highlights is the sixteenth century **Burg Munot**, a castle that may have been designed by Albrecht Dürer, and **Kloster Allerheiligen**, a monastery founded in 1045.

ACCOMMODATION

Basle

Accommodation in Basle is not cheap. Many will find it more economical to stay in Lörrach, or Weil am Rhein in Germany.

Stadthof $$
Gerbergasse 84
☎ (061) 261 8711, Fax (061) 2612584

Steinenschanze $$$
Steinengraben 69
☎ (061) 2725353, Fax (061) 2724573
Quiet, central location.

Colmar

Jardin Du Bonheur $
23, route de Neuf-Brisach
☎ (0389) 236336, Fax (0389) 249442
Central location.

Turenne $$
10, route de Bâle
☎ (0389) 411226, Fax (0389) 412764
Near la Petite Venise.

Hôtel Beau Séjour $$
25, rue du Ladhof
☎ (0389) 413716, Fax (0389) 414307
Pleasant hotel close to the sights.

Hostellerie Le Maréchal $$$
4, place des Six-Montagnes-Noires
☎ (0389) 416032, Fax (0389) 245940
Rooms in a sixteenth century house, central location.

Heidelberg

Pension Jeske $
Mittelbadgasse 2
☎ (06221) 23733
Central location, breakfast not included in price.

Burgfreiheit $$
Neue Schloßstrasse 52
☎ (06221) 22062,
Fax (06221) 164800
Central location.

Ibis Hotel $$
Lessingstrasse 3
☎ (06221) 9130, Fax (06221) 913300

Romantik Hotel zum Ritter St Georg $$$
Hauptstrasse 178
☎ (06221) 1350, Fax (06221) 135230
Right in the middle of the Altstadt, in a magnificent Renaissance building.

Konstanz

Gästehaus Holzer $$
Fischerstrasse 6
☎ (07531) 31546, Fax (07531) 32124
Rooms for non-smokers, indoor pool, sauna, solarium.

Parkhotel am See $$$
Seestrasse 25a
☎ (07531) 8990, Fax (07531) 899400
Next to the lake, sauna, solarium.

Strasbourg

Le Grillon $
2, rue Thiergarten
☎ (0388) 327188, Fax (0388) 322201
Not far from railway station, soundproofed rooms.

Hotel Du Rhin $/$$
7-8, Place de la Gare
☎ (0388) 323500, Fax (0388) 235192
Near railway station, soundproofed rooms.

Hotel Beaucour $$$
5, rue des Bouchers
☎ (0388) 767200, Fax (0388) 230392
Comfortable rooms in historic surroundings.

EATING OUT

Basle

Hirscheneck $
Lindenberg 23
☎ (061) 6927333
Good food, youthful crowd.

Charon $$/$$$
Schützengraben 62
☎ (061) 2619980
Near Spalentor, fish specialities.
Closed Saturday and Sunday.

Stucki Bruderholz $$$
Bruderholzallee 42
☎ (061) 3618222
Gourmet restaurant.
Closed Sunday and Monday.

Colmar

L'Auberge-Brasserie $/$$
7, Place de la Gare
(at Grand Hôtel Bristol)
☎ (0389) 235959
Good, traditional Alsation cooking
at reasonable prices. Open: seven
days a week.

Restaurant Wistub Flory $/$$$
1, Rue Mangold
☎ (0389) 417880
Alsation specilaities and wine.
Closed Tuesday evening and
Wednesday.

Maison Des Têtes $$/$$$
19, Rue des Têtes
☎ (0389) 244343,
Fax (0389) 245834
A top address in Colmar, also
accommodation. Closed Sunday
evenings and Monday.

Au Fer Rouge $$$
52, Grand-Rue
☎ (0389) 413724
Excellent gourmet fare.
Closed Sunday.

Heidelberg

Zum Roten Ochsen $$
Hauptstrasse 217
☎ (06221) 20977
Traditional student inn.
Closed Sunday and holidays.

Simplicissimus $$$
Ingrimstrasse 16
☎ (06221) 183336
One of the best restaurants in
town. Closed Tuesday.

Strasbourg

Le Baeckeoffe D'Alsace $
14, Rue des Moulins
☎ (0388) 321442
Good, traditional fare.
Open: seven days a week.

Zum Strissel $
5, Place de la Grande-Boucherie
☎ (0388) 321473
Pleasant *Winstub*.
Closed Sunday and Monday.

Relaxing at a restaurant in La Petite Venice

Bierstub L'Ami Schutz $$
1, Ponts-Couverts
☎ (0388) 327698
Traditional dishes and an excellent selection of beer. Open: seven days a week from 12 noon.

Maison Kammerzell $$$
16, Place de la Cathédrale
☎ (0388) 324214,
Fax (0388)230392
Excellent Alsatian cuisine, also accommodation. Open: seven days a week.

PLACES TO VISIT

Basle

Historisches Museum
Barfüsserplatz
A collection of medieval art and artefacts in the old Franciscan Church. Open: daily except Tuesday 10am-5pm.

Kunstmuseum
St Alban-Graben 16
Largest art collection in Switzerland. Open: Tuesday to Sunday 10am-5pm.

Münster
The cathedral is situated on a hill overlooking the Rhine
Open: Monday to Saturday 11am-4pm, Sunday 2-4pm.

Museum der Kulturen
Augustinergasse 2
An excellent ethnological/ anthropological museum with the emphasis on Oceania. Open: Tuesday to Sunday 10am-5pm.

Zoo
Basle's excellent zoo is well worth a visit. Open: daily 8am-6.30pm; in winter 8am-5.30pm.

Colmar

Église des Dominicains
Place des Dominicains
Church contains a painting by Schongauer. Open: end of March to 31 December, daily 10am-1pm and 3-6pm.

Musée Bartholdi
30, Rue des Marchands
Home of the man who created the Statue of Liberty. Open: 1 March to 31 December, every day except Tuesday 10am-12noon and 2-6pm.

Musée d'Unterlinden
1, Rue d'Unterlinden
Highlight is the famous Issenheim Altar. Open: 1 April to 31 October, daily 9am-6pm; 1 November to 31 March, daily except Tuesday 10am-5pm.

Heidelberg

Apothekenmuseum
In the Ottheinrichbau of the Schloss
An interesting pharmacy museum. Open: daily 10am-5.30pm. Ticket is also valid for the Schlosshof (castle courtyard).

Heidelberger Schloss
Heidelberg's famous castle is perched on a hill above town. Open: daily 8am-5pm. An extra ticket must be purchased for a tour of the castle interior.

Karzer
Augustinergasse
Student detention room. Open: 1 April to 31 October, Tuesday to Saturday 10am-12noon and 2-5pm; 1 November to 31 March, Tuesday to Friday 10am-12noon and 2-5pm, Saturday 10am-1pm.

Kurpfälzisches Museum
Hauptstrasse 97
Contains the jawbone of
Heidelberg man.
Open: Tuesday to Sunday 10am-
5pm, Wednesday until 9pm.

Universitätsbibliothek
Plöck 107-109
Collection of medieval
manuscripts. Open: Monday to
Saturday 10am-7pm.

Zoo
Tiergartenstrasse 3
Open: April to September, daily
9am-7pm, , October to March,
daily 9am-5pm. Seals are fed at
11am and 4pm, except Fridays.

Konstanz

Insel Mainau
This small island in the lake is
famed for its flower gardens. Also
of interest is the Schmetterlinghaus
(Butterfly House with tropical
butterflies and vegetation).
Open: daily 7am-8pm. The same
times apply to the Schmetterlinghaus.

Münster Unserer Lieben Frau
Beautiful medieval church.
Open: daily 8am-5.30pm.
Closed during church services.

Rosgartenmuseum
Rosgartenstrasse 5
Collection of medieval art.
Open: Tuesday to Thursday 10am-
5pm, Friday, Saturday and Sunday
10am-4pm.

Maulbronn

Kloster Maulbronn
Medieval monastery complex, now a
World Heritage Site. Open: 1 March
to 31 October, daily 9am-5.30pm;

1 November to 28 February, Tuesday
to Sunday 9.30am-5pm. Guided
tours at 11.15am and 3pm.

Strasbourg

Cathédrale Notre-Dame
Place de la Cathédrale
Open: the tower can be climbed
from 9am-6pm daily.

European Parliament
(on the III Canal)
Groups of no less than 15 (max 40)
can visit the European Parliament.
Applications must be made in
writing to:
European Parliament
Strasbourg Unit
BP 1024
F-67070 Strasbourg Cedex
Fax (0033) 388175184

Maginot Line
At Schoenenbourg,
north of Strasbourg
Open: 1 May to 30 September,
Monday to Saturday 2am-4pm,
Sunday 9.30am-11am and 2-4pm.

Musée de l'Oeuvre Notre Dame
3, Place du Château
An important collection of medieval
art. Open: Wednesday to Sunday
10am-12noon and 1.30-6pm.

Palais Rohan
2, Place du Château
This impressive palace houses
three interesting museums.
Open: Wednesday to Monday
10am-12noon and 1.30-6pm.

TOURIST INFORMATION OFFICES

Basle

Basel Tourismus
Schifflände 5
☎ (061) 2615050,
Fax (061) 2615944
Open: Monday to Friday 8.30am-6pm, Saturday 10am-1pm.

Colmar

Office de Tourisme de Colmar
4, Rue d'Unterlinden
☎ (0389) 206892,
Fax (0389) 413413
Open: April to October, Monday to Saturday 9am-6pm, Sunday and public holidays 10am-2pm. In winter, Monday to Saturday 9am-12noon and 2-6pm, Sunday and public holidays 10am-2pm.

Heidelberg

Tourist-Information Heidelberg
At the main railway station, Willy-Brandt-Platz 1
☎ (06221) 19433 (24 hour information and hotel reservation service), Fax (06221) 1388111
Room reservations, bookings for guided city walks and information about local transport. Also sell the **HeidelbergCard** which includes free use of local buses/trams and free or reduced entry to many of Heidelberg's attractions.
Open: Monday to Saturday 9am-7pm, Sunday and public holidays 10am-6pm.

Tourist-Information am Neckarmünzplatz
Neckarmünzplatz
Open: 9am-6.30pm, closed in winter.

Tourist-Information am Schloss
Neue Schloßstrasse 54
Open: 10am-5pm, closed in winter.

Medieval Rathaus, Basle

Konstanz

Tourist-Information Konstanz
Bahnhofplatz 13
☎ (07531) 133030,
Fax (07531) 133060
Open: November to March,
Monday to Friday 9.30am-
12.30pm and 2-6pm; April to
October, Monday to Friday 9am-
6.30pm, Saturday 9am-4pm,
Sunday 10am-1pm.

Strasbourg

Office de Tourisme de Strasbourg
17, Place de la Cathédrale
☎ (0388) 522828,
Fax (0388) 522829
Open: daily 9am-6pm.

Below: On Mainau, the Island of Flowers

Bottom: Detail of the main portal, Strasbourg cathedral

ACCOMMODATION

Information about hotel accommodation can be obtained from the German National Tourist Office or your local travel agent. Extensive lists containing a wider variety of accommodation such as holiday flats and the many privately run small hotels or inns (*Gasthof*) can be obtained in Germany from regional or local Tourist Offices. Many local Tourist Offices will arrange accommodation for visitors, but not every office will do this over the telephone.

Note that it is quite possible to find accommodation on arrival in the Black Forest, without pre-booking it at home. When touring the region simply watch out for the *Zimmer frei* (vacancies) sign. The advantage of this method, of course, is that one is flexible and can stay at whatever spot looks nicest. When doing this, however, try and make sure that you start looking before 7pm. This is especially recommended for those who seek accommodation at small bed and breakfasts (*Privatzimmer*), as in the villages people tend to turn in early for the night. The authors have always managed to find a bed for the night like this, even at the height of summer. However, it is a good idea to book accommodation for the first couple of nights when arriving from abroad – there is nothing worse than searching for a bed after a long drive or with jet-lag.

Schwarzwald Gästekarte

Every visitor who spends a few nights in the Black Forest can benefit from this 'guest card'. It is usually given to guests by their hosts on arrival, or can be obtained from the local Tourist Information Office. The card is free and enables its user to receive reductions at various shops, restaurants and attractions throughout the region. Many businesses and attractions advertise the fact that they accept the cards, otherwise the Tourist Office will be able to tell visitors where it can be used in their area.

It is possible to get a double room with breakfast in a cheap pension or Privatzimmer for less than DM80. The moderately priced places might cost up to DM150 for two people.

In the Additional Information section at the end of each chapter, the various forms of accommodation are graded as follows (for double rooms):

$ = inexpensive $$ = moderate $$$ = expensive

Camping

There are around 66 camping grounds (*Campingplatz*) spread around the Black Forest, but they are especially common in the southern region. For the most part they are beautifully situated in the countryside, usually outside town. Facilities are good and one can expect to find a small restaurant and shop attached to the camp site, as well as facilities for camper vans and caravans. Many sites have children's playgrounds and some even have their own (or are close to) swimming pool and hire out bicycles.

Camping grounds in Germany are normally open between April and October, but many in the Black Forest are close to winter sport resorts and remain open throughout the year. There are camping grounds at both Freiburg and Karlsruhe, two of the most important entry points to the Black Forest. Note that camping rough is illegal in Germany.

A list of camping grounds is available from the German National Tourist Office or from the Schwarzwald Tourismus Verband – see Tourist Offices.

Guesthouses and Bed & Breakfasts

Known in Germany as *Gasthöfe, Gästehäuser, Pensionen* or *Privatzimmer* the range and quality of the accommodation they offer is as varied as the terminology. The common denominator linking all, however they are called, is that one usually gets breakfast included in the price of a room.

Generally speaking a *Gasthof* or *Gästehaus* is a small, privately run hotel or inn and is usually more expensive, but also offers more facilities, than a *Pension* (pension) or room in a private house (*Privatzimmer*). Apart from breakfast it is often possible to get an evening meal or even full board at these places. Many *Gasthöfe* have attached restaurants and a few have beautifully furnished rooms and facilities, such as an indoor swimming pool, which would then easily place them in the luxury category. Obviously the price will then be similar to that of a large first-class hotel. What distinguishes them from the big hotels is the more personal service and the cosier atmosphere.

Though a pension can also sometimes be in the 'small hotel' category the *Privatzimmer* are always just that; a room in a private home. Once again the standards and prices can vary greatly but they are definitely the cheapest form of accommodation in the Black Forest, apart from camping or the rental of a holiday flat. At the cheaper places one will often have to share bathroom facilities but there is usually a sink with hot and cold water in the room. Some rooms are equipped with a television set and a fridge, whereas others might even provide a proper kitchen for their guests. Breakfasts can be quite substantial and usually consist of a selection of breads, salami, cheese, jam and of course a pot of coffee or tea. At some places they will also offer fruit or some kind of cereal, such as muesli.

Many *Gasthöfe* and *Privatzimmer* offer reductions for stays of three days or longer. Quite a few also offer reductions for children – usually these reductions apply to children up to 12 years old, but it is best to inquire beforehand. At some places there will be a surcharge for a stay of only one night.

Holiday flats

Self-catering holiday flats (*Ferienwohnung*) are excellent value if one wants to stay in a place for at least 3 days or longer – some landlords will only rent out flats for a minimum of 7 days. Some of the cheaper flats might cost no more than a *Privatzimmer*, but once again prices vary quite a lot according to the size of the flat and the facilities it rs. However, all flats are provided with cooking facilities and many e equipped with a television and a private balcony.

Holidays on farms

A holiday on a farm (*Urlaub auf dem Bauernhof*) is often great value for families. Many Black Forest farmers supplement their incomes by renting out rooms or holiday flats to guests. In general what applies to *Privatzimmer* also applies to staying on a farm. The main difference is that one often gets fresh farm produce served at breakfast and the children can sometimes lend a hand with farm work.

A list of addresses for farm holidays is available from German National Tourist Offices overseas or from the following address in Germany:

Verein zur Förderung des Urlaubs auf dem Bauernhof
Friedrichstrasse 41
79098 Freiburg, Germany
☎ (0761) 2713390, Fax (0761) 287775

Hotels

All the main holiday resorts in the Black Forest offer a good range of hotels from the simple economy class to international standard first-class and luxury class establishments. Some of the very best hotels are found at Baden-Baden, Baiersbronn, Freiburg and Karlsruhe.

Those who wish to stay at one of the larger hotels should inquire as to possible special offers and holiday packages before leaving home. For instance many of Baden-Baden's top hotels offer short (2-7 nights) discount holiday packages that might include a candle-lit dinner in an exclusive restaurant, free entry to the casino or one of the town's luxurious thermal spas.

Internet Hotel Reservation Services

It is possible to book accommodation in the Black Forest (and elsewhere in Germany) at one of the following web addresses:

Bookings De: www.bookings.org/de/cgi-bin/homepage.pl

DZT (German National Tourist Office): www.tourismus-service.com/f_i_d/index_engl.html

IHA-Hotel Verband: www.hotels-germany.com

Minotel: www.hotelnet.co.uk/minotel

Schwarzwald Tourismusverband: www.schwarzwald-tourist-info.de

Youth Hostels

There is a good network of hostels in the Black Forest. German Youth Hostels are listed in the International Youth Hostels' *Guide to Budget Accommodation Handbook, Volume 1, Europe and the Mediterranean*. Hostels in Germany are identified by a green triangle with the letters DJH.

Farmhouse near Hausach

Some of the best cross-country ski trails are found in the Black Forest

For detailed information about hostels in the Black Forest contact:
Deutsches Jugendherbergswerk
Landesverband Baden e V
Weinweg 43
76137 Karlsruhe, Germany
☎ (0721) 962100, Fax (0721) 613470

ARRIVAL AND CUSTOMS

Nationals of the UK and other EU countries require a valid passport but no visa. Holders of Australian, USA, Canadian and New Zealand passports do not need a visa provided they do not take up employment and their stay does not exceed 3 months. Nationals of other countries should contact the nearest German consulate for details.

At the present time vaccination certificates are not required.

Pets (dog/cat) need a health certificate, issued by a licensed veterinarian more than 30 days, but less than 12 months prior to entry. A notarised German translation of the document is also required.

As entry requirements and customs regulations are subject to change it is always wise to check the current situation with your airline, travel agent or a German embassy or consulate before departing.

CUSTOMS REGULATIONS

There are no longer customs controls at borders for visitors from EU countries – on the border between France and Germany they usually do not even control one's passport. Visitors from EU countries can bring in or take out goods without any limits on quantity or value, as long as these goods are for personal use only. In other words these goods may not be imported or exported for commercial purposes. For visitors from outside the EU the following restrictions are applicable:

All personal belongings needed for a visit are duty-free. The maximum duty-free quantities are as follows:

- 200 cigarettes or 100 cigarillos or 50 cigars or 9oz (250g) tobacco;
- 0.26gal (1l) of spirits (22 proof or higher), or 0.52gal (2l) of spirits (less than 22 proof), or 0.52gal (2l) of sparkling or fortified wine and 0.52gal (2l) of still wine;
- 17$\frac{1}{2}$oz (500g) of coffee or 7oz (200g) of freeze-dried coffee;
- 3$\frac{1}{2}$oz (100g) of tea or 1.4oz (40g) of concentrate;
- 1.7oz (50g) of perfume or $\frac{1}{2}$pt (0.25l) of eau de toilette.
- Please note that tobacco and alcoholic beverages are only duty-free for persons 17 years of age and older and coffee only for persons over 15.

BANKS

Banks are usually open during the week from 8.30am-1pm and from 2.30-4pm (Thursdays to 5.30pm). They are closed Saturday and Sunday.

Currency exchange offices (bureaux de change) are found at main railway stations in the cities, airports and at border crossings. They are usually open from 6am-10pm.

BUSINESS HOURS

Official opening hours are from 6am-8pm Monday to Friday and to 4pm on Saturdays. On Sundays and statutory holidays shops are closed. Within the framework of the legal opening times there is, however, some variation. Large retail stores are often open from 8.30am or 9am right through to 8pm. In many small towns shops may already close by 6.30pm. Bakeries are always the first to open (often closing by 6pm) and some may even remain open on Sunday mornings. Hairdressers and many restaurants and museums are closed on Monday. On the first Saturday of the month, and in the 4 weeks before Christmas, shops may remain open until 6pm.

For the most part village churches are open during the day, if locked then check the notice board for the address of the *Küster* (sexton), or whoever else might hold the key (*Schlüssel*). Large churches, cathedrals and monasteries may have set opening times and if they are not pinned up by the main entrance then inquire at the local Tourist Office.

CHEMIST (*APOTHEKE*)

Open during normal business hours. Information about after-hour emergency and weekend services (*Apothekennotdienst* or simply *Notdienst*) is always displayed at the front of the shop. This information is also found in local newspapers.

Medicines are only available on doctor's prescription from the chemist. No prescription is necessary for aspirins and other mild medication. A *Drogerie* (Drug Store) sells things like insect repellents, vitamin tablets etc.

CLIMATE

While the Upper Rhine plain is one of the warmest regions in Germany, some of the towns on the higher slopes of the Black Forest mountains have average annual temperatures comparable to Scandinavian settlements near the Polar circle. It can be wet anywhere in the Black Forest at any time of the year (mountains tend to trap rain clouds), but it is wettest in the north and in the high country regions. Towards the east it is drier and because the Vosges mountains act as a rain shadow for the southern Black Forest it gets less rain than in the north, despite the fact that it is slightly higher.

But before prospective visitors throw up their hands in dismay, it is worth mentioning that all the good wine that is grown along the Rhine means lots of sunshine too. The sunniest areas are the western foothills, the summit regions and the high plateau (Hotzenwald) of the southern Black Forest. The views from the mountain tops in autumn and winter, when the valleys are obscured by mist, can be fantastic.

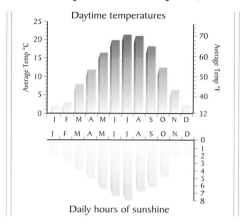

Daily hours of sunshine

Best time to come

The Black Forest is a year round destination whatever the weather. Summer is of course high season everywhere which means, on the positive side, that all the tourist facilities are certainly open, but also that some major attractions can be rather overcrowded. The region along the Rhine can get quite hot at this time of the year (temperatures in or near the 86°F/30°C mark are common on the Kaiserstuhl), though it is never far to the cooler air on the mountain summits. In winter the snow-covered Black Forest landscape can take on an almost fairy-tale quality; the villages that dot the slopes with their quaint churches and large-roofed farmhouses look like they might have been taken directly from the pages of the Brothers Grimm. In spring the weather can be a bit wet, but this is also the time when one can experience the blossoming of the fruit trees in the valleys, while the mountain tops are still brushed with winter snow. Autumn is particularly good for walking as the days are not so hot and, with a bit of luck, the weather is more stable than at other times of the year.

CRIME

Visitors to the Black Forest region will find that they need take no more than the normal precautions they would at home to guard against theft. Never leave valuables lying about in your car and always make sure that it is locked. Theft from cars is mainly a problem at car parks near major attractions or at popular *Wanderparkplätze* (car parks near walking trails outside town, specially provided for hikers).

CURRENCY AND CREDIT CARDS

The German unit of currency is the German mark or Deutsche Mark (DM). 100 Pfennige (Pf) = 1DM. It is freely convertible, i.e. it can be exchanged for any foreign currency at the going rate. You can bring as much currency as you wish into Germany.

The Deutsche Mark comes in **notes** of DM5, DM10, DM20, DM50, DM100, DM200, DM500 and DM1,000; **pfennig coins** of DM0.01, DM0.02, DM0.05, DM0.20, DM0.50 and **mark coins** of DM1, DM2 and DM5.

From the 1 March 2002 the euro will replace the German mark as official currency.

The most widely accepted credit cards are Eurocard and Mastercard. However, other international credit cards such as American Express, Diners Club and Visa are also commonly accepted. Some small restaurants, bed & breakfasts and individual retailers (especially in smaller towns) accept no credit cards.

EC cards and international credit cards can be used for 24-hour access to cash from the cashomats (ABM terminals) located in or near banks. Operating instructions for these machines are usually also provided in English.

All banks exchange traveller's cheques. If the cheques are in German marks the full face value will be given. If they are in a foreign currency the bank will make a service charge of around 2 per cent.

Eurocheques, together with a cheque card, are used like ordinary domestic cheques and must be made out in the local currency. Eurocheques can be used for all business transactions but filling stations make a small additional charge. These cheques can only be cashed up to a value of DM400 per transaction. Scottish bank notes are not accepted for exchange, nor are foreign coins.

The Deutsche Verkehrsbank will give a cash advance against major credit cards, subject to a DM100 minimum.

ELECTRICITY

The mains electricity supply operates at 220 volts (AC), 50 Hertz. Round-ended, two-pronged continental adapters are needed for UK/USA appliances.

EMBASSIES

Main foreign Embassies (Botschaften) in Germany:

Australian Embassy

Godesberger Allee 105-107
53175 Bonn
☎ (0228) 81030,
Fax (0228) 376268

Kempinski Plaza 4
10623 Berlin
☎ (030) 8800880,
Fax (030) 88008899

Fact File

Canadian Embassy
Friedrich-Wilhelm-Strasse 18
53113 Bonn
☎ (0228) 9680,
Fax (0228) 9683900

Friedrichstrasse 95
10117 Berlin
☎ (030) 203120,
Fax (030) 20312590

New Zealand Embassy
Bundeskanzlerplatz 2-10
53113 Bonn
☎ (0228) 228070,
Fax (0228) 221687

UK Embassy
Friedrich-Ebert-Allee 77
53113 Bonn
☎ (0228) 91670,
Fax (0228) 9167200

Unter den Linden 32-34
10117 Berlin
☎ (030) 201840,
Fax (030) 20184158

USA Embassy
Deichmanns Aue 29
53170 Bonn
☎ (0228) 3391,
Fax (0228) 3392663

Neustädtische Kirchstrasse 4-5
10117 Berlin
☎ (030) 2385174,
Fax (030) 2386290

Main German Embassies Overseas:

Australia
Yarralumla
119 Empire Circuit
Canberra, ACT 2600
☎ (062) 701911,
Fax (062) 701951

Canada
1 Waverley Street
Ottawa, ON K1N 8V4
☎ (613) 2321101,
Fax (613) 5949330

New Zealand
90-92 Hobson Street
Wellington
☎ (04) 4736063,
Fax (04) 4736069

UK
23 Belgrave Square
London SW1X 8PZ
☎ (171) 8241300, Fax (171) 8241435

USA
4645 Reservoir Rd. N.W.
Washington, D.C. 20007-1998
☎ (202) 2984000, Fax (202) 2984249

EMERGENCIES

For police and accidents ☎ 110, for the fire brigade ☎ 112. The automobile breakdown service number throughout Germany is ☎ 0180 2 222222.

FACILITIES FOR THE DISABLED

Facilities for the disabled are usually indicated by the blue pictogram of a person in a wheelchair. Most motorway service stops (*Autobahnraststätten*) have toilet facilities for the handicapped and there are always reserved parking places for people in wheelchairs in multi-storey car parks and elsewhere. Most important museums and public buildings are accessible for the handicapped. Town guides for the handicapped are available at Tourist Offices in major cities and are mostly bilingual.

Disabled persons who plan to travel by train should contact a DER Travel Service office in their country of origin – see addresses under 'Trains'. Available at these offices is the *Reiseführer für unsere behinderten Fahrgäste* ('Travel Guide for Disabled Passengers' – partly in English). This guide is also available at train stations, DB (German Rail) agencies or a DER-*Reisebüro* in Germany.

FESTIVALS

Listed here are only some of the more important or interesting festivals and local events. Local Tourist Information Offices will have more details on these and other events.

February

- **Fasnet** or carnival celebrations take place throughout the Black Forest. The most spectacular processions are in Elzach, Gengenbach, Rottweil, Villingen and Wolfach.

April

- International **Jazz-Festival** in Villingen-Schwenningen.

May

- **Internationale Galoppwoche** (International Race Meeting) at Iffezheim, near Baden-Baden.

June

- **Freiburger Weintage**, a wine festival in Freiburg.
- **Fronleichnam** (Corpus Christi) processions in traditional costumes in a number of Black Forest towns, for instance in Bad Peterstal-Griesbach.
- **Hornberger Schiessen** (June to September), an open-air performance commemorating an embarrassing moment in the town's history.

- **Zeltmusikfestival** in Freiburg with performances of jazz, rock and classical music.

July

- **Firework display** at the Triberg Waterfall (last weekend of the month).
- **Schwyzertag,** a Swiss-German festival in Tiengen (1st weekend of the month).

August

- **Breisacher Weinfest**, wine festival in Breisach (last weekend in August). As is the case at every wine festival (there are many more than can be listed here); a great chance to try the local wines and good home cooking from the numerous food stalls.
- **Breisgauer Weinfest**, wine festival in Emmendingen on the Kaiserstuhl (3rd weekend of the month).
- **Markgräfler Weinfest**, a wine festival in Staufen with the accent on wines from Markgräflerland (1st weekend of the month).

The Zwetschgenfest (Plum Festival) in Bühl is just one of the many festivals celebrated throughout the Black Forest during the year

A watermill near Bad Rippoldsau

- **Waldshuter Chilbi**, a festival in Waldshut with processions of people dressed in traditional costumes (3rd weekend of the month).

September

- **Ortenauer Weinfest**, an important wine festival in Offenburg (last weekend of the month).

- **Zwetschgenfest** (Plum Festival) in Bühl celebrating a famous local product with parades and good local wine from the street stalls (2nd weekend of the month).

October

- **Donaueschinger Musiktage**, a festival of contemporary music in Donaueschingen.

- **Erntedankfestzug** (Harvest Festival Procession) in Gutach. A chance to see women wearing the famous *Bollenhut* hat (1st Sunday in October).

December

- **Weihnachtsmärkte** or Christmas Markets are held in most larger towns in the weeks leading up to Christmas. Some of the prettiest are in Gengenbach, Freiburg (Black Forest) and Heidelberg (north of Karlsruhe). Also worth visiting are the traditional Christmas Markets in Colmar and Strasbourg in Alsace.

HEALTH

The Black Forest is a region where visitors have to take care concerning tick bites. These blood-sucking parasites can (in rare cases) transmit a dangerous viral infection known as tickborne encephalitis, as well as various bacterial diseases. An effective deterrent to ticks is the insecticide permethrin, sprinkled over one's clothes. Also avoid walking through long grass with bare legs, or brushing against bushes with bare arms etc.

After a walk (better, during the walk) in a forested area one should always check for ticks. If one is found remove it immediately with special *Zeckenzange* (tick tweezers). These tweezers can be bought at a chemist's shop (*Apotheke*). Ask how it works when buying it. Should a circular rash develop around the bite, or symptoms appear that resemble those of influenza, consult a doctor. A doctor should also be consulted as to the possibility and risks of immunisation.

When walking through forested areas beware of eating wild berries. Eating these berries brings with it the risk of ingesting a tapeworm spread by foxes known as *Fuchsbandwurm*.

Health Insurance

Visitors from the UK are covered by reciprocal agreements when in Germany. They require an E111 form which can be obtained from their local post office or DHSS office. Nationals of other countries should ensure that they have adequate medical cover before departing.

Fact File ↑

KURTAXE

All visitors who overnight in one of the region's spa towns or health resorts are required to pay a so-called 'spa tax' (*Kurtaxe*). This varies according to the facilities that the resort provides for its guests and usually ranges from DM1 to DM3 per person per day.

LANGUAGE

Although English is quite widely spoken a decent phrase book will prove useful. Even mastery of the very simplest phrases produces a positive response and helps break the ice between visitors and locals. Note that 'ß' is sometimes used in German to represent a double 's'.

Some common greetings and polite phrases:

Auf Wiedersehen	goodbye
Bitte	please, or after somebody has thanked someone for something 'not at all' or 'don't mention it'
Danke* or** ***Dankeschön	thanks or thank you very much
Entschuldigung	excuse me
Guten Morgen	good morning
Guten Tag	hello
Guten Abend	good evening
Gute Nacht	good night
Ja, bitte	yes, please
Nein, danke	no thanks

Words encountered in the text and while travelling:

Abtei	abbey
Altstadt	old quarter of town
***Autobahn* (A-)**	motorway
Bad	in front of a town indicates its status as a spa, e.g. Bad Wildbad
***Bundesstrasse* (B-)**	Federal road, i.e. main road
Burg	castle or fortress
Busbahnhof	bus station
Dom	cathedral
Freibad	outdoor swimming pool
Fremdenverkehrsamt/ Verkehrsamt	tourist office
Gaststätte	restaurant
Hallenbad	indoor swimming pool
Hauptbahnhof	main railway station

Heimatmuseum	local history museum
Kapelle	chapel
Kirche	church
Kloster	monastery, abbey, nunnery or convent
Kurpark	no self-respecting German spa is without its own well-tended park
Luftkurort	climatic health resort
Marktplatz	market square
Münster	minster; in south Germany can also mean cathedral
Naturschutzgebiet	nature reserve
Rathaus	town hall
Schloss	castle, residential palace or what, in England, may be referred to as a stately home
See	lake
Strasse	street
Tal	valley, e.g. Albtal or Alb valley
Tierpark	zoo
Wanderparkplatz	car park specially situated near walking area
Wallfahrtskirche	pilgrimage church
Wildgehege	forest enclosure, usually for native animals

MAPS

A detailed map of the region is well worth the price. A good choice for touring in the Black Forest and adjacent regions is the Shell/Marco Polo map *Vogesen, Elsass, Schwarzwald 1:200,000* in the *Die General Karte* series. This map shows not only the main roads, but also the many secondary and country roads quite clearly. Other good maps to the same scale are published by the oil companies and are available at most filling stations. Reliable maps at various scales are also published by RV-Verlag and Hallwag and can be purchased at any bookshop.

MEASUREMENTS

The metric system is used in Germany:

1 kilogram (1,000 grams) = 2.2lb
1 litre = 1$\frac{1}{2}$ pints
4.5 litres = 1 gallon
1 kilometre = 0.62 miles (10km = approximately 6 miles)

POST OFFICES

Post offices are usually open from Monday to Friday from 8am-6pm; on Saturdays from 8am-12noon. At airports and railway stations in large towns and cities they often stay open longer, and some are open on Sundays. Post offices can also change currency. Foreign money orders are paid out in German marks.

PUBLIC HOLIDAYS

1 January	**Neujahr** (New Years Day)
6 January	**Heilige Drei Könige** (Epiphany)
March/April	**Karfreitag** (Good Friday) and
	Ostermontag (Easter Monday)
1 May	**Tag der Arbeit** (Labour Day)
May/June	**Christi Himmelfahrt** (Ascension Day)
	Pfingstmontag (Whit Monday)
June	**Fronleichnam** (Corpus Christi)
3 October	**Tag der deutschen Einheit**
	(Day of German Unity)
1 November	**Allerheiligen** (All Saints Day)
25 & 26 December	**Weihnachten** (Christmas)

RESTAURANTS

Most restaurants open for lunch around 12 noon or a bit earlier. Between 2-6pm the restaurants usually only serve cold dishes – outside main resorts and in small villages they may be closed then. The evening meal is served from about 6pm. In large towns and in cities they may remain open until past midnight, in small towns they might already be closed by 10pm. Many restaurants have their *Ruhetag* (day when they are closed) on Monday and quite a few restaurants close from November until shortly before Christmas.

A tip for restaurants is to look out for the economical *Mittagstisch* or 'menu of the day' at lunchtime. Any restaurant advertising *Gutbürgerliche Küche* can generally be relied upon to serve reasonably priced, down-to-earth home cooking. Early risers will find that many bakeries sell not only bread but also hot cups of coffee early in the morning. Some cafés (especially at railway stations) are also open quite early.

The tourist resorts of the Black Forest are well endowed with a wide range of restaurants and cafés to suit all budgets and tastes. International fast food restaurants such as McDonalds, Burger King and Pizza Hut are found in many of the larger towns. An inexpensive meal in a local restaurant might cost no more than DM15 (not including drinks and dessert), while restaurants in the moderately priced category serve mains from around DM15 to DM25. The categories used in the Additional Information section at the end of each chapter are intended only as a rough guide. They are:

$ = inexpensive $$ = moderate $$$ = expensive

SOUVENIRS

Obviously a genuine Black Forest cuckoo clock belongs at the top of many souvenir lists. They come in all shapes and sizes and may be reasonably cheap or quite expensive. Expect to pay at least DM500 for an elaborately carved model. Also traditional are the wooden wall clocks with beautifully painted dials. Those who like it a bit more modern can buy a Black Forest wristwatch (without cuckoo) from the Kienzle factory in Villingen-Schwenningen. There are numerous opportunities to study what is available throughout the Black Forest, but the best area to look is along the German Clock Road around Triberg.

The famous Black Forest cherry cake will have to be eaten on the spot, but a portion of tasty Black Forest ham or a jar of pine honey (*Tannenhonig*) could be taken home – North American visitors will need to check their country's customs regulations. Those who have journeyed along the Baden Wine Road will no doubt have a few bottles of good local wine with them. Another good souvenir is a bottle of *Kirschwasser* (for instance from Oberkirch or Ottenhöfen) or some other kind of fruit brandy in a designer bottle.

Other souvenirs from the Black Forest include wood carvings (Bernau, near Todtnau in the southern Black Forest is a good place to look), dolls dressed in traditional costumes, or glassware from one of the region's glassworks. A good place to buy high quality ceramic articles is direct from the Zeller Keramik factory outlet at Zell, near Gengenbach.

SPORTS AND PASTIMES

Angling

The Black Forest, along with Bavaria, offers the best trout fishing in Germany. Good fishing streams (trout and grayling) include the Kinzig, Murg, Obere Wolf and Nagold. There is also good fishing in lakes such as Titisee and Schluchsee.

Foreigners who wish to fish in the Black Forest require permits:

- *Fischereischein* (national permit), which is obtainable from the *Landratsamt* (rural district council) or the *Stadtverwaltung* (town council) – the office where one has to go may also be referred to as the *Ordnungsamt* or *Bürgermeisteramt*. The permit is valid for foreigners for 1 month.

- *Fischereierlaubnisschein* or *Angelkarte* (local fishing permit) from the owner or lease-holder of the body of water where one wishes to fish. These permits may be valid for a day, a week or a month.

The local Tourist Information Offices will be able to provide further information about fishing in their locality and will help visitors who wish to obtain angling permits.

Boat trips

During the summer season boat trips are offered on the Rhine or on lakes such as Titisee and Schluchsee. Towns on the Rhine where boat trips are offered include Breisach and Bad Säckingen. Particularly interesting are the trips by punt through the Taubergiessen Nature Reserve and the short trip out to the rocky island in the middle of the Rhine Falls near Schaffhausen.

For trips by punt through the Taubergiessen Nature Reserve contact the Tourist Office in Rust or:

Rudolf Deibel
Karl-Friedrich-Strasse 35
Rust
☎ (07822) 61331

Bertram Spoth
Hinter den Gärten 4
Rust
☎ (07822) 61501,
Fax (07822) 78231

Cycling

Cycling in the Black Forest, especially on a mountain bike, has enjoyed increasing popularity in recent years. Bicycles of all types (also children's bikes) can be hired in just about every town in the region and at a number of railway stations as well. If the local Tourist Offices do not actually offer cycles for hire themselves, they will at least be able to provide the addresses of places that do. On top of this most Tourist Offices are well stocked with *Radwanderkarten* (bike touring maps) and can offer plenty of tips for the best cycling routes in their locality.

An interesting alternative to the 'Westweg' long-distance walk through the Black Forest is the long-distance cycle path **Schwarzwald-Radweg Karlsruhe – Lörrach**. Around 250 miles (400km) long this bike trail leads from Karlsruhe to Lörrach, near the Swiss border at Basle. For the most part the route avoids busy roads and runs parallel to the Westweg walk. The entire trail can be done in 6 days, with the distances that have to covered daily varying between 27 to 42 miles (43 to 67km). For more information contact the Schwarzwaldverein (see address under hiking below) or, if you read German, buy the following guide: '*Radwanderweg Schwarzwald*', published by Fink-Kümmerly and Frey.

Bicycles on public transport

Bicycles can be carried on *Nahverkehrszüge* (local trains) such as the **StadtExpress** (SE), **Regionalbahn** (RB) and **RegionalExpress** (RE). Before carrying a bike onto the train it is necessary to purchase a *Fahrrad-Karte* (bicycle ticket) in addition to a ticket for oneself. On many local trains one has to stand with one's bicycle in the entrance area of the carriage – with this in mind try to avoid weekends, especially when going from Freiburg through the Höllental! Some long-distance trains will also allow cyclists to take their bikes with them. They include the InterRegio (recommended) and some InterCity trains. Inquire at the station beforehand as to which trains offer this service.

The Südbaden Bus bus company has an interesting service for cyclists in the southern Black Forest. From the 30 May to 1 November the 'SBG-VeloBus' takes cyclists and their bikes from Freiburg to the start of cycle routes at Denzlingen, Waldkich and Furtwangen. The bus departs from Freiburg's main bus station (ZOB) near the Hauptbahnhof. More information and touring tips are available at the information desk at the bus station.

Hiking

Walking is one of Germany's great national pastimes. The number and length of waymarked trails in the Black Forest is accordingly immense. For the motorist the numerous *Wanderparkplätze* (car parks specially situated close to a network of walking trails) are ideal. They are almost always marked by the pictogram of a couple walking, are free, and there is usually an information board with a map, including length and duration of the walks. These trails or *Wanderwege* are mostly of a circular nature and might take from an hour to a full day.

For longer walks a *Wanderkarte* (walking map) showing the various trails is recommended, as the many different symbols used along some trails can get confusing. The best scales are from 1:75,000/1:50,000 for covering a fairly large area and 1:25,000 for those who want to do a lot of walking in the area where they are based. Good walking maps for the Black Forest are the *Schwarzwaldverein* (Black Forest Club) maps and those published by Atlasco. These and other maps can be bought at any local bookshop or from many Tourist Information Offices. Walking guides such as the '*Kompass Wanderführer*' are useful for visitors with a good knowledge of German, as they give very detailed descriptions of walks. An English language hiking guide to the region is '*Walking in the Black Forest*' by Fleur and Colin Speakman, published by Cicerone Press.

Long-distance walks

A long-distance walk through the Black Forest is a great way to get to know the land and people. Numerous camping grounds and a good range of hotel accommodation along most trails make finding a place to sleep relatively easy. Apart from being a cheap way to spend one's leisure time it is also very healthy; the cool air in the mountain forests has proven medicinal qualities. This is the reason why there are so many *Luftkurorte* (climatic health resorts) in the upper regions of the forest. Air quality is regularly tested and if a resort can no longer meet the requirements it loses its title immediately.

There are 16 long-distance walks in the Black Forest, covering a total distance of 4,350 miles (7,000km). What follows is a selection of a few of the most popular routes.

Kandel Höhenweg

Along picturesque mountain ridges from the wine-growing region of the Ortenau to the lovely Black Forest 'capital' of Freiburg im Breisgau.
Route: Oberkirch to Freiburg
Length: 83 miles (133km)
Time: 5 days

Ostweg

The trail takes hikers south along the eastern borders of the Black Forest to Switzerland.
Route: Pforzheim to Schaffhausen
Length: 148 miles (238km)
Time: 10 days

Querweg 'Hotzenwald'

A beautiful walk through a lesser known region of the Black Forest.
Route: Schopfheim to Waldshut
Length: 30 miles (49km)
Time: 2 days

Westweg

This trail was waymarked in 1900, making it the first long-distance walk in the Black Forest. The trail divides into two variants after the Feldberg, a.) via the Belchen b.) via the Hochkopf. The latter variant is slightly longer. See also the Feature Box 'Black Forest on Foot: the Westweg' in Chapter 1.
Route: Pforzheim to Basle
Length: 174 miles (280km)
Time: 11-12 days

Wandern ohne Gepäck (walking without luggage)

This was first offered in the Black Forest over 25 years ago and remains a popular alternative for those who do not want to lug their heavy backpacks up steep mountain slopes. What it basically involves is a hike along a pre-defined route where certain *Gasthöfe* not only offer accommodation but also transfer luggage to the next *Gasthof* on the trail. Organised tours of this type (where hotel reservations, etc, are all taken care of) often have to be booked at least 3 weeks in advance. It is of course possible to organise everything yourself, but this is probably too time consuming for most visitors.

Wandern ohne Gepäck and **Radeln ohne Gepäck (cycling without Luggage)** are organised on a regional and local basis. If DER travel offices or German National Tourist Offices overseas cannot provide sufficient information then it is best to contact the relevant regional or local Tourist Offices. They should be able to provide specific information (some of the material may only be in German) on the nature of the walk, along with route descriptions, maps and costs. To be sure of a reply it is best to include an International Reply Coupon if writing. Those who decide to organise such a walk when in the Black Forest will find that many local Tourist Offices will be quite helpful in this respect.

Specially prepared cycle paths make it easy to explore the region by bicycle

A cable railway provides a comfortable ascent of the Schauinsland

Some suggestions for Walking without Luggage are:

**Murgtalwanderweg
(Murg Valley Trail)**

This trail follows the River Murg through the lovely Murg valley.
Route: Murg-Quelle (source of the Murg) to Gernsbach
Length: 59 miles (95km)
Time: 5 days
Information and bookings: Tourist Office Gernsbach (see
Additional Information, Chapter 1)

Ortenauer Weinpfad (Ortenau Wine Trail)

This is the perfect trail for those who prefer to drink and walk,
rather than drive.
Route: Baden-Baden to Diersburg (via Oberkirch and Gengenbach)
Length: 62 miles (100km)
Time: 3-6 days
Information and bookings: Stadtinformation Offenburg
(see Additional Information, Chapter 2). Also bookings.

Rund um den Feldberg (Around the Feldberg)

A tour around the peaks of the southern Black Forest.
Route: Titisee via Todtnau-Fahl back to Titisee
Length: 99 miles (160km)
Time: 3, 5 or 9 days
Information and bookings: Tourist Information Titisee-Neustadt
(see Additional Information, Chapter 5)

**Schwarzwald – Wutachschlucht – Rundwanderweg
(Black Forest – Wutach Gorge Circular Walk)**

This trail goes through the Wutach Gorge, one of the Black
Forest's most famous natural features.
Route: Marbach via Wutach Gorge back to Marbach
Length: 97 miles (156km)
Time: 6 days
Information and bookings: Arge Wandern ohne Gepäck, Bahnhof
Schwenningen, c/o Deutsche Uhrenstrasse, 78054 Villingen-
Schwenningen, ☎ (07720) 810278, Fax (07720) 810279

Some useful addresses for hikers in the Black Forest are:

Schwarzwaldverein e V
Wilhelmstrasse 1e
79098 Freiburg im Breisgau
☎ (0761) 380530,
Fax (0761) 3805320
Information about the Westweg
and other long distance walks in
the Black Forest. Also maps and
guides.

**Touristenverein 'Die
Naturfreunde'**
Landesleitung Baden
Alte Weingartener Strasse 37
76227 Karlsruhe
☎ (0721) 405096,
Fax (0721) 496237
Information about
accommodation in *Naturfreunde*
(Friends of Nature) huts in the
Black Forest.

Golf

Visitors are generally welcome at local golf courses and the local Tourist Offices will be able to provide addresses.

Golf courses with 18 holes are located at Bad Dürrheim, Bad Liebenzell, Baden-Baden, Badenweiler, Donaueschingen, Freiburg-Munzingen, Freudenstadt, Karlsruhe, Kirchzarten, Königsfeld, Rastatt, Rheinmünster, Rickenbach and Stühlingen.

Keen golfers might be interested in the 7-day package deal offered by the Fairway Hotel (category: $$$) at Baden-Baden. Situated right on the 18 hole golf course the package includes 7 nights with breakfast buffet, entrance to both the Caracalla and Friedrichsbad thermal spas, a massage and use of the hotel sauna. Contact the Baden-Baden Marketing GmbH, Schloss Solms, 76530 Baden-Baden, ☎ (07221) 275221, Fax (07221) 275260.

Skiing

Though downhill skiing is possible in the Black Forest the ski slopes are comparatively short compared to those in the Alps. Therefore foreign visitors to the region are more likely to be interested in the possibilities for cross-country skiing or *Langlauf,* as the Germans call it. There are good cross-country circuits (*Loipen*) along the Schwarzwald-Hochstrasse near Hotel Sand, the Mummelsee, Kniebis and Freudenstadt. In the central Black Forest there are circuits around Triberg and St Georgen. In the southern Black Forest (where the skiing is generally best) there are circuits on the Feldberg, around Titisee, Todtnau, Todtmoos and Herrischried. For more information on the various circuits and other winter sport possibilities contact the Schwarzwald-Tourismusverband (see under Tourist Offices below) or the relevant local Tourist Office.

Equipment can be hired at most of the winter sports resorts and the Tourist Offices will be able to provide maps showing the length and location of the various circuits and downhill slopes. Note also that there is usually a specific entry point for the cross-country circuits and that some trails may only be followed in a certain direction.

How good the skiing will be in any particular year obviously depends on the amount of snow that falls. The lower regions can be a bit problematic in the Black Forest, but one can generally be certain of snow at altitudes of 2,600ft (800m) or more. The best months for skiing are between December and March. Locations such as the Feldberg, Schauinsland and Kniebis can usually offer good conditions at this time of the year.

Interesting for experienced cross-country ski enthusiasts are the long-distance trails (*Skifernwanderwege*). Like some long-distance walks they can also be done without having to carry a backpack. They are:

**Skifernwanderweg Nördlicher Schwarzwald
(Northern Black Forest)**
Route: Rote Lache (south of Gernsbach) to Freudenstadt.
Difficulty: easy to difficult
Length: 37 miles (59km)
Information: Touristik Nördlicher Schwarzwald
(see under Tourist Offices)

**Skifernwanderweg Mittlerer und Südlicher Schwarzwald
(Central and Southern Black Forest)**
Route: Schonach to Belchen
Difficulty: very difficult
Length: 62 miles (100km)
Information: Arbeitsgemeinschaft Skiwanderwege
Schwarzwald, Haus des Gastes, 78136 Schonach,
☎ (07722) 964810, Fax (07722) 2548

**Skifernwanderweg Südlicher Schwarzwald
(Southern Black Forest)**
Route: Hinterzarten to Schluchsee
Difficulty: moderate
Length: 20 miles (32km)
Information: Kurverwaltung Hinterzarten
(see Additional Information, Chapter 3)

Swimming

Swimming is possible in lakes such as the Titisee, Schluchsee and the
Nagoldtalstausee. Just about every town has its own indoor
(*Hallenbad*) or outdoor swimming pool (*Freibad*). Some towns,
especially the larger spa towns, can offer luxurious bathing complexes
with saunas, water slides and so forth. The Tourist Offices will have
more details on what is available locally.

TELEPHONES

Every telephone booth has a local directory. Phone books covering all
Germany are found in the post offices. Local and national long-distance
calls can be made from any post office or phone booth. International
calls can also be made from post offices or international phone booths
marked 'International'. Unit fees for calls from hotels are about twice as
expensive as the standard call units. Telephoning within Germany and
to Great Britain and Ireland is cheaper after 6pm and on weekends.
Reduced rates to the USA and Canada apply from 3am to 2pm.

To make a reverse charges call (*R-Gespräch*) to North America dial
01802 001033. The person at reception will then give further details.
Those who wish to charge the call directly to their home number at US
or Canadian long-distance rates (North American rates are cheaper
than those in Germany) can use the AT&T or CanadaDirect services.

The toll free numbers in Germany are 01300010 for AT&T and
01300014 for CanadaDirect.

Coin-operated telephones are becoming very rare in Germany. Far
more common are card operated phones. Telephone cards
(*Telefonkarten*) can be bought at any post office and some stores, for
instance bookshops or stalls at railway stations. They are available for
either DM12 or DM50.

Instructions on how to use payphones are written in English in
phone booths for international calls. Otherwise the principle is simple.
Lift up the receiver, insert the telephone card and dial the number. A
display shows how much credit is left.

International direct dialling codes

When making an international call, dial the international code you
require and drop the first zero of the number you are ringing.

Australia 0061
Britain 0044
Germany 0049

Irish Republic 00353
New Zealand 0064
USA and **Canada** 001

Other services

National directory 11833
International directory 11834

TIME

In Germany the clocks run according to Middle European Time. This
means that Germany is 1 hour ahead of Britain (Greenwich Mean
Time), 9 hours ahead of Pacific Standard Time and 6 hours ahead of
Eastern Standard Time. Daylight Saving Time prevails between the end
of March to the end of October, which means that the clocks are put
ahead 1 hour.

TIPPING

Not a must but is customary for good service. Small sums are rounded
off, large sums (over 100DM) might include a tip of around DM2.

TOURIST OFFICES

The local Tourist Offices are excellent sources of information and will
be able to help visitors find accommodation when they arrive. Apart
from selling maps (town plans are usually free) and guides to their
area, some Tourist Offices may also have bicycles for hire. They are
usually open during normal shop hours, though in major tourist areas
some are also open at weekends. Tourist Offices can be recognised by
the international 'i' symbol.

German National Tourist Offices (GNTO) Overseas

Australia
GNTO, PO Box A 980,
Sydney South NSW 1235
☎ (02) 92678148,
Fax (02) 92679035

Canada
GNTO, 175 Bloor Street East
North Tower, Suite 604
Toronto, Ontario M4W 3R8
☎ (416) 9681570,
Fax (416) 9681986
E-mail: germanto@idirect.com

Great Britain
GNTO, PO Box 2695
London W1A 3TN
☎ (020) 4956129 (50 pence per
minute), Fax (020) 73170908
E-mail:
gntolon@d-z-t.com

USA
GNTO, 122 East 42nd Street
Chanin Building, 52nd Floor
New York, N.Y. 101 68-00 72
☎ (212) 6617200,
Fax (212) 6617174
E-mail: gntony@aol.com

Regional Tourist Offices in Germany

**Deutsche Zentrale für
Tourismus e V (DZT)**
Beethovenstrasse 69
60325 Frankfurt am Main
☎ (069) 974640,
Fax (069) 751903
General information about
Germany.

**Schwarzwald
Tourismusverband e.V.**
Bertoldstrasse 45
79098 Freiburg im Breisgau
☎ (0761) 31317,
Fax (0761) 36021
E-mail: mail@schwarzwald-tourist-
info.de,
website: www.schwarzwald-
tourist-info.de
This is the best address for
detailed information about the
Black Forest.

**Tourismus Südlicher
Schwarzwald e.V.**
Stadtstrasse 2
79104 Freiburg im Breisgau
☎ (0761) 2187304,
Fax (0761) 2187534
Information on the southern
Black Forest.

**Tourismus-Verband Baden-
Württemberg e.V.**
Esslinger Strasse 8
70182 Stuttgart
☎ (0711) 238580,
Fax (0711) 2385899
For information about the Black
Forest and the state of Baden-
Württemberg in general.

**Tourist-Information
Mittlerer Schwarzwald**
Schwenninger Strasse 3
78048 Villingen-Schwenningen
☎ (07721) 846410,
Fax (07721) 846411
E-mail: tourismus@schwarzwald-
baar-kreis.de
Information on the central
Black Forest.

**Touristik Nördlicher
Schwarzwald e.V.**
Am Waisenhausplatz 26
75172 Pforzheim
☎ (07231) 314052,
Fax (07231) 357691
Information about the northern
Black Forest.

TRAVELLING TO THE BLACK FOREST

By sea, road and rail

Visitors coming from Great Britain to the Black Forest can choose one
of the various ferry services across the English Channel and North Sea
to continental Europe. Now, of course, there is also the possibility of
taking the train through the Eurotunnel. Local travel agents will be able
to supply all the necessary details about sailings and so forth. Those
travelling by train will find a DER Travel Service agent useful for
planning a rail journey to and around the Black Forest – see also
Travelling within the Black Forest. The distance by road from the Hook
of Holland to Baden-Baden in the northern Black Forest is roughly 443
miles (713km).

By air

With over 100 international airlines flying to Germany there will be
little difficulty in finding a ticket to suit your personal needs. Lufthansa,
Air Canada and United Airlines (to name but a few) all have daily non-
stop services between many North American cities and Germany.
There are also direct flights with Lufthansa, Qantas and Air New
Zealand from Australasia.

British travellers who want to leave their car behind might find that
it is cheaper to fly to Germany than it is to take a train. Scour the
newspapers or ask your travel agent about any bargain tickets that
might be on offer. In any case there are regular daily flights to
Germany from London and other airports with a number of airlines,
including British Airways and Lufthansa.

There are several international airports that can be conveniently
used when flying to the Black Forest. Most transatlantic visitors will
probably fly to Frankfurt. From here they can quickly reach the northern
Black Forest on the A5 motorway or with an InterCity or high-speed
ICE train from the station at the airport. Both rental car and train ticket
can be booked prior to departure at your travel agent.

Other international airports close to the Black Forest are the
EuroAirport near Basle (good for Freiburg and the south), the Aéroport
de Strasbourg-Entzheim at Strasbourg and the airport at Stuttgart on
the eastern side of the region. Like Frankfurt, all these airports are
connected by bus or train to the cities they serve. As at all important
airports one will also find representatives of the major car rental
companies such as Avis, Europcar, Hertz and Sixt. Reaching any
destination, anywhere in the Black Forest, is quick and easy from all
these airports, though one can save a little bit of time by picking that
airport closest to the point where you wish to start exploring.

TRAVELLING WITHIN THE BLACK FOREST

BUS SERVICES

Visitors using public transport will find that comfortable modern buses connect most of the smaller and larger towns in the region. The bus connections are generally very good between the main towns, but can be a bit infrequent to the small villages. However, in general it is fairly easy to get to wherever one wants by using a combination of bus and train.

The SBG (SüdbadenBus GmbH) bus company has a very reasonably priced holiday bus pass for visitors to the region. The **7-Tage-SüdbadenBus-Paß** (7 Day SBG Bus Pass) is valid for a period of 7 consecutive days for unlimited travel on the entire SBG bus network in the southern Black Forest. The bus pass can be bought from the driver or at the main SBG bus station next to Freiburg's main railway station.

In the northern Black Forest the SüdwestBus bus company also has a few good deals for tickets. More information about what is on offer can be obtained from their offices (*ServicePunkte*) at Pforzheim, Poststrasse 10; Freudenstadt, Am Stadtbahnhof 1 and Offenburg, Hauptstrasse 24a.

CAR

There is a very good network of roads throughout the Black Forest. The fast motorways (*Autobahn*) are restricted to the region's fringes, while the interior can be explored on slower (but far more scenic) *Bundestrassen* (federal trunk roads) or winding country roads. When driving through the mountainous areas keep your speed down and watch out for hikers, cyclists and motorbikes. At night beware of deer crossing the roads through areas of forest.

Car rental

This is available from the major car rental companies at airports, major train stations and in the cities. Minimum age to rent a car varies from 19 to 25 years, depending on the rental company and the type of car. Maximum age is usually 70. A valid national driving license that has been held for at least 1 year is required. Major credit cards and cash are accepted in Germany, though overseas visitors will generally find that prepayment of the rental car in their own countries works out cheaper.

Central reservation services in Germany:

Avis	☎ 0180 55577
Europcar	☎ 0180 5221122
Hertz	☎ 0180 5333535
Sixt	☎ 0180 5252525

Breakdown services

A 24-hour breakdown service is offered by the ADAC automobile club. On motorways and main roads help can be called from one of the

Traditional costumes of the Gutachtal with the famous Bollenhut hat

Above: Black Forest Cake

Right: Typical sign hanging outside a Strausswirtschaft

orange emergency telephone boxes. Small arrows on the posts
bordering the road show the way to the nearest telephone.
The universal breakdown service number is ☎ 0180 2 222222.

Driving regulations

The German automobile clubs have offices at major border crossings
and will be able to provide useful information for tourists touring the
country by car. Automobile clubs and travel agents in one's own
country will also be able to provide tips about driving in Germany and
Europe.

UK, USA, Canadian and Australasian citizens only require their valid
national driving licenses or an international driver's licence – the latter
is recommended. This enables the motorist to drive for a period of up
to 1 year in Germany. National or international vehicle registration
papers should also be carried. Vehicles from outside Germany must
display their country's national identification plate on the back.

Third party insurance is compulsory in Germany and foreign visitors,
other than nationals of EU countries, must have an international
insurance certificate (Green Card) or take out third party insurance at
the border. This is obtainable for 15 days or 1 month. On expiry this
temporary insurance can be extended, like the Green Card, at any
office of the ADAC automobile club.

Germans drive on the right-hand side of the road. Other than on
minor roads in rural areas, priority is always indicated on signs
approaching a junction. Traffic on a *Bundesstrasse* (main federal road)
always has priority. *Bundesstrassen* are recognised by a small
rectangular yellow plate bearing a road number – the recommended
maps for the Black Forest indicate these roads quite clearly. Priority is
shown elsewhere by a yellow square with white border set on its
corner, while the same sign with diagonal black line indicates the end
of priority. In general, however, easy to understand international road
signs are used throughout the country.

There is no speed limit on German *Autobahnen* (motorways) for
cars, unless a sign indicates otherwise. The recommended speed on
the motorways is 130kph (81mph). Cars towing a trailer on motorways
are subject to a speed limit of 80kph (50mph). Outside built-up areas
the speed limit is 100kph (62mph), and in towns and villages 50kph
(31mph), unless posted differently.

Parking is forbidden near traffic lights, intersections, taxi ranks, on or
near pedestrian crossings, bus or tram stops and on main roads or
those with fast flowing traffic. It is also forbidden to park on the
'wrong' side of the road, except in *Einbahnstrassen* (one-way streets).

Important safety regulations are:

- Warning triangles are compulsory and must be placed 109yd (100m)
  behind a broken down vehicle and 219yd (200m) on an Autobahn.

- Seat belts must be worn at all times in both the front and back seats.
  Children 12 years and younger must sit in the back on seats that

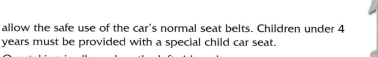
allow the safe use of the car's normal seat belts. Children under 4 years must be provided with a special child car seat.

- Overtaking is allowed on the left side only.
- The blood alcohol limit is 0.5 per millilitre. Do not drink and drive!
- Dipped headlights are required at night, in fog, heavy rain and snowfalls.

Fuel

Fuel is considerably more expensive in Germany than it is in North America. It is always cheaper to refuel at self-service stations and off the *Autobahnen* – though the motorway stations are often open 24 hours.

The types of fuel available are *Normal Bleifrei* (Regular unleaded), *Super Bleifrei* (Super unleaded), *Super Plus Bleifrei* (Super Plus unleaded) and Diesel. Remember when tanking the car yourself to note the number of the pump, as you have to quote this when paying.

Tourist roads

There are numerous tourist roads through the Black Forest, some of which are clearly sign-posted. Maps at a scale of 1:200,000 will show these roads quite clearly. They always follow scenically attractive or historically interesting routes, though using them means, for the most part, following a well-beaten path. Here is a brief description of the most interesting roads.

Badische Weinstrasse (Baden Wine Road)
99 miles (160km)
This route runs along the western fringe of the Black Forest mountains from Baden-Baden to Lörrach. The enthusiastic wine drinker has numerous opportunities on the way to taste the wonderful red wines of the Ortenau, the Burgunder wines of the Kaiserstuhl and the fine Gutedels from Markgräflerland.

Deutsche Uhrenstrasse (German Clock Road)
193 miles (310km)
The route begins in Villingen-Schwenningen, continues via Vöhrenbach to Titisee-Neustadt, moves north-west to St Peter and Waldkirch, then slowly winds its way through the towns of Triberg, Schramberg and St Georgen back to Villingen-Schwenningen. A shorter version of this tour through towns associated with the history of clock-making is described in this guide.

Schwarzwald-Bäderstrasse (Black Forest Spa Road)
168 miles (270km)
This circular route takes visitors to many of the most important spa towns of the northern Black Forest. It starts in Pforzheim, moves south via Neuenbürg, Bad Herrenalb, Bad Wildbad and

Fact File

Baiersbronn to Freudenstadt and then circles back via
Altensteig, Nagold, Calw and Bad Liebenzell to Pforzheim.

Schwarzwald-Hochstrasse (Black Forest Summit Road)
40 miles (65km)
This is the oldest of the Black Forest's tourist roads. It follows
the B500 from Baden-Baden, past the Mummelsee, to
Freudenstadt.

Schwarzwald-Panoramastrasse (Black Forest Panoramic Road)
31 miles (50km)
One of the loveliest routes through the Black Forest, it goes
from Waldkirch via St Peter to Hinterzarten. It is a good
alternative to the more well known Summit Road.

Useful road signs

Ausfahrt	exit from motorway or dual carriageway
Bankett nicht befahrbar	soft verges
Einordnen	get in lane
Einbahnstrasse	one-way street
Freie Fahrt	end of restrictions, usually after passing roadworks
Gegenverkehr	oncoming traffic
Glatteisgefahr	danger of ice on roads
Langsam fahren	drive slowly
Links/Rechts fahren	drive on the left/right
Rollsplit	loose chippings
Stau	traffic jam, shown on neon signs on motorways
Umleitung	traffic diversion
Vorfahrt	right of way, priority

TRAINS

Railway lines circle the entire Black Forest, with the interior of the
northern and central regions being also fairly well served by trains. In
the south there is only a railway line from Freiburg through to
Donaueschingen, otherwise the mountainous interior can only be
explored by bus. Towns with good train connections to other places in
the Black Forest and further afield are Karlsruhe, Rastatt, Offenburg,
Freiburg, Villingen-Schwenningen and Pforzheim. A number of river
valleys can also be easily explored by train. **Northern and Central
Black Forest**: Albtal, Murgtal, Renchtal, Kinzigtal, Gutachtal and
Nagoldtal. **Southern Black Forest**: Elztal, Höllental, Münstertal and
Wiesental.

Railway timetables for planning your route can be obtained from a German National Tourist Office or a DER Travel Service office in your home country. Timetables (*Städteverbindungen*) can also be obtained for free at any German railway station. Those with an internet connection can seek information on individual train routes and book tickets at the following web address (in English): http://bahn.hafas.de/bin/detect.exe/bin/query.exe/d

There are all sorts of reduced fare tickets available for travelling by train in Germany. Space precludes a detailed description of every fare that is currently obtainable but German National Tourist Offices, DER Travel Service offices and travel agents in your home country will able to provide more information. German Rail also offers information (in English) about tickets and trains at the following website: www.bahn.de

Interesting for those who plan to use trains not only in the Black Forest, but throughout Germany, is the **German Rail Pass**. These rail passes must be purchased prior to departing for Germany. They allow unlimited First or Second Class rail travel in Germany for from 4 to 10 days within a 1 month period. Additional days may be added.

Very useful for those using public transport in the Black Forest is the **Ferien-Ticket** (Holiday Ticket). It allows unlimited travel on trains and certain bus lines within the chosen transportation network (the Black Forest is divided into three regions for this purpose). It is valid for a week within one region but this can be extended for another week at only half the price of the original ticket. The ticket can also be extended at half price to include the adjoining region. Up to five people can travel on one ticket. The first person pays full price (DM40 in Second Class at the time of writing), the others pay half. Children between 6 to 11 years pay only a quarter of the full price. Children under 6 years pay nothing.

The *Ferien-Ticket* can only be bought in combination with a long-distance **German Rail Return Ticket** to a destination in the Black Forest. This return ticket can be bought in Germany but (at the time of writing) it must have a minimum value of DM199 (in Second Class). On arrival at your destination go to the railway ticket counter and ask for the *Ferien Ticket-Karte*. This map shows the area where your ticket is valid and what forms of transport you may use. Get them to explain all the details – with this in mind the large railway stations at places like Karlsruhe or Freiburg are good, as one can be fairly sure to find someone who speaks good English.

For railway tickets in general it is useful to know that children up to 5 years travel free and that children from 6 to 11 years pay only half the adult fare.

Most trains have First and Second Class compartments, as well as *Raucher/Nichtraucher* (smoking/non-smoking) compartments. All have toilets (WC). Reservations are recommended for ICE trains and also for the InterCity and EuroCity trains. Some of the main types of train are shown on the next page.

Nahverkehrszug
(Regional Express or RE, RegionalBahn or RB, StadtExpress or SE, S-Bahn)
These local trains stop nearly everywhere and are therefore comparatively slow. They are very good for visiting smaller towns and villages.

D-Zug/InterRegio
These long-distance trains stop only in the larger towns or cities. The InterRegios are equipped with a Bistro Café and a telephone which accepts telephone cards. This is the rule with all telephones on trains. *Telefonkarten* (telephone cards) can be bought from the train personnel.

InterCity/EuroCity
These fast trains stop in the main German cities.They are equipped with a dining car and telephones.

ICE
The InterCityExpress is a high speed train (up to 174mph/280kph) that travels to a number of important German towns and cities including Karlsruhe, Baden-Baden, Offenburg and Freiburg. It is very comfortable with dining car, telephones on board and various facilities catering to the wishes of business travellers. Just as on a plane music, or even videos, can be enjoyed at your seat.

NachtZug
Many of the overnight trains are equipped with comfortable sleeper compartments and couchettes.

For further information about rail tours and travel contact:

Canada
DER Travel Service
904 The East Mall
Etobicoke, Ontario M9B 6K2
☎ (416) 6951209,
Fax (416) 6951210
E-mail der@dercanada.com

Great Britain
DER Travel Service
18 Conduit Street
London W1R 9TD
☎ (0171) 290 1111,
Fax (0171) 6297442 or 6297501
E-mail sales@dertravel.co.uk

USA
DER Travel Service
9501 Devon Ave
Rosemont, IL 60018
☎ (847) 4300000 or
(888) 3377350,
Fax (847) 6924165 or
(800) 2827474

Steam trains

There are a number of opportunities to enjoy a nostalgic steam train ride in the Black Forest. These old trains usually run during the summer months and on weekends. As the timetables are subject to variation it is best to inquire at the relevant Tourist Offices or to contact one of the addresses given below.

The **Achertalbahn** runs between Achern and Ottenhöfen. A small steam locomotive pulls carriages along 7 miles (11km) of track. Contact the Tourist Offices in Achern or Ottenhöfen.

The **Albtalbahn** line runs between Ettlingen and Bad Herrenalb in the northern Black Forest. Contact the Tourist Office in Ettlingen or Ulmer Eisenbahnfreunde ☎ (07247) 21230 or ☎/Fax (0711) 2261958.

Wine lovers will love the **Kaiserstuhlbahn**. While the 'Rebenbummler' steam locomotive makes its leisurely way through the Kaiserstuhl vineyards one can sip a good vintage in a vintage carriage. The 31-mile (50km) trip from Riegel to Breisach can be capped off with a short trip on the Rhine at Breisach. Contact the Tourist Office in Breisach or the Eisenbahnfreunde Breisgau, c/o Rolf Roestel, Moltkestrasse 10, 79312 Emmendingen, ☎/Fax (07641) 573918.

The 100-year old locomotive 'Chanderli' puffs its way from Kandern to Haltingen near Basle on the **Kandertalbahn** railway. There are plenty of chances to take snapshots as the train stops at a number of quaint stations on the way. Contact the Tourist Office in Kandern or Museums und Erlebniszüge Kandern – Haltingen ☎/Fax (07626) 89960, E-mail: info@kandertalbahn.de, web site: www.kandertalbahn.de.

The **Sauschwänzlebahn** or Wutachtalbahn is mentioned in the main text. Contact the tourist office in Blumberg for timetable details (see Additional Information, Chapter 5).

Finally, the *Romantische Tunnelfahrten* (Romantic Tunnel Trips) on the **Schwarzwaldbahn** (Black Forest Railway) are not with a steam locomotive, but are nevertheless interesting for those who want to experience one of the great achievements of railway engineering. The engineer Robert Gerwig overcame an altitude difference of 1,470ft (448m) between Hornberg and St Georgen by using two double horseshoe curves and 39 tunnels. In so doing he artificially increased the distance between the two towns from 7 miles (11km) 'as the crow flies' to 16 miles (26km). Contact the Tourist Information Office in Triberg (see Additional Information, Chapter 2) for details of the trip.

LANDMARK
VISITORS GUIDES

US & British Virgin Islands

US & British VI*
ISBN: 1 901522 03 2
256pp,
UK £11.95 US $15.95

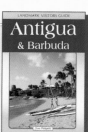

Antigua & Barbuda

Antigua & Barbuda*
ISBN: 1 901522 02 4
96pp,
UK £5.95 US $12.95

Jamaica

Jamaica*
ISBN: 1 901522 31 8
160pp
UK £7.95 US $12.95

Barbados

Barbados*
ISBN: 1 901522 32 6
160pp,
UK £7.95 US $12.95

St Lucia

St Lucia*
ISBN: 1 901522 82 2
144pp,
UK £6.95 US $13.95

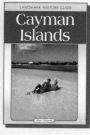

Cayman Islands

Cayman Islands*
ISBN: 1 901522 33 4
160pp
UK £7.95 US $12.95

Dominican Republic

Dominican Republic*
ISBN: 1 901522 08 3
160pp,
UK £7.95 US $12.95

Orlando & Central Florida

Orlando*
ISBN: 1 901522 22 9
256pp,
UK £9.95 US $15.95

Florida: Gulf Coast

Florida: Gulf Coast*
ISBN: 1 901522 01 6
160pp
UK £7.95 US $12.95

Florida: The Keys

Florida: The Keys*
ISBN: 1 901522 21 0
160pp,
UK £7.95 US $12.95

Gran Canaria

Gran Canaria*
ISBN: 1 901522 19 9
160pp
UK £7.95 US $12.95

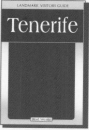

Tenerife

Tenerife
ISBN: 1 901522 17 2
160pp,
UK £7.95

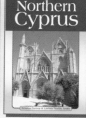

Northern Cyprus

North Cyprus
ISBN: 1 901522 51 2
192pp
UK £8.95

Madeira

Madeira
ISBN: 1 901522 42 3
192pp,
UK £8.95

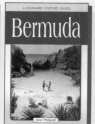

Bermuda

Bermuda*
ISBN: 1 901522 07 5
160pp,
UK £7.95 US $12.95

To order send a cheque (check)/Visa/MasterCard details to: Landmark Publishing,
Waterloo House, 12 Compton, Ashbourne, Derbyshire DE6 IDA England
Tel: 01335 347349 Fax: 01335 347303 e-mail: landmark@clara.net
web site: www.landmarkpublishing.co.uk

* In USA order from **Hunter Publishing**
130 Campus Drive, Edison NJ 08818, Tel (732) 225 1900 or (800) 255 0343
Fax: (732) 417 0482 www.hunterpublishing.com

   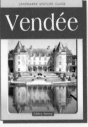 

Provence*	Côte d'Azur*	Dordogne	Vendée	Languedoc
ISBN: 1 901522 45 8	ISBN: 1 901522 29 6	ISBN: 1 901522 67 9	ISBN: 1 901522 76 X	ISBN: 1 901522 79 2
240pp,	144pp,	224pp,	96pp,	144pp,
UK £10.95 US $17.95	UK £6.95 US $13.95	UK £11.95	UK £4.95	UK £7.95

Bruges*	Ticino	Italian Lakes*	Riga*	Cracow
ISBN: 1 901522 66 0	ISBN: 1 901522 74 1	ISBN: 1 901522 11 3	ISBN: 1 901522 59 8	ISBN: 1 901522 54 7
96pp,	192pp	240pp,	160pp,	160pp,
UK £5.95	UK £8.95	UK £11.95 US $15.95	UK £7.95	UK £7.95

 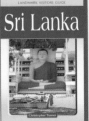   

Iceland*	Sri Lanka	India: Kerala	India: Goa	New Zealand*
ISBN: 1 901522 68 7	ISBN: 1 901522 37 7	ISBN: 1 901522 16 4	ISBN: 1 901522 23 7	ISBN: 1 901522 36 9
192pp,	192pp,	256pp,	160pp,	320pp
UK £9.95	UK £9.95	UK £10.99	UK £7.95	UK £12.95 US $18.95

Published in the UK by
Landmark Publishing Ltd,
Waterloo House, 12 Compton, Ashbourne, Derbyshire DE6 1DA England
Tel: (01335) 347349 Fax: (01335) 347303
e-mail: sales@landmarkpublishing.co.uk
website: landmarkpublishing.co.uk

Published in the USA by
Hunter Publishing Inc,
130 Campus Drive, Edison NJ 08818
Tel: (732) 225 1900, (800) 255 0343 Fax: (732) 417 0482
website: www.hunterpublishing.com

ISBN 1 901 522 39 3
© **Grant Bourne & Sabine Körner-Bourne 2001**

1st Edition

The rights of Grant Bourne & Sabine Körner-Bourne as authors of this work
have been asserted by them in accordance with the Copyright,
Design and Patents Act, 1993.

All rights reserved. No part of this publication may be reproduced, stored in a retrieval system
or transmitted in any form or by any means, electronic, mechanical, photocopying, recording
or otherwise without the prior permission of Landmark Publishing Ltd.

British Library Cataloguing in Publication Data: a catalogue record for this
book is available from the British Library.

Print: Gutenberg Press Ltd, Malta
Editor: Pat Fielding
Cartography: Mark Titterton
Design: Samantha Witham

Front cover: Traditional costume of the Gutachtal. With its distinctive red
pompoms the *Bollenhut* has become a symbol of the Black Forest
Back cover top: Staufen is one of the prettiest towns in the Black Forest;
bottom: Waterfall at Triberg

Picture Credits:
All photography provided by the authors.

DISCLAIMER
While every care has been taken to ensure that the information in this book
is as accurate as possible at the time of publication, the publishers
and authors accept no responsibility for any loss, injury or inconvenience sustained
by anyone using this book.